D1519654

"Across the Indo-Pacific, states are turning to minilateral groupings to address issues of common concern, and away from traditional multilateral institutions. This timely book analyses why this has occurred and what consequences it may have for the security of the region. Bringing together an expert team of scholars, it makes an incisive contribution to our understanding of minilateralism as an evolving phenomenon and emerging practice."

– Ian Hall, Professor, Griffith University

"The S. Rajaratnam School of International Studies in Singapore has long been the world's leading authority on Asian security cooperation. This volume, edited by two of its rising stars, brings together a stellar lineup to study an increasingly central, but underexamined, form of collaboration. As multilateralism and traditional alliances each confront existential challenges in this increasingly important region, minilateralism is coming to the fore. This excellent book is thus a must read for scholars, practitioners, journalists and students of Asian security alike."

– Brendan Taylor, Professor of Strategic Studies, Australian National University

"In this prescient volume, Singh and Teo bring together leading experts in the field to explore an understudied but important aspect of Asia's evolving regional architecture: the rise and prevalence of minilateral initiatives in the Indo-Pacific. In a period of increasing uncertainty and dissatisfaction with current bilateral and multilateral arrangements, *Minilateralism in the Indo-Pacific* is a must read for any serious student, scholar, and policymaker interested in Asian affairs."

– Andrew Yeo, Associate Professor of Politics, The Catholic University of America

MINILATERALISM IN THE INDO-PACIFIC

While US-centred bilateralism and ASEAN-led multilateralism have largely dominated the post-Cold War regional security architecture in the Indo-Pacific, increasing doubts about their effectiveness have resulted in countries turning to alternative forms of cooperation, such as minilateral arrangements. Compared to multilateral groupings, minilateral platforms are smaller in size, as well as more exclusive, flexible and functional.

Both China and the United States have contributed to minilateral initiatives in the Indo-Pacific. In the case of the former, there is the Lancang-Mekong Cooperation mechanism—involving China, Cambodia, Laos, Myanmar, Thailand and Vietnam—established in 2015. In the case of the latter, there has been a revival of the Quadrilateral Security Dialogue in 2017—involving the United States, Australia, Japan and India. This book examines the rise of these arrangements, their challenges and opportunities, as well as their impact on the extant regional security architecture, including on the ASEAN-led multilateral order.

This is a valuable guide for students and policymakers looking to understand the nature and development of minilateralism in the Indo-Pacific region.

Bhubhindar Singh is Associate Professor, Coordinator of the Regional Security Architecture Programme, and Head of Graduate Studies at the S. Rajaratnam School of International Studies, Nanyang Technological University, Singapore.

Sarah Teo is a Research Fellow with the Regional Security Architecture Programme at the S. Rajaratnam School of International Studies, Nanyang Technological University, Singapore.

MINILATERALISM IN THE INDO-PACIFIC

The Quadrilateral Security Dialogue, Lancang-Mekong Cooperation Mechanism, and ASEAN

Edited by Bhubhindar Singh and Sarah Teo

LONDON AND NEW YORK

First published 2020
by Routledge
2 Park Square, Milton Park, Abingdon, Oxon OX14 4RN

and by Routledge
52 Vanderbilt Avenue, New York, NY 10017

Routledge is an imprint of the Taylor & Francis Group, an informa business

British Library Cataloguing in Publication Data
A catalogue record for this book is available from the British Library

Library of Congress Cataloging-in-Publication Data
Names: Singh, Bhubhindar, editor. | Teo, Sarah, editor.
Title: Minilateralism in the Indo-Pacific : the Quadrilateral Security Dialogue, Lancang-Mekong Cooperation Mechanism, and ASEAN / edited by Bhubhindar Singh, Sarah Teo.
Description: Abingdon, Oxon ; New York, NY : Routledge, 2020. | Includes bibliographical references and index.
Identifiers: LCCN 2019058566 (print) | LCCN 2019058567 (ebook) | ISBN 9780367430375 (hardback) | ISBN 9780367430382 (paperback) | ISBN 9781003000839 (ebook)
Subjects: LCSH: Lancang-Mekong Cooperation Special Fund. | ASEAN. | Quadrilateral Security Dialogue (2007) | Regionalism–Indo-Pacific Region. | Security, International–Indo-Pacific Region. | Indo-Pacific Region–Foreign relations.
Classification: LCC JZ1720.A5 M56 2020 (print) | LCC JZ1720.A5 (ebook) | DDC 355/.0310959–dc23
LC record available at https://lccn.loc.gov/2019058566
LC ebook record available at https://lccn.loc.gov/2019058567

ISBN: 978-0-367-43037-5 (hbk)
ISBN: 978-0-367-43038-2 (pbk)
ISBN: 978-1-003-00083-9 (ebk)

Typeset in Bembo
by Taylor & Francis Books

CONTENTS

ILLUSTRATIONS

Figures

Table

ACKNOWLEDGEMENTS

We would like to express our gratitude to the S. Rajaratnam School of International Studies, Nanyang Technological University, Singapore, for giving us the time and support to work on this project. We wish to express our deepest appreciation to the authors for their contributions. Special thanks go to Shang-su Wu for agreeing to contribute a chapter at short notice. We are grateful to Alison Phillips for painstakingly copyediting the manuscript. Last but not least, we would like to thank Simon Bates, Tan ShengBin and Cherry Allen, as well as the anonymous reviewers, for their support of this project.

CONTRIBUTORS

Bhubhindar Singh is Associate Professor, Coordinator of the Regional Security Architecture Programme, and Head of Graduate Studies at the S. Rajaratnam School of International Studies, Nanyang Technological University, Singapore.

Sarah Teo is a Research Fellow with the Regional Security Architecture Programme at the S. Rajaratnam School of International Studies, Nanyang Technological University, Singapore.

Vannarith Chheang is serving as President of Asian Vision Institute, a leading think tank on geopolitical risk analysis and governance innovation.

Xue Gong is a Research Fellow in the China Programme at RSIS.

Huong Le Thu is a Senior Analyst at the Australian Strategic Policy Institute and she can be contacted at huonglethu@aspi.org.

Andrew O'Neil is Professor of Political Science and Research Dean at the Griffith University Business School.

Tomohiko Satake is a Senior Research Fellow in the Policy Studies Department, the National Institute for Defense Studies, Japan.

See Seng Tan is President/CEO-elect of International Students Inc, a US-based non-profit organisation. He is concurrently Professor of International Relations at RSIS.

William T. Tow is Professor Emeritus in the Department of International Relations, Coral Bell School of Asia Pacific Affairs, the Australian National University.

Lucy West is a Research Associate at the Griffith Asia Institute and a sessional lecturer in the School of Government and International Relations, Griffith University.

Shang-su Wu is a Research Fellow at RSIS.

INTRODUCTION

Minilateralism in the Indo-Pacific

Bhubhindar Singh and Sarah Teo

Introduction

This volume seeks to understand and explain the increased presence of minilateral arrangements in the Indo-Pacific, focusing particularly on the time period since the late 2000s. During the post-Cold War period the regional security architecture in the Indo-Pacific has generally been viewed as revolving around two primary axes of security cooperation, namely bilateralism and multilateralism. The former, to a large extent, has been a continuation of the San Francisco System of US alliances established during the Cold War, although their functions have evolved along with changing geopolitical circumstances. These alliances between the United States and Australia, Japan, the Philippines, South Korea and Thailand have been the bedrock of US presence in and engagement with the Indo-Pacific. In contrast to the strong emphasis on US-centred bilateralism, other types of relations among regional countries—both bilateral and multilateral—were initially slow to develop, due to the mistrust stemming from past conflicts. Nevertheless, as Cold War tensions wound down, a nascent multilateral architecture emerged in the Indo-Pacific with arrangements centred mainly on the ten-member Association of Southeast Asian Nations (ASEAN), as well as its associated platforms such as the eighteen-member East Asia Summit and the 27-member ASEAN Regional Forum. Since the 2000s, however, another mode of cooperation has appeared to be gaining ground in the Indo-Pacific security architecture. Between narrow bilateralism and broad multilateralism, regional countries have increasingly relied on minilateral platforms to achieve their security objectives.

While the literature has yet to come to a consensus on the definition of minilateralism, our treatment of the concept encompasses both its quantitative and qualitative dimensions. Taking reference from the scope and objectives of regional multilateralism and bilateralism, minilateralism in the Indo-Pacific therefore refers to cooperative relations that usually involve between three and nine countries, and are relatively exclusive, flexible and functional in nature. More importantly, mini-lateral initiatives follow a critical mass approach—meaning that they comprise only countries that are the most relevant to or that are able to make the biggest impact on the issue in question (see Eckersley 2012, p. 32; Falkner 2016, p. 89). The Trilateral Strategic Dialogue (TSD) that began in 2002 among Australia, Japan and the United States, the original Quadrilateral Security Dialogue (QSD) convened in 2007, as well as the Malacca Straits Sea Patrol in 2004 involving Indonesia, Malaysia and Singapore, were early examples of minilateral cooperation in Indo-Pacific security. Such efforts have appeared to intensify in recent years, for instance with the establishment of the Lancang-Mekong Cooperation (LMC) mechanism—involving Cambodia, China, Laos, Myanmar, Thailand and Vietnam—in 2015, the revival of the QSD—involving Australia, Japan, India and the United States—in 2017, as well as the Sulu Sea trilateral patrols launched in 2017 among Indonesia, Malaysia and the Philippines. The formation of the LMC and resurrection of the QSD, in particular, present interesting case studies to examine how and why minilateralism has emerged against the backdrop of growing Sino-US rivalry in the Indo-Pacific. Broadly, we argue that the emergence of minilaterals in the regional security architecture has been fuelled chiefly by two factors—specifically the rising doubts over the sustainability of the US leadership and its alliance network in the region, as well as the inadequacies of the extant multilateral arrangements in resolving strategic regional challenges. Consequently, the appeal of minilateral 'coalitions of the willing' in addressing security problems has increased among regional countries.

The idea of minilateralism itself is admittedly not new. Kahler (1992) notes, for instance, that bilateralism, minilateralism and multilateralism have co-existed in global governance since 1945, while others add that these three modes of security cooperation are also not unfamiliar to the Indo-Pacific (see also Cha 2003, p. 117; Medcalf 2008, pp. 25–6). However, as Green (2014, p. 758) correctly points out in a 2014 chapter on 'Asian strategic triangles', there is a paucity in the literature regarding security minilateralism in the region. Moreover, most works that have explored minilateralism in the regional security architecture, including Green (2014), have tended to focus primarily on either trilateralism or the US perspective of minilateral initiatives (see also Cha 2003; Nilsson-Wright 2017). Arguably, this has simply been an extension of actual geopolitical dynamics, whereby trilateral initiatives among the United States and its allies have appeared to dominate the space between bilateralism and multilateralism. Nevertheless, this edited volume aims to add to the existing body of work by examining the more recent minilateral mechanisms, such as the QSD 2.0 and the LMC, in the current strategic climate framed by uncertainty about US commitment to the region alongside a rising China, as well as scepticism about the effectiveness of regional multilateralism. Dominated by non-ASEAN powers, these minilateral groupings could indeed hold important consequences for the evolution of the regional security architecture. Within the context of ASEAN-centric multilateralism, the minilateral-multilateral nexus is also explored using the case of the ASEAN Defence Ministers' Meeting (ADMM)-Plus. The remainder of this introductory chapter will discuss the treatment of minilateralism in the extant literature, and offer some context that has framed the emergence of minilateralism in the Indo-Pacific security architecture. The chapter concludes with an overview of the edited volume.

Conceptualising minilateralism

To define what minilateralism is, we first need to understand the features that make it different from multilateralism. This is because in many aspects, the concept of minilateralism draws upon the literature on multilateralism. Both forms of cooperation involve an indeterminate number of parties—although evidently more than two—and in purely numerical terms minilateralism can be treated as a subset of multilateralism. In Keohane's (1990, p. 731) influential article, for instance, his definition of multilateralism as 'the practice of co-ordinating national policies in groups of three or more states, through ad hoc arrangements or by means of institutions', could certainly also apply to minilateralism. Following the arguments of Ruggie (1992, pp. 566–7) and others, qualitative characteristics are thus as important as the quantitative dimension in distinguishing between minilateralism and multilateralism (see also Tago 2017, p. 2). In this section, we explore the defining features of minilateralism, particularly vis-à-vis multilateralism.

In his extensively quoted definition of multilateralism, Ruggie (1992, p. 571) acknowledges its numerical aspect—'three or more states'—but contends that it is the qualitative dimension that makes the concept distinctive. According to Ruggie (ibid., pp. 571–2), the qualitative dimension of multilateralism should entail three features, namely generalised organising principles, indivisibility and diffuse reciprocity. For the most part, Ruggie contrasts these features with those of bilateralism. Generalised organising principles refer to 'principles which specify appropriate conduct for a class of actions, without regard to the particularistic interests of the parties or the strategic exigencies that may exist in any specific occurrence' (ibid., p. 571). This even applies to the bigger powers, which 'otherwise may prefer to follow their own interests … at the expense of explicit institutional rules' (Tow 2019, p. 235). In contrast, bilateralism allows for relations to be conducted on a case-by-case basis, tailored to the requirements and needs of the respective sets of relations between the two parties (Ruggie 1992, p. 571; Tago 2017, p. 2). Indivisibility involves the recognition of and acceptance by participants in multilateralism that public goods exist, even if they are socially constructed (Ruggie 1992, p. 571). Last but not least, diffuse reciprocity means that 'the [multilateral] arrangement is expected … to yield a rough equivalence of the benefits in the aggregate and over time' (ibid.; see also Keohane 1986, pp. 19–24). Bilateralism, on the other hand, involves specific reciprocity, which involves 'the simultaneous balancing of specific quids-pro-quos by each party with every other at all times' (Ruggie 1992, p. 572). Similarly, Ikenberry (2003, p. 534) makes the case that multilateralism could be differentiated from other types of interstate relations such as bilateralism based on numbers, as well as the presence of 'agreed-upon rules and principles' which leads to 'some reduction in policy autonomy' of the participating states.

Considering these premises of multilateralism and bilateralism, the task of introducing the minilateral concept into the literature should underscore how the latter is a distinctive category on its own that is different from existing forms of interstate cooperation. Distinguishing minilateralism from bilateralism is relatively straightforward; given that bilateralism is associated with a specific numerical figure, any type of relations or platform that does not fulfil the criteria of two participants would not, by default, qualify as bilateralism. Our concern is thus more with differentiating between minilateralism and multilateralism, given that both forms of cooperation involve an unspecified number of states—as long as there are more than two—and, on the surface, appear quite similar in form. Taking the above definitions of multilateralism as a starting point, it appears that minilateralism should differ from multilateralism in both quantitative and qualitative ways. In terms of numbers, minilateralism logically suggests a smaller group of participants compared to multilateralism. The specific sizes of minilateral groupings vary depending on the issue at hand. Naim (2009), whose definition of minilateralism has been cited at length in the literature, highlights that in issues of global economy, climate change and nuclear proliferation, the 'magic number' for effective action is about twenty. Within the context of an Indo-Pacific region, the number is logically much smaller given that regional multilateralism arguably ranges from ten (in ASEAN itself) to 27 members (in the ASEAN Regional Forum). Indeed, Cha (2003, pp. 116–17) suggests that regional minilaterals in the Indo-Pacific have typically comprised three or four members. Nilsson-Wright (2017) and Green (2014) explore various trilateral relationships in the context of minilateralism, while Emmers (2013, p. 88) defines the Five Power Defence Arrangements—involving Australia, Malaysia, New Zealand, Singapore and the United Kingdom—as a 'minilateral defense coalition'.

The numerical dimension relates to the second, more qualitative aspect of minilateralism, specifically that it differs from multilateralism in terms of relative exclusivity. While the latter works on the basis of indivisibility and generalised organising principles—thus necessitating a broad and inclusive approach—minilateralism focuses on gathering 'critical mass' (Eckersley 2012, p. 32; Falkner 2016, p. 89). This means 'bring[ing] to the table the smallest possible number of countries needed to have the largest possible impact on solving a particular problem' (Naim 2009). This conceptualisation implies two things. First, minilateral arrangements acknowledge and accommodate the discriminatory nature of power. Minilateralism recognises that only a select few countries are able to potentially resolve a particular issue, and incorporates them in decision making to the exclusion of all others. Hence, it is viewed as a more realistic and effective option—especially when compared to multilateralism's emphasis on equality—for driving action (Falkner 2016, pp. 88, 94). In other words, minilateralism does not necessarily follow multilateralism in having a levelling effect on interstate cooperation; in some instances, it may instead deliberately promote power asymmetries.

Second, unlike the problems associated with larger multilateral mechanisms, minilateral arrangements are conceivably more flexible due to the smaller number of stakeholders—and consequently fewer sets of interests—involved (Eckersley 2012, p. 32; Falkner 2016, p. 89; Lee-Brown 2018, p. 168). On the other hand, this perceptibly 'undemocratic and exclusionary' feature of minilateralism could deepen divisions and mistrust (Naim 2009). An opinion piece in China's *Global Times*, for instance, highlighted that the QSD had been described as 'the Asian NATO [North Atlantic Treaty Organization]' and warned that it would 'divide the Asia-Pacific into hostile armed blocs' (Li 2017). The emphasis on shared values in the QSD—a grouping that the Japanese Prime Minister Shinzo Abe describes in an article as 'Asia's democratic security diamond'—has also underscored differences between those four countries and others in terms of political ideology and governance, especially vis-à-vis China (Abe 2012). As Green (2014, p. 759) observes, minilateralism could either 'contribute to a stable balance of power or pose the risk of competing blocs that would fuel a security dilemma in the region'.

The third feature of minilateralism involves its informality and functionality. In many instances, minilateralism is meant to be a more nimble and targeted approach to address specific challenges in ways that existing mechanisms are unable to. This feature of minilateralism sets it apart from multilateral platforms, which—due to their larger numbers and institutional processes—typically see drawn-out negotiations before taking action. In this sense, minilateralism arguably offers an additional middle-ground approach to states that find their security interests not fully served by bilateral alliances or multilateral institutional processes. Amid declining commitment to multilateralism from some states, minilateralism could thus buttress global multilateralism by supplementing the latter's existing inadequacies (Teo 2018). For instance, minilateral initiatives such as the Malacca Straits Sea Patrol, the Sulu Sea trilateral patrols, and the 'Our Eyes' initiative which facilitates intelligence sharing among six Southeast Asian countries, are essentially concrete operationalisations of multilateral-level discussions in ASEAN. ASEAN member states located in the Mekong sub-region have also formed their own minilateral groupings to manage challenges arising from their geopolitical context, given that the ASEAN agenda has typically not appeared to pay much attention to those issues (Ho and Pitakdumrongkit 2019). On the other hand, minilateral initiatives could sideline broader multilateral processes, particularly if they come across as more effective and less costly.

The functional nature of minilateralism also suggests that such arrangements typically tend to form and disband 'without an institutional legacy', distinguishing it both from multilateral platforms that are built around rules and long-term reciprocity, as well as from bilateral alliances that are often grounded in formal treaties (Cha 2003, p. 117). While this could prove expedient for driving collective action, the lack of institutional linkages means that the sustainability of a particular minilateral mechanism depends very much on the commitment and interest of its participating governments. A good example of this would be the original version of the QSD in 2007, which faded into obscurity following Abe's resignation, and the withdrawal of support from Kevin Rudd's newly elected Australian government which had concerns about provoking China.

As reflected in the above discussion, this edited volume advocates for an analytically eclectic approach towards the concept of minilateralism that incorporates elements from various International Relations paradigms (see Katzenstein and Sil 2010). Such an approach helps us to consider the rise of minilateralism in the Indo-Pacific in a realistic and comprehensive manner. Indeed, despite its pitfalls, minilateralism has intensified in the region in recent times. In regional (and global) agendas, minilateralism's primary contribution has been to convene resources from a few specific actors that have the greatest ability to make a difference to the issue of concern. Its relative exclusivity, institutional flexibility and functionality indicate that minilateralism in general represents a distinct form of interstate cooperation. In the next section, we focus on the rise of minilateralism in the Indo-Pacific security architecture.

Rising minilateralism in the Indo-Pacific

To a considerable degree, the increasing prominence of minilateralism in the Indo-Pacific has been a response to the shortcomings of both US bilateral alliances and ASEAN-centric platforms in addressing regional challenges. Ongoing structural change, including the waning of US hegemony and the rapid strategic rise of China, have put pressure on the San Francisco System. Although there continues to be strong support for the US leadership and commitment from its allies and partners, questions have been raised about the sustainability of the US alliance network and leadership in the region. This questioning moved to the forefront in 2008 following the global recession—the worst economic downturn experienced by the United States since the Great Depression—and reached a new peak during President Donald Trump's administration, particularly given its 'America First' policy and transactional approach to foreign affairs (Nilsson-Wright 2017, p. 2). To be sure, the United States retains its military, economic and technological superiority in the world. Yet evidence suggests that the gap between the United States and other rising powers, specifically China, is narrowing. Since 2010, China has been the world's second largest economy, and, by some accounts, is on track to surpass US economic dominance as long as it maintains its growth trajectory (Smith 2018; Wesley 2017, p. 6). Increasingly, Indo-Pacific countries, US allies among them, find themselves caught between Chinese economic benefits and US security guarantees—with the latter arguably appearing to be more tenuous under the Trump administration (Fisher and Carlsen 2018).

Another challenge that could affect the sustainability of the US 'hub-and-spokes' system relates to the Trump administration's approach towards US bilateral alliances. Trump has repeatedly complained about free-riding allies, and has insisted on 'fair burden sharing' with 'wealthy countries' (The White House 2019). Trump administration officials have reportedly asked both Seoul and Tokyo to increase their contributions towards maintaining US forces on their respective territories by up to five times the current amount (Jo 2019; Johnson 2019). As Wesley (2017, p. 12) observes, 'the relatively costless nature of alliances is starting to be questioned' by US allies around the world. It may be premature to predict the demise of US bilateral alliances in the Indo-Pacific, but there certainly appears to be increasing uncertainty about Washington's commitment to its allies and partners. Given these pressures on the system of US bilateral alliances, Indo-Pacific countries have sought alternative modes of cooperation to reinforce a positive US presence in the region, as well as to ensure the existence of other channels for dialogue and collaboration among regional countries.

The second key axis of the regional security architecture—ASEAN-centric multilateralism—has also come under fire for its perceived ineffectiveness in resolving key strategic challenges in the region. For the last two decades, ASEAN has been the main convener of multilateral dialogue and cooperative platforms that include major and regional powers such as China, Japan and the United States. This is arguably surprising, given that ASEAN comprises ten of the smallest or weakest states in the Indo-Pacific. Perhaps even more astonishing is that the other more powerful countries have, at least in diplomatic terms, committed to the 'ASEAN way' of cooperation, which emphasises consensus building and process over outcomes. ASEAN-led platforms such as the ADMM-Plus, the ASEAN Regional Forum and the East Asia Summit have served to facilitate dialogue and confidence building among regional countries.

From the late 2000s, however, doubts over the ASEAN way and the association's unity have deepened as regional challenges, such as the South China Sea territorial disputes, started to come to the fore. Green (2014, p. 760) argues, for example, that ASEAN's failure to issue a joint communiqué in 2012 due to member states' disagreements over the South China Sea disputes showed that 'any advantages of a lowest-common-denominator, consensus-based approach are offset by the inability to produce meaningful results on controversial issues contested by a determined power'. Jones and Smith (2007, p. 184) contend, similarly, that despite rhetorically committing themselves to ASEAN centrality and the ASEAN way, major powers such as China and Japan have in fact 'manipulate[d] ASEAN's shared norms and nonbinding processes for their own strategic advantage'. Additionally, Trump has appeared to show little interest in Southeast Asia, skipping both of the annual East Asia Summits that were held in the first two years of his presidency. The oft-cited critique of ASEAN-led institutions, as elegantly summarised by Medcalf (2008, p. 25), is that there are 'too many arrangements' in a multilateral architecture that 'generally does too little'. The inability of ASEAN-led multilateralism to address regional security problems, alongside the structural shifts in Sino-US dynamics and consequently the changes in the US hub-and-spokes system, have created a conducive context for the rise of regional minilateral arrangements that are supposedly more flexible and more effective in responding to strategic challenges.

This volume focuses on two recent minilateral initiatives, namely the QSD and the LMC. It also explores the impact of the 'rise of minilaterals' on the ASEAN-led multilateral structure. This is carried out through unpacking ASEAN's responses to the QSD and assessing the relationship between minilaterals and the ASEAN framework.

The idea of a quadrilateral cooperative platform involving Australia, India, Japan and the United States was first proposed by Abe in early 2007, with a subsequent low-profile meeting of the four countries on the sidelines of the ASEAN Regional Forum Senior Officials' Meeting taking place in May that same year. Later in September, the annual India-US naval drill, Exercise Malabar, was expanded for the first time to include Australia and Japan, along with Singapore. Following Abe's resignation and the election of Rudd—who sought a less confrontational approach towards China—as Australia's prime minister in late 2007, however, the QSD lost steam. It would be a decade later, in 2017, that officials from the four nations met again on the sidelines of the East Asia Summit in Manila, Philippines. From the US perspective, the QSD is one way to counter expanding Chinese influence. For its allies and partners, however, the QSD has also re-emerged as a result of declining US leadership in the region and the subsequent efforts of US allies and partners to ensure that Washington remains committed to the Indo-Pacific, as well as to find alternative ways to maintain a favourable regional architecture even in the absence of a strong US presence. While all four countries have emphasised the importance of a free and open Indo-Pacific, some doubts remain over the QSD's purpose and sustainability, on the one hand, and the challenges it could pose to ASEAN centrality, on the other.

The LMC presents a slightly different case to the QSD. Launched in 2015, the LMC comprises Cambodia, China, Laos, Myanmar, Thailand and Vietnam. Unlike the QSD, the LMC process provides an overarching framework—encompassing the three pillars of political-security issues, economics and sustainable development, as well as sociocultural exchanges—to strengthen collaboration between the six participating nations. While the LMC officially focuses on non-traditional security issues such as water resource management, agricultural development and infra-structural connectivity, it is also part of a larger drive by Beijing to enhance its neighbourhood diplomacy and cultivate its profile as a 'responsible major power' (Yang 2019, pp. 108, 112; see also LMC 2016). Crucially, the LMC also serves as one key element of China's Belt and Road Initiative (Chheang 2018, p. 1). This is perhaps why China has provided high levels of financial support and efforts to ensure the success of the mechanism (Yang 2019, pp. 114–17; Nguyen 2018). More importantly for China, the success of the LMC would mean the success of 'the first Chinese-built Southeast Asian institution' (Nguyen 2018). Through the LMC, China's ability to exercise influence over the Mekong sub-regional coun-tries—all of which are ASEAN member states—and potentially over ASEAN processes in the longer term, highlights the risks that the mechanism could pose to ASEAN centrality. Yet the LMC has arguably emerged from ASEAN's neglect of issues that the Mekong countries deem important to their interests. In this sense, there remains the possibility that synergies could be created between the LMC and broader ASEAN-centric multilateralism.

Based on the subsequent discussion of the case studies in this volume, a few broad trends are apparent. First, minilateralism is generally treated as complementary with both bilateral and multilateral forms of regional cooperation. Most meetings of the QSD, for instance, have taken place on the sidelines of ASEAN-centric forums. Moreover, the agendas of the QSD and the LMC do not overlap completely with those of ASEAN. That said, for the LMC in particular, its focus on infrastructure building and development in the Mekong sub-region could potentially help to bolster ASEAN's community-building process. Second, despite the complementarities between minilateralism and multilateralism, there is a need to carefully manage the proliferation of minilateral initiatives, particularly when major powers are involved. It is important to avoid a situation in which minilateral mechanisms merely serve as platforms for major powers to extend their influence. It may be a fact that specific major powers are particularly dominant in these smaller and more functional groupings, but in the interest of regional stability it is necessary to ensure that minilateralism is not simply used as a tool of major power politics. Last but not least, regional actors, ASEAN included, should be realistic about ASEAN centrality. As a grouping of ten medium-sized and small countries, ASEAN may be able to offer a neutral platform for various dialogue processes, but it is unlikely to take on a strategic role in the same way that the major powers could.

Overview of the volume

The book is divided into three parts, with the first section focusing on US-centric minilateralism in the Indo-Pacific. In Chapter 1, Tow discusses how minilateral initiatives such as the TSD and the QSD could potentially supplement the hub-and-spokes system of US alliances. At the same time, he reminds us that regional minilateral groupings have thus far been effective mostly as platforms for 'cooperative interaction' (this volume, p. 22) rather than in resolving or managing security dilemmas, and it remains to be seen if minilateralism emerges as the region's primary mode of security cooperation. The next two chapters examine specifically the QSD. In Chapter 2, O'Neil and West explain that the QSD's resurgence has been driven by perceptions of rising Chinese assertiveness and, for Australia, India and Japan, by Trump's uncertain commitment to the region. They argue, nevertheless, that there remains 'little evidence of coherent strategic intent' among the four QSD countries, suggesting that the quadrilateral is likely to be 'a very distant second' to US bilateral alliances and trilateral arrangements among US allies and partners (this volume, pp. 27, 28). Like O'Neil and West, Satake points out in Chapter 3 that the QSD faces challenges arising from differences among its four participating countries regarding strategic priorities and intensifying Sino-US rivalry. Satake, however, offers a slightly more optimistic view of the QSD's future, arguing that if effectively managed, the QSD could help to establish an 'open, inclusive and more pluralistic order in the Indo-Pacific' (this volume, p. 53).

The second section in this volume examines minilateralism in the Mekong sub-region, focusing particularly on the LMC mechanism in which China is arguably the most dominant member. In Chapter 4, Gong highlights that China has extended its influence over the Mekong sub-region by embracing water resource management cooperation through the LMC—something which is largely absent from the agenda of the other sub-regional mechanisms. She argues that the LMC's launch reflects a new recognition by Beijing that minilateralism could very well complement its preferred strategy of bilateralism. Eventually, Gong expects the LMC to contribute towards increasing multipolarity in the region. In Chapter 5, Wu similarly highlights the LMC's potential to reshape the geopolitical landscape in mainland Southeast Asia. Despite existing challenges that may limit the LMC's success, Beijing has irreversibly gained the upper hand in Mekong sub-regional dynamics through its dam-building activities. As such, the Southeast Asian Mekong states are left with no feasible alternative to China's dominance in the Lancang-Mekong.

The final section in the volume focuses on the impact of minilaterals, such as the QSD and Mekong sub-regional platforms, on ASEAN-centric multilateralism. Based on primary data from surveys and interviews, Le Thu in Chapter 6 unpacks the (mis)perception that ASEAN is wary of the QSD threatening its centrality in the regional security architecture. On the contrary, a considerable number of survey respondents viewed the QSD as being complementary to ASEAN rather than competing with it. Le Thu attributes this (mis)perception to equally misplaced assumptions about ASEAN centrality, particularly given the perennial contestation over the concept. In Chapter 7, Chheang observes that while economic mini-lateralism has been largely complementary to ASEAN-centric multilateralism, the impact of political-security minilateralism on ASEAN has been more mixed. In particular, political-security minilateral mechanisms dominated by extra-regional major powers amid geopolitical rivalry could potentially challenge ASEAN cen-trality and unity. To ensure that regional political-security minilateralism benefits ASEAN, Chheang underscores the need to align the former with ASEAN Com-munity blueprints and principles. In the final chapter in this volume, Tan offers a novel perspective on regional minilateralism using the case of the ADMM-Plus. In contrast to juxtapositions of regional minilaterals against ASEAN-centric multi-lateralism, Tan argues that the ADMM-Plus itself is an example of a minilateral arrangement. At a time when doubts are being raised over the effectiveness of ASEAN-centric multilateralism, Tan's analysis of the ADMM-Plus is instructive on the potential convergences between multilateralism and minilateralism in the regional security architecture.

References

Abe, S 2012, 'Asia's democratic security diamond', *Project Syndicate*, 27 December, viewed 19 September 2019, www.project-syndicate.org/commentary/a-strategic-alliance-for-japan-and-india-by-shinzo-abe.

Cha, VD 2003, 'The dilemma of regional security in East Asia: multilateralism versus bila-teralism', in PF Diehl and J Lepgold (eds), *Regional Conflict Management*, Lanham, MD, Rowman & Littlefield, pp. 104–122.

Chheang, V 2018, 'China's economic statecraft in Southeast Asia', *Perspective*, no. 45, viewed 20 September 2019, www.iseas.edu.sg/images/pdf/ISEAS_Perspective_2018_45@50.pdf.

Eckersley, R 2012, 'Moving forward in the climate negotiations: multilateralism or minilateralism?' *Global Environmental Politics*, vol. 12, no. 2, pp. 24–42.

Emmers, R 2013, 'The role of the Five Power Defence Arrangements in the Southeast Asian security architecture', in WT Tow and B Taylor (eds), *Bilateralism, Multilateralism and Asia-Pacific Security: Contending Cooperation*, London, Routledge, pp. 87–99.

Falkner, R 2016, 'A minilateral solution for global climate change? On bargaining efficiency, club benefits, and international legitimacy', *Perspectives on Politics*, vol. 14, no. 1, pp. 87–101.

Fisher, M and Carlsen, A 2018, 'How China is challenging American dominance in Asia', *New York Times*, 9 March, viewed 19 September 2019, www.nytimes.com/interactive/2018/03/09/world/asia/china-us-asia-rivalry.html.

Green, M 2014, 'Strategic Asian triangles', in SM Pekkanen, J Ravenhill and R Foot (eds), *The Oxford Handbook of the International Relations of Asia*, Oxford, Oxford University Press, pp. 758–774.

Ho, S and Pitakdumrongkit, K 2019, 'Can ASEAN play a greater role in the Mekong sub-region?' *The Diplomat*, 30 January, viewed 19 September 2019, https://thediplomat.com/2019/01/can-asean-play-a-greater-role-in-the-mekong-subregion/.

Ikenberry, GJ 2003, 'Is American multilateralism in decline?' *Perspectives on Politics*, vol 1, no. 3, pp. 533–550.

Jo, H 2019, 'S. Korea faces prospect Trump may be seeking "alliance fee"', *Korea Herald*, 27 August, viewed 9 September 2019, www.koreaherald.com/view.php?ud=20190827000744.

Johnson, J 2019, 'Trump's push for South Korea to pay more for U.S. troops puts Japan on notice', *Japan Times*, 8 August, viewed 9 September 2019, www.japantimes.co.jp/news/2019/08/08/asia-pacific/trumps-push-south-korea-pay-u-s-troops-puts-japan-notice/#.XYLt_2kza71.

Jones, DM and Smith, MLR 2007, 'Making process, not progress: ASEAN and the evolving East Asian regional order', *International Security*, vol. 32, no. 1, pp. 148–184.

Kahler, M 1992, 'Multilateralism with small and large numbers', *International Organization*, vol. 46, no. 3, pp. 681–708.

Katzenstein, PJ and Sil, R 2010, 'Analytic eclecticism in the study of world politics: reconfiguring problems and mechanisms across research traditions', *Perspectives on Politics*, vol. 8, no. 2, pp. 411–431.

Keohane, RO 1986, 'Reciprocity in international relations', *International Organization*, vol. 40, no. 1, pp. 1–27.

Keohane, RO 1990, 'Multilateralism: an agenda for research', *International Journal*, vol. 45, no. 4, pp. 731–764.

Lancang-Mekong Cooperation (LMC) 2016, 'Sanya Declaration of the First Lancang-Mekong Cooperation (LMC) Leaders' Meeting', Beijing, 23 March, viewed 20 September 2019, www.lmcchina.org/eng/zywj_5/t1513793.htm.

Lee-Brown, T 2018, 'Asia's security triangles: maritime minilateralism in the Indo-Pacific', *East Asia*, vol. 35, no. 2, pp. 163–176.

Li, Y 2017, 'Australia rejoining Quad will not advance regional prosperity, unity', *Global Times*, 15 November, viewed 19 September 2019, www.globaltimes.cn/content/1075382.shtml.

Medcalf, R 2008, 'Squaring the triangle: an Australian perspective on Asian security minilateralism', in R Medcalf, WT Tow, SW Simon, A Tanaka, M Auslin and F Zhu, *Assessing the Trilateral Strategic Dialogue*, Washington, DC, The National Bureau of Asian Research, pp. 23–31.

Naim, M 2009, 'Minilateralism', *Foreign Policy*, 21 June, viewed 19 September 2019, https://foreignpolicy.com/2009/06/21/minilateralism/.

Nguyen, KG 2018, 'China is making Mekong friends', *East Asia Forum*, 19 May, viewed 20 September 2019, www.eastasiaforum.org/2018/05/19/china-is-making-mekong-friends/.

Nilsson-Wright, J 2017, 'Creative minilateralism in a changing Asia: opportunities for security convergence and cooperation between Australia, India and Japan', Research Paper, London, Chatham House, viewed 19 September 2019, www.chathamhouse.org/sites/default/files/images/2017-07-28-Minilateralism.pdf.

Ruggie, JG 1992, 'Multilateralism: the anatomy of an institution', *International Organization*, vol. 46, no. 3, pp. 561–598.

Smith, N 2018, 'Get used to it, America: we're no longer no. 1', *Bloomberg*, 18 December, viewed 9 September 2019, www.bloomberg.com/opinion/articles/2018-12-18/china-as-no-1-economy-to-reap-benefits-that-once-flowed-to-u-s.

Tago, A 2017, 'Multilateralism, bilateralism, and unilateralism in foreign policy', in WR Thompson (ed.), *Oxford Research Encyclopedia of Politics*, viewed 20 August 2019, Oxford, Oxford Research Encyclopedias.

Teo, S 2018, 'Could minilateralism be multilateralism's best hope in the Asia Pacific?' *The Diplomat*, 15 December, viewed 9 September 2019, https://thediplomat.com/2018/12/could-minilateralism-be-multilateralisms-best-hope-in-the-asia-pacific/.

The White House 2019, 'Remarks by President Trump and Vice President Pence announcing the missile defense review', Washington, DC, White House, 17 January, viewed 9 September 2019, www.whitehouse.gov/briefings-statements/remarks-president-trump-vice-president-pence-announcing-missile-defense-review/.

Tow, WT 2019, 'Minilateral security's relevance to US strategy in the Indo-Pacific: challenges and prospects', *Pacific Review*, vol. 32, no. 2, pp. 232–244.

Wesley, M 2017, 'Global allies in a changing world', in M Wesley (ed.), *Global Allies: Comparing US Alliances in the 21st Century*, Acton, ANU Press, pp. 1–13.

Yang, X 2019, 'The Lancang-Mekong Cooperation mechanism: a new platform for China's neighbourhood diplomacy', *China: An International Journal*, vol. 17, no. 2, pp. 106–126.

1

MINILATERALISM AND US SECURITY POLICY IN THE INDO-PACIFIC

The legacy, viability and deficiencies of a new security approach

William T. Tow

Introduction

As 2018 drew to a close, events underlining US President Donald Trump's 'America First' policy and rendering uncertain the United States' long-standing post-war alliance politics accelerated. The resignation of Trump's Secretary of Defense, James N. Mattis, followed the president's decision, apparently without prior consultation, to withdraw US troops from Syria. However, ongoing events and trends pertaining to US alliance politics in Asia clearly contributed to Mattis's disillusionment. Uncertainties also intensified over the future of US–South Korean and US–Japanese alliance relations in the aftermath of Trump's June 2018 summit with North Korean leader Kim Jong Un in Singapore and his spontaneous decision to suspend a major US–South Korean military exercise. This was the case even in the absence of hard evidence that North Korea was following through with Kim's pledge to implement North Korea's comprehensive denuclearisation. As Mattis observed in his resignation letter to the president:

> My views on treating allies with respect and also being clear-eyed about both malign and strategic competitors are strongly held ... Because you have the right to have a Secretary of Defense whose views are better aligned with yours, and other subjects, I believe it is right for me to step down from my position.
>
> (New York Times *2018*)

In August 2019, US strategic interests were further undermined when South Korea terminated a bilateral defence intelligence-sharing agreement with Japan over a reparations dispute involving Korean labourers being forced to work under the Japanese during the occupation of Korea in the Second World War (Lind 2019;

Richardson 2019). An increasingly powerful China was likewise relentlessly asserting its territorial claims and strategic interests in the South China Sea and throughout Asia.

Notwithstanding the machinations and dramas associated with the Trump administration, it is doubtful that US post-war alliance politics in Asia or Europe is close to being relegated to the dustbin of history. One American president (not even Trump) cannot completely overturn 70 years of systematic collaboration between like-minded states who either relate to or support post-war Western values and norms. Most traditional US allies and security partners continue to view Washington as a useful counter to great power hegemonic aspirations in their regions. Their key policy calculation is to identify, explore and implement other forms of security collaboration with Washington and with each other that are less binding but still effective in realising mutual security objectives. This imperative helps to explain the rise of minilateral security politics as one means for operationalising such a vision.

The nature and rationales underlying minilateral politics will initially be considered here. It is fully acknowledged that minilateralism is not exclusively applicable to security politics. Indeed, it has been adapted for several decades as a means for advancing the politics of climate change, arms control, institution building and trade. Its recent emergence as a form of collective security and/or collective defence implementation, however, is an important aspect of contemporary international security that warrants closer examination, especially in an Indo-Pacific regional context. A second section in this chapter examines recent initiatives to introduce minilateral security as a complement to US alliance politics in the region. This trend has become increasingly notable as the Cold War system recedes further into history and as structural change in the Indo-Pacific's power politics requires Washington to adopt new approaches for maintaining the relevance of alliances and security partnerships in a rapidly changing world. A third section reviews and examines an intensifying debate over the advantages and liabilities of minilateral security politics from both American and regional perspectives. If the regional and global balance of power is indeed transforming, members of the Association of Southeast Asian Nations (ASEAN) and other regional states may either reject US minilateral security approaches as inappropriate for their own regional security planning or may prefer to adapt variants of minilateral security which are a better fit for their own national and regional priorities.

The main argument advanced in this chapter is that minilateralism—if effectively applied—can indeed supplement US alliance politics in the Indo-Pacific region. It remains to be seen, however, whether US policymakers will adopt and implement this approach by design or merely as an afterthought in their quest to salvage what remains of the traditional US 'hub-and-spokes' alliance network that has endured throughout much of Asia over the past 70 years. Or, alternatively, Washington may elect to modify current US minilateral security approaches as part of its quest to achieve a neo-isolationist, offshore balancing, or other variant of an 'America First' strategic posture.

Definition

What is 'minilateralism'? Perhaps the most widely accepted definition of the concept was offered by Naim (2009), a distinguished economist and journalist writing for the journal *Foreign Policy* a decade ago: bringing together 'the smallest possible number of countries needed to have the largest impact on solving a particular problem'. Until recently, the minilateralism concept was largely applied to discussions about international trade and about deriving greater flexibility in global governance and international diplomacy (Brandi *et al.* 2015; Brummer 2014; Hampson and Heinbeker 2011; Patrick 2014). In part such discussions were fuelled by a dawning realisation that American global hegemony may be drawing to a close, and that the multilateral institutions that US predominance spawned such as the International Monetary Fund, the World Bank and, indeed, the United States itself were suffering increasingly from 'middle age' and potential irrelevance. As Brummer (2014, pp. 1–2, emphasis in the original) has observed, such multilateralism has been gradually supplanted by 'an array of more modest and seemingly less ambitious joint ventures … to coordinate diverse sectors of the international economy and export shared policy preferences of member governments … [they] can be described distinctively as *mini*lateral strategies of economic statecraft'.

Without relinquishing the entire post-war multilateral framework cultivated for more than half a century and credited with generating greater prosperity for many of those developing states associated with it, the United States, along with its friends and allies in both Europe and greater Asia, began to implement selective minilateral security initiatives to complement and revitalise the multilateral framework. Four distinct approaches to minilateral politics, addressing specific economic and security issues, initially emerged. Haass (2010) has described them collectively as 'messy multilateralism' but they are perhaps more accurately viewed as minilateral typologies (see also Moret 2016). Haass included (1) *elite minilateralism* in which great and middle powers formalise groupings within the G20 framework to address specific issues; (2) *regional minilateralism* within trading arrangements such as the Asia-Pacific Economic Cooperation (APEC) (and, more specifically, that organisation's annual summit involving member states' heads of government) or utilisation of the European Union's individual trading arrangements with African states; (3) *functional minilateralism* in which states coalesce to address a specific task or issue at hand without intending to permanently maintain such an arrangement once the issue is either resolved or proven to be implacable (that is, the North Atlantic Treaty Organization's (NATO) 'smart defence' initiatives to coordinate greater cooperation in such areas as cyber and ballistic missile defence or the Six-Party Talks on Korean denuclearisation); and (4) *informal multilateralism* whereby national governments collaborate to promote or reinterpret global norms (that is, various arms control arrangements or China-ASEAN deliberations over shaping a 'code of conduct' in the South China Sea). A fifth variant, *minilateral* security, specifically applicable to US alliance adaptation, has materialised over the past two decades, most prominently in the Indo-Pacific sphere.

Minilateralism's development and history

Minilateral security politics intensified as the post-Cold War era unfolded. The viability of the United Nations, NATO and the ASEAN Regional Forum and other multilateral groupings was increasingly questioned as their member states' national interests diverged more sharply in the Middle East, Europe and the Indo-Pacific. These diverse interests often obfuscated multilateral institutions' original principles and norms while minimising prospects for collective gains—critical pre-conditions for the successful management of regional and international security. With the global balance of power shifting from a Soviet-American global bipolar rivalry to a more complex multipolar configuration, the longevity of a stable 'international liberal order' appeared to become increasingly tenuous.

Unlike its ongoing adherence to multilateral security in Europe via NATO, the United States has traditionally favoured engaging its Indo-Pacific allies and security partners bilaterally. Various observers have pointed to the United States' higher levels of 'collective identity' with post-war Europe than with an Asia that was wrestling with the challenges of decolonisation and development politics (Hemmer and Katzenstein 2002). US policymakers have asserted that a bilateral alliance net-work in the Indo-Pacific, underpinned by US power and commitments to its friends and allies, fits the 'geopolitical realities' of that region where 'no single threat [has been] commonly perceived', unlike the Soviet Union's danger to the Atlantic community which was the rationale for maintaining and strengthening NATO. The Indo-Pacific area has multiple security concerns 'that differ from country to country and within the sub-regions of this vast area' (Baker 1991, p. 5). As the Cold War receded, China's power and ambitions evolved in ways which encouraged the United States' post-war bilateral treaty allies—Australia, Japan, the Philippines, South Korea and Thailand— either to remain solidly within the US hub-and-spokes system or (in the case of Thailand and an increasingly nationalist Philippines) to at least hedge against growing Chinese power by maintaining their alliance affiliation with Washington. North Korea's nuclear aspirations reinforced the logic of America continuing its deterrence guarantees on behalf of its Northeast Asian allies, Japan and South Korea.

The North Korean example

Minilateral security politics was pursued in earnest in response to North Korea's intensified nuclear weapons programme in Northeast Asia during the late 1990s. A Trilateral Cooperation and Oversight Group (TCOG) was established in 1999 by the United States, Japan and South Korea to coordinate responses by the three allies to the North Korean nuclear weapons programme. However, this early initiative to apply an inter-alliance approach to a major emerging threat in the Indo-Pacific was short-lived and, arguably, fell short of its formulative purpose. This initiative was impeded by progressive South Korean governments' efforts led by President Kim Dae-jung and his immediate successor, Roh Moo-hyun, to pursue independent diplomatic initiatives with the North Korean government. This 'Sunshine Policy' arguably decoupled South Korea's approach to North Korea from American and Japanese efforts to preserve a credible deterrent against future North Korean nuclear aggression in Northeast Asia. Kim and Roh maintained that North Korea felt threatened by the George W. Bush administration's efforts to eradicate the regimes of Saddam Hussein in Iraq and Muammar al-Gaddafi in Libya, due to their efforts to build a nuclear weapons capacity in their own countries (Lee 2018, p. 8; see also Kang 2013, pp. 59–102). (Prior to President Bush's inauguration in January 2001, independent American negotiations with the North Koreans had appeared to complement South Korea's reliance on diplomacy for interacting with its northern neighbour.) Subsequent non-minilateral approaches such as an independent bilateral consultation process between the United States and North Korea, and the Six-Party Talks (from 2003 to 2009) were equally unsuccessful.

The TCOG also floundered because South Korea and Japan were hardly natural allies. Both countries are democratic and beholden to the post-war international liberal order for their impressive economic growth. However, they have been unable to overcome their historical animosities, territorial disputes and diverse outlooks on North Korea—even with substantial and long-standing American mediation efforts—to the extent that their bilateral politico-security ties could overcome such impediments. As Heginbotham and Samuels (2019) state, 'TCOG meetings continued for a time, but only informally, at lower levels, and without generating actionable recommendations' (see also Tow 2018, p. 3). The recent hardening of tensions between Seoul and Tokyo (including South Korea's cancellation of a bilateral intelligence agreement with Japan) renders any American role of arbitrating a modus vivendi between its two key Northeast Asian allies extremely difficult. However, if left untended, the recent deterioration of Japanese-South Korean ties is a risk for the overall American strategic position in Asia (Silverberg and Park 2019). In this context, the revival of a minilateral approach to modify this crisis may be an appropriate US policy response.

The Trilateral Strategic Dialogue

The Trilateral Strategic Dialogue (TSD) has been a relatively more successful venture in multilateral security policy. The TSD was the product of a consultation process initiated in 2001 by Japanese, Australian and American defence officials as the 'Trilateral Security Dialogue', conferring at the vice-ministerial level. It was characterised by the three participating countries' policymakers as providing a complementary instrument to the TCOG in deriving policy responses to the emerging North Korean nuclear threat (Tow 2017, p. 28). In mid-2005, TSD consultations were upgraded to full ministerial status and this was fully implemented when US Secretary of State Condoleezza Rice met with her Australian and Japanese counterparts in Sydney. On her way to Australia, Rice made it clear that she and Japanese Minister for Foreign Affairs Taro Aso 'shared concerns about

Australia's growing accommodation with China' and implied that the TSD could be employed as a balancing or containment mechanism directed against China (White 2017, p. 109; see also Terada 2013, p. 134). However, Australian efforts to soften this posture were successful and the inaugural TSD statement issued at the end of the Sydney meeting actually 'welcomed China's constructive engagement in the region'—a statement clearly designed to modify Chinese concerns about the TSD constituting a de facto 'mini-NATO' (Jain 2006).

The Sydney summit represented a benchmark in the Indo-Pacific's minilateral security politics, signalling that the TSD would gravitate towards primarily addressing non-traditional security issues such as humanitarian assistance and disaster relief, development politics, climate change and counter-terrorism. Nuclear non-proliferation issues such as the Korean peninsula's denuclearisation remained an important agenda item, but they were pursued in line with international norms created to address this problem. The 2018 joint statement released at the end of the TSD's eighth ministerial meeting was instructive in this regard:

> The Ministers reiterated that the international community needs to achieve the dismantlement of North Korea's weapons of mass destruction and ballistic missile programs in accordance with United Nations Security Council (UNSC) resolutions ... The Ministers called on all members of the international community to maintain pressure on the DPRK, including through the full implementation of UNSC resolutions.
>
> *(US Department of State 2018)*

'Traditional security' concerns were directed towards the South China Sea. But these were again expressed in the context of urging China to conform with established international law of the sea and to comply with the July 2016 Philippines-China arbitral tribunal's decision that China's island reclamation programme in those waters did not constitute Chinese sovereign territory. Much of the 2018 TSD joint statement was preoccupied with maritime security and safety in Southeast Asia and the Pacific Island countries, sustainable infrastructure throughout the Indo-Pacific, cyberspace security, and counter-terrorism. In 2019, the TSD summit declared that Australia, Japan and the United States would coordinate efforts to upgrade infrastructure efforts throughout the South Pacific. This was an obvious response to the substantial growth of the Chinese presence and development assistance efforts directed towards various South Pacific countries (Payne 2019; Sheridan 2019).

The Quadrilateral Security Initiative

Along with the TCOG and the TSD, the Quadrilateral Security Dialogue (QSD) (also known as the Quadrilateral Security Initiative) involving Australia, India, Japan and the United States unfolded as a third significant Indo-Pacific minilateral security project in 2007–8 and in a revised version during 2017. Japanese Prime Minister

Shinzo Abe spearheaded the original QSD with the support of his Australian and Indian counterparts, John Howard and Manmohan Singh, and the notably strong backing of US Vice-President Dick Cheney. A variety of factors drove this initiative, including Abe's long-standing infatuation with India as a natural 'democratic partner' for Japan, Australian fears of growing Chinese military capabilities and several influential studies in the United States envisioning the creation of a Concert of Democracies to preserve and promote liberal democratic systems throughout Eurasia and beyond (Daalder and Lindsay 2007; Slaughter and Ikenberry 2006). China anticipated this initiative even prior to an exploratory meeting between Australian, Indian, Japanese and US officials in May 2007 by protesting that Abe's rhetoric praising the idea of democracies in Asia uniting to plan their national security strategies and to conduct joint naval exercises such as Malabar was nothing more than the implementation of a full-fledged containment policy against itself (Madan 2017). Chinese pressure combined with domestic political developments in several QSD countries to affect the demise of this initiative: Abe's resignation in September 2007, the election of a QSD sceptic, Kevin Rudd, as Australia's new prime minister in November, and protests by various left-wing and nationalist Indian political factions against Singh's closure of a nuclear energy deal with the United States led to this version of the QSD dying a relatively quiet death.

However, low-key trilateral security dialogues were maintained and even expanded in the aftermath of the quadrilateral experiment (Madan 2017). An India–US–Japan trilateral was formed in 2011 and an Australia–India–Japan trilateral was created in 2015. These have been complemented by an intensification of bilateral and trilateral military exercises. Some strains in India–Australia bilateral relations, however, have been evident due to New Delhi's concerns about the growing intimacy of Sino-Australian economic relations, India's tendency to rank the importance of its bilateral relationship with Australia lower than the one that it cultivates with both the United States and Japan, and its exclusion of Australia in the annual Malabar naval exercises held in the Bay of Bengal (Australia's omission was due to Indian sensitivities about alienating China further in the aftermath of a 2017 skirmish involving Chinese and Indian forces in the Doklam border area between China and India) (Bachhawat 2018).

In November 2017, with Abe once again serving as Japan's prime minister and the Trump administration searching for ways to support and operationalise its support for his 'Free and Open Indo-Pacific' concept, senior officials from the original QSD countries met on the sidelines of the East Asia Summit in Manila. Each country released a separate statement outlining their interpretation of this consultation, with India downplaying specific references to freedom of navigation and overflight in deference to its sensitivity about not directly challenging Chinese interests in a post-Doklam context and Japan modulating its commentary on China's Belt and Road regional economic initiative. All four powers focused on the need to curtail North Korea's nuclear weapons programme, advancement of a rules-based order in the Indo-Pacific, strengthening counter-terrorism cooperation, and promoting democratic values in the region (Panda 2017).

Advocates of a QSD approach to the Indo-Pacific insist that it is not a replacement for the US post-war hub-and-spokes alliance system which has balanced Soviet and now Chinese hegemonic behaviour by offering formal security guarantees to its participant states nor a competitor to the notion of 'ASEAN centrality' as the basis for defining regional norms and managing regional order building. It is, they insist, just another offshoot which serves as a viable forum for discussion and coordination of like-minded states over issues that have been around for years (Envall and Hall 2016; Hall 2018, p. 13). Its future relevance, however, depends on the degree of common interests that are entertained and sustained by its member states.

Minilateral security politics: advantages and liabilities

Minilateral security politics in the Indo-Pacific can be regarded as a compromise—a 'satisficing' regional security strategy—implemented by the United States and its Indo-Pacific allies when the post-war US hub-and-spokes bilateral alliance network—also known as the San Francisco System—was viewed as becoming potentially outdated, and multilateral order building appeared too cumbersome to replace it. Cha's (2010) widely acclaimed work on 'powerplay strategy', for example, argues that the United States, as the region's senior ally, cultivated bilateral alliance relationships with less powerful regional security partners in order to exert greater asymmetrical control over them and to prevent them from entrapping it into conflicts it preferred to avoid. As the post-war era has evolved, however, economic and geopolitical changes in the Indo-Pacific meant that the initially sparse material resources or limited military capacities of Washington's bilateral allies were transformed into more formidable capabilities. By the late 1970s, US policymakers were pressuring their bilateral allied counterparts to contribute *greater* amounts to the San Francisco System's collective defence burden. Seventy-plus years into the post-war era, Trump during his presidential campaign directly linked the future of US forward defence commitments and force presence to Japanese and South Korean willingness to enhance their own defence and deterrence capabilities (Sevastopulo 2016). Concurrently, growing Chinese and North Korean nuclear weapons and delivery capacities have directly challenged the traditional US extended deterrence strategy and have shaken allied confidence about American strategic supremacy (Smith 2017).

Trump's decision to pull the United States out of the Trans-Pacific Partnership multilateral trade initiative graphically displayed his disdain for multilateral politico-economic order-building approaches and reinforced his scepticism for multilateral security institutions such as NATO. His decision to miss the 'Asian summit season' in 2018 (dispatching his Vice-President, Mike Pence, in his place) specifically reflected his frustration over ASEAN's adherence to advancing free trade negotiations through multilateral institutions and his growing scepticism about 'ASEAN centrality' as the key determinant to future regional order building. In late August 2019, the United States conducted its first joint maritime exercise with all ten

ASEAN members (after China had conducted three such exercises with ASEAN during 2018-19). The main significance of this development, however, was less about the United States projecting a confidence-building measure to assure the Southeast Asians about its continued force presence in the region, than about the latter signalling to China their own determination to keep what they perceive as an increasingly reluctant Trump administration strategically present and active in their region. Washington remains more comfortable in working with *selected* ASEAN members such as Vietnam, Singapore and Indonesia in identifying and oper-ationalising specific missions consistent with those favoured by a large offshore power than in directly countering Beijing at every turn (Heydarian 2019).

A major advantage of minilateralism, therefore, lies in its evident flexibility relative to its more unwieldy multilateral counterparts and more discriminate targeting of common strategic interests than bilateral alliance politics. In the Indo-Pacific, minilateralism's exclusivity retains some of the control to which Washington had become accustomed under the hub-and-spokes network, but still allows participants the means to prioritise their own interests relative to those of its security collaborator, the United States. In this context, 'minilateralism could prove more effective than multilateralism in responding to specific issues and move regional cooperation beyond the proverbial low-hanging fruits' (Teo 2018). Minilateralism may at least partially address intra-alliance tensions between the United States and its various allies emanating from the asymmetrical nature of hub-and-spokes bilateral alliances.

In minilateralism, an informal coalition of three security partners formed to address a specific security problem should ideally 'act like caucuses in a legis-lature' rather than confronting the danger of allied abandonment and entrapment if a specific conflict situation overwhelms the capacity for alliance unanimity on what a specific alliance treaty commitment actually means or how it should be specifically interpreted (Green 2014, p. 761). Preferably, minilateral security pol-itics can be viewed as a bridge-building tool which acts to complement and reinforce more formal and long-standing bilateral alliances. It encourages junior allies to selectively collaborate with each other in ways that would not be the case if the issue-areas where they discover that they share common interests must be suppressed or subordinated to the predominant interest orientation of the senior security partner.

As a minilateralism risk, security partners could at times be lured into interpret-ing priority issues defined in minilateral settings as the core business of formal alli-ance collaboration. Formal security allies would be ill-served to view minilateral coalitions as adequately replacing their longer-standing formal alliances or security institutions. Once those issues compelling minilateralism's application are addressed or resolved there may be little credible or enduring motivation for sustaining longer-term security or defence minilateral arrangements in view of long-term instruments for maintaining deterrence, power balancing and other strategies enabling a senior ally to protect and advance its own interests in the Indo-Pacific region.

A second risk in minilateral security politics relates to its latent political fragility. This is particularly subject to changes in the domestic politics of affiliate participant states. It is thus susceptible to being co-opted or 'morphed' into different postures supported by those states' successive leaderships. Abe's resignation as Japan's prime minister and Rudd's election as Australia's new leader in 2007 spelled the demise of the initial QSD while US President Barack Obama's 'rebalancing strategy' was dismantled by the implementation of Trump's 2016 campaign rhetoric which called for an exploration of Japan and South Korea financing and developing more self-reliant defence and deterrence postures. While US alliance commitments have indeed been maintained the prospects for new minilateral defence arrangements coming into being are currently remote unless America's Northeast Asian allies can implement far more significant self-defence postures in response to Trump's 'America First' stance. The future defence postures of Japan and South Korea may constitute a seminal test of minilateral security cooperation's viability in this regard, especially if those two states are unable to modify their incessant hostility over issues of history and trade.

Conclusion

The overall lesson of the minilateral security experience in the Indo-Pacific thus far is that these groupings seem to have functioned more effectively where cooperative interaction is prioritised as the main purpose for their creation. The 2004 Core Group experience, and the evolution of the TSD into a predominantly non-traditional security-oriented body, are illustrative. The Core Group involved four key Indo-Pacific powers—Australia, India, Japan and the United States— coalescing and coordinating disaster relief efforts in the aftermath of a massive tsunami that hit South and Southeast Asian countries in late December of that year. Together these four countries contributed over 40,000 military personnel and substantial levels of military equipment to carry out this very notable exercise of humanitarian assistance. Although the Core Group's formal framework was quickly dissolved (in early January 2005) in deference to the United Nations taking over assistance efforts, a significant precedent for non-traditional security cooperation among US allies and partners had been established. It proved to be a model that Australia, Japan and the United States adopted as the major rationale for TSD cooperation the following year, trumping the usual 'threat-centric' (that is, anti-China) calculus for traditional security collaboration (Grossman 2005).

This trend does not necessarily preclude minilateralism's relevance to more competitive situations but does indicate that a 'functional multilateralism' typology seems to have prevailed in the region since the end of the Cold War. On the other hand, the United States applying minilateral security politics to buttress alliances and coalitions or balance against other regional powers is more likely to occur if regional security dilemmas intensify or if US regional allies and powers are amenable to counter-measures to support American security interests and policies. Even under such conditions, however, US regional security allies such as Japan and South Korea, and any other ally or American security partner in the region, need to modify their ongoing animosities in ways that will enable minilateral approaches to be effective.

Mak (2004, p. 128) has presciently observed that both broader security cooperation and more constricted defence cooperation (such as minilateral coalitions) can be tailored in response to both conventional threat-centric and non-military threats from 'within or without' a state's sovereign territory. Issues that have motivated various forms of minilateral collaboration in the Indo-Pacific include nuclear non-proliferation and nuclear-free zone negotiations, humanitarian assistance and disaster relief coordination, and consultations on environmental hazards, pandemics, maritime security and forced peoples' movements. Minilateral interaction in the economics sector can likewise overlap in ways that have security implications. Both the China-Japan-South Korea Trilateral Summit (formed on the sidelines of the 1999 ASEAN Plus Three meeting in Manila) as well as various minilateral preferential trading agreements embodied within ASEAN (such as ASEAN Plus Three) and APEC exemplify precedents to and processes for trust building and cooperative security behaviour (see Aggarwal and Govella 2013, p. 8).

Minilateral defence cooperation is perhaps most relevant when generating 'second-order traditional security effects' that supplement existing bilateral security alliances such as the hub-and-spokes system (Cha 2003, pp. 117–18, emphasis in the original). However, this is not always the case. As noted above, the TCOG initiative represented an unsuccessful effort by Washington to combine the extended deterrence components of its bilateral alliances with Japan and South Korea, respectively, notwithstanding its basic mission to cultivate meaningful security policy coordination between Japan and South Korea on a specific and critical security issue in Northeast Asia (ibid.).

Ultimately, American-led minilateral security politics in the Indo-Pacific can be viewed as having reached an important crossroads. Functional minilateralism has accrued a relatively positive track record in the region as evidenced by the Core Group and TSD episodes. Efforts incorporating regional minilateralism have been mixed in the economic sector with some spillover into security politics occurring in an APEC summit context but with the Trans-Pacific Partnership initiative proving less efficacious. Informal multilateralism such as the Six-Party Talks to denuclearise the Korean peninsula or to implement a 'code of conduct' in the South China Sea has fallen short. Elite multilateralism—mainly pursued by the United States—and regional minilateralism in which formal US alliance politics has been complemented by minilateral projects addressing issues such as smart defence collaboration and intra-alliance force interoperability have dovetailed logically in some instances. Yet elite minilateralism in this part of the world has failed to produce the type of arms control, order-building norm identification or other breakthroughs in strategic reassurance that were successfully realised in Europe towards the end of the Cold War. Certainly, the US hub-and-spokes alliance system will be more subject to challenge as a result of the domestic political trends now unfolding in South Korea, the Philippines and Thailand. Informal security collaborators such as India, Singapore and Vietnam have simultaneously become more important for the United States to pursue its regional interests at a time when China is growing stronger. It remains to be seen whether minilateralism's flexibility and bridge-building properties will be enough to complement or even supplant either bilateralism or multilateralism as the region's predominant mode of security organisation in the near future or beyond.

References

Aggarwal, VK and Govella, K 2013, 'The trade-security nexus in the Asia-Pacific', in VK Aggarwal and K Govella (eds), *Linking Trade and Security: Evolving Institutions and Strategies in Asia, Europe and the United States*, New York, Springer Science, pp. 1–22.

Bachhawat, A 2018, 'India still wary of the Quad amid its own China "reset"', *ASPI The Strategist*, 24 August, www.aspistrategist.org.au/india-still-wary-of-the-quad-amid-its-own -china-reset/.

Baker, JA 1991, 'America in Asia: emerging architecture for a Pacific community', *Foreign Affairs*, vol. 70, no. 5, pp. 1–18.

Brandi, C, Berger, A and Bruhn, D 2015, 'Between minilateralism and multilateralism: opportunities and risks of pioneer alliances in international trade and climate politics', *Briefing Paper*, 16/2015, Bonn, German Development Institute, www.die-gdi.de/en/ briefing-paper/article/between-minilateralism-and-multilateralism-opportunities-and-risks -of-pioneer-alliances-in-international-trade-and-climate-politics/.

Brummer, C 2014, *Minilateralism: How Trade Alliances, Soft Law and Financial Engineering Are Redefining Economic Statecraft*, Cambridge, Cambridge University Press.

Cha, V 2003, 'The dilemma of regional security in East Asia: multilateralism versus bilateralism', in PF Diehl and J Lepgold (eds), *Regional Conflict Management*, Lanham, MD, Rowman & Littlefield, pp. 104–122.

Cha, V 2010, 'Powerplay: origins of the US alliance system in Asia', *International Security*, vol. 34, no. 3, pp. 158–196.

Daalder, I and Lindsay, J 2007, 'Democracies of the world, unite', *Brookings Institution*, 1 January, www.brookings.edu/articles/democracies-of-the-world-unite/.

Envall, HDP and Hall, I 2016, 'Asian strategic partnerships: new practices and regional security governance', *Asian Politics & Policy*, vol. 8, no. 1, pp. 87–105.

Green, MJ 2014, 'Strategic Asian triangles', in S Pekkanen, J Ravenhill and R Foot (eds), *The Oxford Handbook of the International Relations of Asia*, New York, Oxford University Press, pp. 758–774.

Grossman, M 2005, 'The tsunami core group: a step toward a transformed diplomacy and beyond', *Security Challenges*, vol. 1, no. 1, pp. 11–14.

Haass, R 2010, 'The case for messy multilateralism', *Financial Times*, 6 January.

Hall, I 2018, 'Meeting the challenge: the case for the Quad', in A Carr (ed.), *Debating the Quad*, Centre of Gravity series, paper 39, Canberra, Strategic and Defence Studies Centre, pp. 12–15.

Hampson, FO and Heinbeker, P 2011, 'The "new" multilateralism of the twenty-first century', *Global Governance*, vol. 17, no. 3, pp. 299–310.

Heginbotham, E and Samuels, R 2019, 'With friends like these: Japan-ROK cooperation and US policy', *The Asan Forum*, vol. 7, no. 1, www.theasanforum.org/with-friends-like- these-japan-rok-cooperation-and-us-policy/#5.

Hemmer, C and Katzenstein, PJ 2002, 'Why is there no NATO in Asia? Collective identity, regionalism, and the origins of multilateralism', *International Organization*, vol. 56, no. 3, pp. 575–607.

Heydarian, R 2019, 'Heavy traffic in the South China Sea: US vies with China in joint naval drills with ASEAN members', *South China Morning Post*, 7 September.

Jain, P 2006, 'A "little NATO" against China', *Asia Times*, 18 March.

Kang, SN 2013, *The incomplete journey of US-ROK-Japan trilateral cooperation: the establishment and dissolution of the Trilateral Coordination and Oversight Group (TCOG)*, Master's thesis, Graduate School of International Studies, Seoul National University.

Lee, CM 2018, 'Prospects for US-South Korean-Japanese trilateral security cooperation in an era of unprecedented threats and evolving political forces', Report prepared for the Atlantic Council, sponsored by the Korea Foundation, December, www.atlanticcouncil. org/images/publications/Prospects_for_US-South_Korean-Japanese_Trilateral_Security_ Cooperation.pdf.

Lind, J 2019, 'The Japan-South Korea dispute isn't just about the past', *Washington Post*, 30 August.

Madan, T 2017, 'The rise, fall, and rebirth of the "Quad"', *War on the Rocks*, 16 November, https://warontherocks.com/2017/11/rise-fall-rebirth-quad/.

Mak, JN 2004, 'Malaysian defense and security cooperation: coming out of the closet', in A Acharya and SS Tan (eds), *Asia-Pacific Security Cooperation: National Interests and Regional Order*, Abingdon, Routledge, pp. 127–153.

Moret, E 2016, 'Effective minilateralism for the EU: what, when and how?' *EUISS Brief*, no. 17, www.iss.europa.eu/sites/default/files/EUISSFiles/Brief_17_Minilateralism.pdf.

Naim, M 2009, 'Minilateralism: the magic number to get real international action', *Foreign Policy*, 21 June, https://foreignpolicy.com/2009/06/21/minilateralism/.

New York Times 2018, 'Read Jim Mattis's letter to Trump: full text', 20 December.

Panda, A 2017, 'US, Japan, India, and Australia Hold working-level quadrilateral meeting on regional cooperation', *The Diplomat*, 13 November, https://thediplomat.com/2017/11/u s-japan-india-and-australia-hold-working-level-quadrilateral-meeting-on-regional-cooper ation/.

Patrick, S 2014, 'The unruled world', *Foreign Affairs*, vol. 57, no. 1, pp. 58–73.

Payne, M 2019, 'Trilateral Strategic Dialogue Joint Ministerial Statement', Australian Minister for Foreign Affairs, 2 August, www.foreignminister.gov.au/minister/marise-payne/m edia-release/trilateral-strategic-dialogue-joint-ministerial-statement.

Richardson, L 2019, 'Japan and South Korea's diplomatic dispute doesn't need US mediation', *The Interpreter*, 13 August, www.lowyinstitute.org/the-interpreter/japan-and-south-korea -s-diplomatic-dispute-doesn-t-need-us-mediation.

Sevastopulo, D 2016, 'Donald Trump open to Japan and South Korea having nuclear weapons', *Financial Times*, 26 March.

Sheridan, G 2019, 'Allies swing in behind Morrison's South Pacific plan', *The Australian*, 3 August.

Silverberg, E and Park, AI 2019, 'Japan vs. South Korea: Can America save the day?' *The National Interest*, 3 September, https://nationalinterest.org/blog/korea-watch/japan-vs-sou th-korea-can-america-save-day-77726.

Slaughter, A and Ikenberry, GJ (co-directors) 2006, *Forging a World of Liberty under Law: US National Security in the 21st Century: Final Report of the Princeton Project on National Security*, Princeton, NJ, Woodrow Wilson School of Public and International Affairs, Princeton University.

Smith, SA 2017, 'Uncertainty among US allies in Northeast Asia', *Council on Foreign Relations Brief*, 8 May, www.cfr.org/expert-brief/uncertainty-among-us-allies-northeast-asia.

Teo, S 2018, 'Could minilateralism be multilateralism's best hope in the Asia Pacific?' *The Diplomat*, 15 December, https://thediplomat.com/2018/12/could-minilateralism-be-multilateralisms-best-hope-in-the-asia-pacific/.

Terada, T 2013, 'Australia and China's rise: ambivalent and inevitable balancing', *Journal of Contemporary East Asia Studies*, vol. 2, no. 2, pp. 129–145.

Tow, WT 2017, '"Contingent trilateralism": applications for the Trilateral Security Dialogue', in WT Tow, MJ Thomson, Y Yamamoto and SP Limaye (eds), *Asia-Pacific Security: US, Australia and Japan and the New Security Triangle*, Abingdon, Routledge, pp. 23–38.

Tow, WT 2018, 'Minilateral security's relevance to US strategy in the Indo-Pacific: challenges and prospects', *Pacific Review*, vol. 32, no. 2, pp. 232–244.

US Department of State 2018, 'Australia–Japan–United States Trilateral Strategic Dialogue Joint Ministerial Statement', media note, Washington, DC, Office of the Spokesperson, 5 August, www.state.gov/australia-japan-united-states-trilateral-strategic-dialogue-joint-ministerial-statement/.

White, H 2017, 'Trilateralism and Australia: Australia and the Trilateral Strategic Dialogue with America and Japan', in WT Tow, MJ Thomson, Y Yamamoto and SP Limaye (eds), *Asia-Pacific Security: US, Australia and Japan and the New Security Triangle*, Abingdon, Routledge, pp. 101-11.

2

THE QUADRILATERAL SECURITY DIALOGUE AND INDO-PACIFIC MINILATERALISM

Resurrection without renewal?

Andrew O'Neil and Lucy West

Introduction

In this chapter, we examine the Quadrilateral Security Dialogue (QSD)—referred to colloquially as the Quad—from its inception in 2007 up until the most recent meeting of members in May 2019. Recent analyses of the QSD's re-emergence in 2017 have tended to stress its potential role as a bulwark against Chinese assertiveness in the Indo-Pacific and as a force for promoting democracy in the region. In remarks to the Shangri-La Dialogue in 2018, former US Defense Secretary James Mattis characterised the QSD as 'an idea absolutely fit for its time' (US Department of Defense 2018). Others have gone further with one analyst arguing that 'the Quad's most important potential advantage is its geopolitical configuration as a grouping of militarily capable powers on and near the Eurasian littoral that could coordinate national strategies that could prevent the emergence of Chinese regional hegemony' (Tarapore 2018).

We argue in this chapter that although the resurrection of the QSD in late 2017 after a decade-long hiatus confirms that the United States, India, Japan and Australia believe that the initiative retains potential as a geostrategic factor in the Indo-Pacific, there are few signs of a genuine renewal of purpose. In contrast to the optimistic tenor of recent commentary, this chapter demonstrates that while there is a convergence of strategic interests among the four parties, there is little evidence of coherent strategic intent among them. As Nilsson-Wright (2017, p. 20) notes, the twin challenges of a more assertive China and concerns over the depth of the Donald Trump administration's commitment to the Indo-Pacific have united Australia, India, and Japan in seeking a reboot of the QSD. For the Trump administration, the QSD aligns with its increasingly muscular approach to China and its enthusiastic embrace of the Indo-Pacific as a geostrategic template for pressing America's attempts to maintain its dominant presence in the face of a concerted challenge from Beijing.[1]

Despite this convergence of convenience between the four parties, questions remain about the QSD's unity of purpose. This has been exemplified by the absence of unified declarations following the QSD's 2017 and 2018 meetings held on the sidelines of the Association of Southeast Asian Nations (ASEAN) summits in Manila (Philippines) and Singapore, respectively. Tellingly, although individual statements released by Australia, India, Japan and the United States draw attention to the importance of an open and free Indo-Pacific, they overlapped on few points of detail (Gale and Shearer 2018). Following the 2018 meeting, Canberra, Tokyo and Washington endorsed a greater focus on enhancing regional security and underscored the preservation of a 'rules-based order', while New Delhi instead chose to emphasise 'the increasingly inter-connected Indo-Pacific region that the four countries share with each other and with other partners' (Panda 2018). Apart from basic points of priority focus, there is also disagreement concerning procedural priorities. As Smith (2019) noted after the 2018 meeting, 'whereas Canberra, Tokyo and Washington have signalled their interest in promoting the dialogue to the level of minister/cabinet secretary, Delhi has been clear that it prefers to keep it at the level of joint/assistant secretary'.

The QSD is frequently identified as a prominent example of minilateral cooperation, in which 'a small group of interested parties work together to supplement or complement the activities of international organisations in tackling subjects deemed too complicated to be addressed appropriately at the multilateral level' (Moret 2016). In the realm of political economy, as one expert has argued, 'minilateralism is a response to a growing recognition that large-scale multilateral agreements … have all seen deadlines missed and policy execution stalled' (Higgott 2012, p. 26). The appeal of minilateralism has also been evident in the security domain. The acceleration of various groupings outside formal alliances has witnessed the creation of coalitions of the willing and a range of trilateral security partnerships that have proliferated in the Indo-Pacific since the 1990s. As one analyst has recently observed with respect to multilateral security, 'minilateralism's appeal relates to its inherent flexibility, relatively low transaction costs and voluntary rather than mandatory kinds of commitment ordained by major power affiliates' (Tow 2018, p. 6). In the Indo-Pacific at least, the QSD is seen as an archetypal minilateral arrangement; for good or ill, its trajectory will shape future perceptions about the utility or otherwise of minilateralism for managing security challenges in the region.

In this chapter, we challenge optimistic interpretations of the QSD's potential on two grounds. First, despite its heralded revival, the arrangement continues to lack essential unity of purpose. Second, the QSD will remain a very distant second to US alliances in the region and, indeed, to existing trilateral arrangements, most notably (though not exclusively) the US-Japan-Australia Trilateral Strategic Dialogue (TSD). By way of establishing background and context, the chapter first examines the Indo-Pacific concept, before further tracing the rise of minilateralism and the rationale underpinning these arrangements. The third section examines the QSD initiative in more detail—its origins, demise and revival. The final section of the chapter discusses the future prospects of the QSD with particular reference to its unity of purpose.

From Asia Pacific to Indo-Pacific

Since the late 1980s, most governments have used the descriptor 'Asia Pacific' to conceptualise Asian regionalism. The term has denoted the states of North and Southeast Asia and other key countries located around the Pacific Rim that share a range of economic, security and institutional linkages. However, over the last decade, a number of governments—most notably Japan, Australia, India and the United States—have increasingly adopted the term 'Indo-Pacific' to conceptualise Asian regionalism and security arrangements (Birtles 2018).[2] The shift reflects the 'merging' of South Asia and the Asia Pacific, which have previously been seen as separate regions. This modified strategic outlook recognises an increasing number of interactions, strategic concerns and interdependencies that traverse the Indian and Pacific Oceans from East Africa to Oceania (Wilson 2018, pp. 177–8). As one of the leading proponents of the Indo-Pacific has written, 'the Indo-Pacific concept underscores the fact that the Indian Ocean has replaced the Atlantic as the globe's busiest and most strategically significant trade corridor, carrying two-thirds of global oil shipments and a third of bulk cargo' (Medcalf 2015).

Wilson (2018) suggests that this 're-scaling' of the Asian region is indicative of a more fundamental shift in the drivers of regionalism. Previous conceptions of the Asia Pacific, best exemplified by the Asia-Pacific Economic Cooperation (APEC) forum, were mainly concerned with trade liberalisation and economic integration. However, the shift to an Indo-Pacific conception represents movement towards a more explicitly security-based regionalism. This shift has been encouraged by the emergence of India and Japan as more prominent security actors (especially in projecting naval power projection), a more assertive Beijing (including growing Chinese penetration into the Indian Ocean), maritime disputes in the South China Sea that links the Pacific and Indian Oceans, and intensified Sino-US rivalry (ibid., p. 178). One of the most important considerations is the protection of sea lines of communication and transport from the Indian Ocean Rim to East Asia, especially from the Gulf of Aden and Persian Gulf. This includes protection from non-traditional security threats such as piracy, terrorism and natural disasters as well as 'conventional risks arising from India and China's naval modernisation to territorial disputes in the South China Sea' (ibid., p. 181).

The origin of the Indo-Pacific concept is usually traced to the landmark 'Con-fluence of the Two Seas' speech by Japanese Prime Minister Shinzo Abe to India's parliament during his first term of office in 2007. In this speech Abe linked the two maritime spaces, arguing for a concept of 'broader Asia' covering the entire southern and eastern Eurasian littoral (Ministry of Foreign Affairs of Japan 2007). US Secretary of State Hillary Clinton subsequently adopted the Indo-Pacific fra-mework in 2010, which featured prominently in the US pivot to the region announced by President Barack Obama in 2011 (Medcalf 2015). In 2012, then

Indian Prime Minister Manmohan Singh invoked the term on a number of occasions to seek closer Indian ties with ASEAN. Australia has arguably gone the furthest in institutionalising the term in its strategic policy guidance, most recently in the 2016 Defence White Paper and the 2017 Foreign Policy White Paper (Department of Defence, Australian Government 2016; Department of Foreign Affairs and Trade, Australian Government 2017).

For Australia, the Indo-Pacific concept reflects its unique two-ocean geography while providing a conceptual frame for expanding security ties beyond the US 'hub-and-spokes' alliance system to include India. The Indo-Pacific concept recognises the strategic interests shared by Australia and India in maintaining open sea lines of communication, retaining a robust US security (especially naval) presence in the Indian Ocean, and hedging against Beijing's Belt and Road Initiative (BRI) and the People's Liberation Army (PLA) Navy's widening military base footprint. The latter is especially important for the PLA's ability 'to extend its naval combat reach into the Indian Ocean and fulfil its two-ocean strategy encompassing the western Pacific and the northern Indian Ocean' (Ji 2016, p. 12). In the event of intensified Sino-US strategic rivalry, Australia would potentially assume an important role for Washington in allowing troops and equipment to be deployed between the two oceans without having to pass through the Malacca Strait chokepoint in the South China Sea (Yang 2016, p. 2).

For India, as a self-consciously rising power and aspiring peer competitor with China, the benefits of the Indo-Pacific concept are self-evident in that it privileges India's status as a regional power in a way that the Asia Pacific does not. It links India more explicitly with the world's most dynamic region and allows a range of foreign policy initiatives that give substance to its 1991 Look East Policy (LEP) and Prime Minister Narendra Modi's more recent renewal of this idea in the form of the Act East Policy, which was inaugurated at the India-ASEAN summit in Myanmar in November 2014 (Yadav 2016, p. 52). Since the LEP was promulgated, India has joined many ASEAN-led regional arrangements, including the ASEAN Regional Forum (ARF), the ASEAN Defence Ministers' Meeting-Plus, the ASEAN-India Annual Summit and the East Asia Summit (EAS) (ibid., pp. 51–2). Japan was reportedly instrumental in gaining India's entry to the EAS in the face of Chinese opposition (Sharma 2010, p. 238).

Minilateralism in the Indo-Pacific

Minilateralism, predominantly in the form of trilateral security dialogues, has been growing steadily in the Indo-Pacific over the past decade. Lee-Brown (2018, p. 164) argues that the institutionalisation of arrangements between Washington, Tokyo, New Delhi and Canberra has been designed to give substance to the Indo-Pacific strategic framework. These trilateral arrangements are intended to supplement the traditional US bilateral alliance structure in a context whereby member states regard extant multilateral security arrangements as either underdeveloped or unsuited to prosecuting their core security concerns. In what Silove (2016, p. 78) has described as 'the pivot before the pivot', the George W. Bush administration undertook a military-diplomatic reorientation towards the region in 2004 with the overriding purpose of pre-empting a concerted challenge from China for strategic superiority in Asia. A key component in this strategy was a decision by Washington to approve 'unprecedented measures to lay the foundations of enhancing inter-operability among its allies and partners in Asia by encouraging them to forge new formal security relationships with one another' (Silove 2016, p. 78).

In March 2006, the US-Japan-Australia TSD—instituted in 2002—was upgraded to ministerial level. The United States sought more coordination and assistance in the 'war on terror' and in dealing with transnational security issues, whereas for Japan and Australia it was another way of deepening US strategic commitment to the region in which post-9/11 much of Washington's attention was focused on the Middle East. This trilateral relationship has become closer since 2006 with increasing policy coordination and functional cooperation across the Indo-Pacific (Cooper 2018). As China's military capabilities have expanded to complement its economic reach, the TSD has taken on a new level of importance for Washington, Tokyo and Canberra and in many respects was the critical precursor to the advent of the QSD in 2007 (Satake and Hemmings 2018).

The upgrading of the US-Japan-Australia trilateral arrangement in 2006 was followed in December 2011 by the establishment of the US-India-Japan trilateral dialogue at the senior officer level. This was also upgraded to ministerial level in September 2015. The purpose of this grouping was to uphold international law and to promote peaceful dispute settlement, freedom of navigation and unimpeded commerce in the Indo-Pacific (Lee-Brown 2018, p. 171). India, in contrast to China, 'champions the use of international arbitration to settle disputes', and in 2014 accepted a verdict by the Permanent Court of Arbitration that ruled against New Delhi in a 40-year-old maritime dispute with Bangladesh (Lee 2016, p. 27). This trilateral grouping has also been considered instrumental in cementing the bilateral ties between these governments and quadrilateral ties with Australia, which are considered in the following section. The US-Japan-India trilateral arrangement has been viewed as a major initiative in Indo-Pacific strategic affairs—as a counterweight to China's influence and as a means of keeping the United States deeply engaged in the Indo-Pacific by demonstrating that other significant regional powers are willing and able to share the burden with Washington.

One of the latest initiatives in minilateralism is the India-Australia-Japan trilateral security dialogue. This was established at a Department Secretary-level meeting in June 2015 between Australia (Peter Varghese), India (Subrahmanyam Jaishankar) and Japan (Akitaka Saiki) (Lang 2015, pp. 1, 8). This was the first such security dialogue between the three countries since then Australian Prime Minister Kevin Rudd decided in 2008 not to pursue the QSD. The reconvening of a trilateral dialogue in 2015 was seen as a collective response to the challenges posed by China's rise and greater assertiveness. In 2015, there was also considered to be a strong personal chemistry between the three conservative and nationalistic leaders, Abe, Modi and Prime Minister Tony Abbott. Moreover, there has been a growing affinity between Japan and India as the largest and most durable Asian democracies, which has become progressively stronger since Abe's speech to the Indian parliament in 2007.

The quadrilateral initiative

A potential quadrilateral security partnership was foreshadowed as early as 2004, when the maritime forces of the United States, Australia, India and Japan undertook coordinated humanitarian assistance and disaster relief operations following the Indian Ocean tsunami (Chanlett-Avery and Vaughn 2008, p. 3). Japan had been looking to court India as a counterweight to Beijing, and a strategic partnership was negotiated in 2006 during Abe's first year in office (Brewster 2010, p. 2). In September 2014, this was upgraded to a Special Strategic and Global Partnership. Japan was also the first of the four states to foreshadow quadrilateral security cooperation during Abe's 2007 speech to the Indian parliament. This was supported in statements at the time by then US Vice-President Dick Cheney. Ministry of Foreign Affairs officials from the four countries met for an exploratory meeting on the margins of the ARF in Manila in May 2007 (Chanlett-Avery and Vaughn 2008, p. 3). This was followed in August 2007 by trilateral naval exercises between the United States, India and Japan in the Western Pacific. Furthermore, in September of that year, the annual Malabar exercises in the Bay of Bengal between the United States and India (that had been held since 1994) were expanded to include Japan, Australia and Singapore. These developments were met with a formal diplomatic protest from Beijing, with Chinese officials alleging that the newly established 'Quad' was an endeavour to establish an 'Asian NATO [North Atlantic Treaty Organization]' to contain China (Ali 2007).

However, by the end of 2007, momentum for the quadrilateral initiative had stalled. There was growing opposition in New Delhi to any perceived alignment with Washington that might draw India into East Asian conflicts. In addition, there were concerns within the US government that the initiative was unnecessarily provocative to China. Although the QSD had initially attracted strong support from the Pentagon, the White House and the State Department, key Bush administration officials began expressing unease privately about the deleterious impact of the initiative on Sino–US relations (Satake and Hemmings 2018, p. 827). While growing US ambivalence was important in explaining the QSD's loss of momentum, two additional factors ultimately sealed its fate in 2008. The first was Abe's resignation from office in September 2007. In many respects, Abe had been the conceptual architect and driving force behind the initial rise of the QSD, which itself had articulated the increasing Japanese bilateral strategic engagement with India and Australia that complemented Tokyo's deeper involvement in the military dimension of its alliance with the United States. The second factor was the newly elected Rudd government's decision to announce Australia's withdrawal from the QSD in 2008 in what many identified as evidence of Australian bandwagoning with China (Manicom and O'Neil 2010, p. 36).

Despite this, however, Australia maintained its commitment to the TSD with the United States and Japan and continued to develop closer bilateral strategic ties with Tokyo and New Delhi. A Joint Declaration of Security Cooperation was concluded between Canberra and New Delhi during Rudd's visit to India in November 2009. This followed earlier similar declarations with Japan (2007) and South Korea (2009). The Australia-India strategic relationship acquired significant momentum when Modi came to power in 2014 and visited Australia after the G20 summit in November. During this visit the 2009 Joint Declaration was upgraded to a Framework for Security Cooperation, which instituted annual ministerial meetings, maritime exercises and joint military training, defence technology sharing, and cooperation on transnational security issues (Lang 2015, pp. 7–8).

Japan-India ties were also upgraded during a visit by Modi to Tokyo in 2016, which was reflected in the Free and Open Indo-Pacific Strategy outlined in Japan's 2017 Diplomatic Bluebook (Thankachan 2017, pp. 84–5). This was injected with additional substance by the creation of the Asia-Africa Growth Corridor. Seen as Japan's response to the BRI, this 'mega-regional' project is dedicated to increasing connectivity between the two continents through technology improvement, infrastructure projects, trade promotion, and human resource development (Prakash 2018). Reports suggest that Japan is already funding large-scale infrastructure projects such as port facilities upgrades and development in Mozambique, Kenya, Madagascar, Iran, Sri Lanka, Myanmar, Cambodia and West Java, Indonesia. Some of these are in direct competition with China. In Sri Lanka, for example, the Japanese-funded Galle port at the south of the island is located only 118 kilometres from the Chinese-funded Hambantota port (Thankachan 2017, p. 87). In addition, Japan has become a permanent participant in the annual US-India Malabar naval exercises while Australia has yet to be brought back into the fold since its 2008 repudiation of the QSD (Doornbos 2018; Haidar and Peri 2019).

A major step towards closer US-India relations was the conclusion of the so-called 123 Nuclear Agreement in 2007, whereby Washington recognised New Delhi as a de facto nuclear state, thus opening channels for greater bilateral cooperation (Brewster 2010, p. 2). Since then, US policymakers have viewed New Delhi as a critical strategic partner, rather than through the prism of nuclear nonproliferation. This change of orientation towards India has been driven by the rise of China, energy security issues, radical Islam and the 'war on terror', and by 'a de-linking of the U.S.-Pakistan relationship from the U.S.-India relationship' (Chanlett-Avery and Vaughn 2008, p. 8).

The recent revival of the QSD was triggered by the return of Abe to the prime ministership of Japan in 2012. Shortly after returning to office, Abe (2012) wrote an essay promoting a 'democratic Asian security diamond' to forestall Chinese 'coercion'. The proposal endorsed the view that the United States, Japan, Australia and India should cooperate to 'safeguard the maritime commons stretching from the Indian Ocean region to the western Pacific'. While Japan and Australia have formal alliances with Washington and close relationships with one another, the position of India is more ambiguous due to its history of non-alignment and its contemporary foreign policy doctrine of 'strategic autonomy'. However, by 2017, Japan and India had established 2+2 (defence and foreign ministers) meetings and upgraded their relationship to a 'Special Strategic and Global Partnership' (Wilson 2018, p. 183).

India's threat perception regarding China has increased in the decade since the QSD was first initiated, pushing it closer to Washington and US allies in Asia. Growing PLA naval deployments in the Indian Ocean and the rapid modernisation of China's nuclear weapons programme, including its sea-launched ballistic missile capabilities, has exercised Indian planners and provoked a greater emphasis on the link between national strategy and maritime force projection (Roy-Chaudhury and Sullivan de Estrada 2018, p. 184). This has been further underscored by India's 'primarily economics-driven emergence that has seen a marked increase in trade flows and a growing dependence on the transport of energy and raw materials, both of which depend primarily on sea lines of communication' (ibid.). These concerns have been overlaid by India's apprehension regarding the strategic reach of China's BRI. Central to this is the so-called China-Pakistan Economic Corridor, the defining feature of which is Beijing's development of the strategically vital Gwadar port, a deep-sea hub in Pakistan's southwest province of Balochistan. While ostensibly designed 'to enable the movement of Chinese goods from China's western provinces to the Arabian Sea by way of the Indian Ocean', once completed, the Gwadar port development will potentially yield a critical basing option for the PLA to project power into the Indian Ocean (Baruah 2018).

Australia's concerns over China's strategic posture in the Indo-Pacific have been reinforced by revelations of interference by Beijing in Australian domestic affairs. Disclosures of the Chinese Communist Party's (CCP) influence in Australia have included attempts to bribe high-level officials, pressure for Chinese language media outlets to toe the line on key issues, the monitoring of Chinese students in Australian universities, and the recruitment of sympathetic advocates to articulate the CCP's position in media outlets.[3] Recent Australian governments have been vocal in reaffirming their commitment to a rules-based international order when criticising China's militarisation activities in the South China Sea and advocating freedom of navigation throughout the Indo-Pacific. Public pushback by Canberra against Beijing has occurred despite the fact that China has never been more important to Australia in economic terms, a fact that Chinese authorities routinely cite. For Australia, concerns over China's overt militarisation activities in the South China Sea and domestic interference revelations have coalesced to create a more permissive environment for participating in minilateral security initiatives including the QSD. The latter has the support of the opposition Australian Labor Party (ALP) as well as the current Liberal-National Party coalition government.[4] This is a significant change in the ALP's stance given the Rudd government's reluctance to commit Australia to the initiative a decade ago.

For the United States, returning to the QSD after a 10-year hiatus dovetails with the Trump administration's preference for more explicit strategic competition with Beijing, not just in the strategic arena but also in the economic domain. Washington's continuation of naval and air freedom of navigation operations in the South China Sea and the Trump administration's appetite for zero-sum confrontation with Beijing over trade, signals a renewed determination by the United States to contain Chinese great power ambitions. While President Trump is less focused than his predecessors on promoting the idea of a concert of democracies in the Indo-Pacific, the QSD aligns with the president's disdain for large-scale multilateralism and his fixation on burden sharing with allies and security partners. Perhaps more importantly, the QSD maps closely to the Pentagon's vision of developing America's Indo-Pacific alliances and partnerships 'into a networked security architecture capable of deterring aggression, maintaining stability, and ensuring free access to common domains' (Mattis 2018).

Since being resurrected in 2017, QSD ministers of foreign affairs have met on the sidelines of ASEAN Summit meetings, while their respective naval chiefs have met regularly at the annual Raisina Dialogue in India. As noted in the introduction to this chapter, these meetings have not yielded a unified QSD vision statement or communiqué, and although the separate statements released by each party have overlapped in some areas, they remained in many respects quite distinctive in tone and substance. In one of only a handful of public references to the QSD by a senior official from any of the four parties, in May 2018 Australia's former Minister for Foreign Affairs Julie Bishop (quoted in Padmanabhat 2018) captured the QSD's seemingly modest vision:

> Australia already has a trilateral strategic dialogue with the U.S. and Japan, while the U.S. and Japan and India have their established meeting. I think the Quad is a natural extension of these mini-lateral relationships. It's just one of the many ways in which Australia will seek to engage with partners that help shape our region at a time of geostrategic and technological and economic change. So, like many other groupings in the region, if the Quad is established at a higher level, it will allow our four nations to discuss all matters of common interest, as we do in other regional groupings. It's obviously something to which Australia is committed, and I believe it's a bipartisan approach towards the Quadrilateral.

It is unclear whether QSD parties have agreed on a procedural roadmap to take the initiative forward beyond annual meetings on the sidelines of the ASEAN Summit and the Raisina Dialogue. The absence of any progress at the operational level of cooperation could betray a broader lack of enthusiasm, but it may also mirror a preference among the parties, particularly India, to maintain a low profile with respect to specific QSD initiatives. Whatever the case, the absence of detail and rhetorical reticence surrounding the QSD provide a flimsy foundation for meaningful action.

Resurrection without renewal?

Lee (2016) argues that any formal QSD arrangement would be opposed by ASEAN, which still sees itself as the driving force in Asian regionalism. ASEAN member states are unified in not wanting to be displaced from this role and explicit reference to ASEAN's centrality was the one feature that united all four statements by the QSD foreign ministries following the 2018 Singapore meeting (Garekar 2018). ASEAN is concerned that a new multilateral grouping could potentially undermine its centrality and unity in the region and be used as a form of 'soft-containment' of China (Choong 2018). Formal arrangements that include the United States and its treaty allies are also likely to be opposed by important foreign policy constituencies in India, which remain suspicious of Washington and its perceived unreliability as a security partner. A formal arrangement would also antagonise China. Beijing would probably increase pressure on India's northern border and move to tighten ties with India's neighbours, thus increasing New Delhi's security concerns (Malik 2016, pp. 53–4).

Given the QSD's record, there are serious doubts about whether it can be sustained despite the strong motivating factors for the parties to act in concert on core issues. Notwithstanding the commitment of QSD parties to curb China's strategic footprint in the Indo–Pacific, as Bisley (2018) notes 'there is not a single vital national interest that all four share'. Perhaps tellingly, in contrast to 2007, the resurrection of the QSD in 2017 has attracted little evident concern on the part of Beijing. This reflects China's broader reaction to US-led minilateral initiatives, as distinct from specific initiatives taken as part of US bilateral security alliances, which tend to elicit vocal condemnation from China. This may well mirror a view in Beijing that underlying divisions between US allies will prevent an Asian NATO from emerging and that most if not all American allies in the region (and those not allied to the United States such as India and Indonesia) will shy away from formal multilateral security commitments because of their acute dependence on Chinese trade and investment (Wuthnow 2018, p. 2).

The major question mark hanging over the QSD is the degree and depth of India's commitment. There appears to be little chance of Indian entrapment by the QSD. To date there are no signs to suggest that India would act outside the Indian Ocean in support of other QSD members against China in the South China Sea or the Western Pacific. Although, as outlined above, India shares significant concerns about China's muscular projection of military and economic power in the Indo–Pacific, policymakers in New Delhi are nonetheless cautious about alienating Beijing. Beijing's assertiveness was articulated in a June 2018 editorial by the *Global Times*—the CCP's mouthpiece—in response to India obtaining access to Sumatra's Sabang Port. New Delhi was advised not to 'wrongfully entrap itself into a strategic competition with China and eventually burn its own fingers' (quoted in Hodge 2018).[5]

In contrast to the US, Japanese and Australian statements, in its statement following the November 2017 QSD meeting, India 'omitted any reference to freedom of navigation and overflight, respect for international law or maritime security' (Gale and Shearer 2018). At the Shangri-La Dialogue in June 2018, Modi's keynote speech emphasised 'multi-alignment' and noted that 'India does not see the Indo-Pacific Region as a strategy or as a club of limited members' (Ministry of External Affairs, Government of India 2018). During his speech Modi made no reference to the QSD and there was also no direct criticism of Beijing. During the September 2018 India–US 2+2 ministerial dialogue Indian Minister of External Affairs Sushma Swaraj (quoted in Bagchi 2018) stated that: 'We see the Indo-Pacific as a free, open and inclusive concept, with ASEAN centrality at the core and defined by a common rules-based order that both our countries are pursuing'. This statement underscored the sentiment expressed by Modi at the Shangri-La Dialogue that the Indo-Pacific region is neither anti-China nor a closed membership club.

Some analysts have considered India the 'weakest link' in the QSD arrangement (see Grossman 2018). Bachhawat (2018) observes that 'India's behaviour is consistent with its inclusive vision of the Indo-Pacific, in which it exercises strategic autonomy by emphasising a "non-bloc" vision of security cooperation'. New Delhi is also likely to be cognisant of the risk of pushing China too far because India is a partner in the Brazil, Russia, India, China and South Africa (BRICS) grouping and the recent settlement of the India-China-Bhutan border dispute. Last, but by no means least, Sino-Indian economic relations continue to accelerate with India enjoying a major trade surplus (China is India's single largest trading partner), and levels of two-way investment are growing steadily (*Times of India* 2018). The significance of the economic relationship was underscored during Modi's much-publicised 'informal' Wuhan summit with Chinese President Xi Jinping in April 2018, which was intended as a 'reset' of Sino-Indian relations (Bachhawat 2018). India's reluctance to elevate the status of the QSD regarding representation from each country—alluded to in the introduction to this chapter—almost certainly indicates an unwillingness to fully commit to a grouping in which the other three members are in a formal alliance. Indian policymakers may regard the QSD as a multiplier in constraining China's strategic influence in the Indo-Pacific, but they are unwilling to support it acquiring greater prominence in the region.

Conclusion

In this chapter, we have argued that although the QSD is seen by its members as a geostrategic multiplier in the Indo-Pacific, there is no evidence of a genuine QSD 2.0 renewal of purpose since the initiative was scrapped in 2008. All four parties have clear incentives to constrain and, in some cases, push back against Beijing's growing assertiveness, but this will not necessarily sustain the QSD beyond its recent resurrection. There is little evidence that members are serious about mapping in detail the QSD's future. Australia may decide to reassess its commitment as it reverts to an 'honest broker' approach to US-China tensions, India verges on being non-committal, and ASEAN remains at best ambivalent about the QSD and regionalism; ironically, US security partner Singapore appears to be the most ambivalent.[6]

One school of thought might be that QSD parties will only discover a renewed purpose if Beijing uses force in a regional contingency. That may be a credible assumption, but it is more likely that the United States, Japan and Australia will focus all their efforts on leveraging existing bilateral security alliances in response to a major uptick in Chinese military activity. And it is difficult to envisage India seriously buying into a conflict in the South China Sea when even Japan and Australia have placed caveats on how much their alliances with the United States formally commit them to do in certain scenarios. In the final analysis, we are likely to look back on the QSD's resurrection in 2017 as another false dawn for the development of meaningful security arrangements outside formal alliances in the Indo-Pacific. Minilateralism in the security domain may be preferable in an increasing range of contingencies, but when it comes to promoting certainty of commitments among like-minded countries, there remains no substitute for formal security alliances.

Notes

1 In May 2018, US Pacific Command was renamed US Indo-Pacific Command.
2 In March 2018, China's Minister of Foreign Affairs Wang Yi (quoted in Birtles 2018) mocked the Australian and US preference for describing the region as 'Indo-Pacific' instead of 'Asia-Pacific'. Wang stated that it was an 'attention grabbing idea' that will 'dissipate like ocean foam'.
3 For background analysis, see Hamilton (2018) and Fitzgerald (2018).
4 In a statement released ahead of the 2018 ASEAN-Australia Special Summit in Sydney, Shadow Minister for Foreign Affairs Penny Wong and defence spokesperson Richard Marles (quoted in Murray 2018) observed that: 'Maintaining a stable strategic system in our region, anchored in the rule of law, will require stronger partnerships and deeper co-operation … As important as ASEAN is, and will continue to be, there are additional arrangements that enhance regional security … Adding the Quadrilateral to the regional mix of dialogues and defence arrangements can only reinforce ASEAN's central structures and institutions'.
5 The *Global Times* editorial (quoted in Hodge 2018) further stated that 'India's investment in Southeast Asian ports is welcome, but if new infrastructure facilities financed by India in those ports are designed for military use, China can take various counter-measures. At the least, Beijing can adopt the same measures in the Indian Ocean'.
6 For an excellent analysis, see Le Thu (2018).

References

Abe, S 2012, 'Asia's democratic security diamond', *Project Syndicate*, 27 December, viewed 27 August 2019, www.project-syndicate.org/commentary/a-strategic-alliance-for-japan-and-india-by-shinzo-abe?barrier=accesspaylog.
Ali, M 2007, 'New strategic partnership against China', BBC News Online, 3 September, viewed 27 August 2019, http://news.bbc.co.uk/2/hi/south_asia/6968412.stm.
Bachhawat, A 2018, 'India still wary of the Quad amid its own China "reset"', *ASPI The Strategist*, 24 August, viewed 27 August 2019, www.aspistrategist.org.au/india-still-wary-of-the-quad-amid-its-own-china-reset.

Bagchi, I 2018, '2+2 talks: strategic dialogue to combat China's influence', *Times of India*, 6 September, viewed 27 August 2019, https://timesofindia.indiatimes.com/india/22-ta lks-strategic-dialogue-to-combat-chinas-influence/articleshow/65711582.cms.

Baruah, D 2018, 'India's answer to the Belt and Road: a road map for South Asia', *Carnegie India Paper*, 21 August, viewed 27 August 2019, https://carnegieindia.org/2018/08/21/ india-s-answer-to-belt-and-road-road-map-for-south-asia-pub-77071.

Birtles, B 2018, 'China mocks Australia over "Indo-Pacific" concept it says will "dissipate"', ABC News Online, 8 March, viewed 27 August 2019, http://www.abc.net.au/news/ 2018-03-08/china-mocks-australia-over-indo-pacific-concept/9529548.

Bisley, N 2018, 'Is there a problem with the Quad?' *China Matters*, July, viewed 27 August 2019, http://chinamatters.org.au/public-outreach/policy-brief-july/.

Brewster, D 2010, 'The Australia–India security declaration: the quadrilateral redux?' *Security Challenges*, vol. 6, no. 1, pp. 1–9.

Chanlett-Avery, E and Vaughn, B 2008, 'Emerging trends in the security architecture in Asia: bilateral and multilateral ties among the United States, Japan, Australia and India', CRS Report for Congress, 7 January, Washington, DC, Congressional Research Service.

Choong, W 2018, 'Quad goals: wooing ASEAN', *ASPI The Strategist*, 11 July, viewed 27 August 2019, www.aspistrategist.org.au/quad-goals-wooing-asean.

Cooper, Z 2018, 'Building a Pacific order: binding the liberal spokes', in M Heazle and A O'Neil (eds), *China's Rise and Australia-Japan-US Relations: Primacy and Leadership in East Asia*, Cheltenham, Edward Elgar, pp. 91–116.

Department of Defence, Australian Government 2016, *2016 Defence White Paper*, viewed 27 August 2019, www.defence.gov.au/WhitePaper/Docs/2016-Defence-White-Paper.pdf.

Department of Foreign Affairs and Trade, Australian Government 2017, *2017 Foreign Policy White Paper*, viewed 27 August 2019, www.fpwhitepaper.gov.au/foreign-policy-white-paper.

Doornbos, C 2018, 'Navy begins annual Malabar Exercise with India and Japan', *Stars and Stripes*, 7 June, viewed 27 August 2019, www.stripes.com/news/navy-begins-annual-mala bar-exercise-with-india-and-japan-1.531537.

Fitzgerald, J 2018, 'Australia: special forum on Chinese interference in the internal affairs of democratic states', *The Asan Forum*, 24 April, viewed 27 August 2019, www.theasa nforum.org/australia-2/.

Gale, JB and Shearer, A 2018, 'The Quadrilateral Security Dialogue and the Maritime Silk Road Initiative', *CSIS Briefs*, March, viewed 27 August 2019, https://csis-prod.s3.amazon aws.com/s3fs-public/publication/180717_GaleShearer_QuadSecurityDialogue.pdf?csNA9 Z0fB6r4L9KKdBnc.a0LzXdNTr7b.

Garekar, B 2018, 'Quad leaders stress ASEAN's centrality in their Indo-Pacific visions', *Straits Times*, 17 November, viewed 27 August 2019, www.straitstimes.com/singapore/ quad-leaders-stress-aseans-centrality-in-their-indo-pacific-visions.

Grossman, D 2018, 'India is the weakest link in the quad', *Foreign Policy*, 23 July, viewed 27 August 2019, https://foreignpolicy.com/2018/07/23/india-is-the-weakest-lin k-in-the-quad.

Haidar, S and Peri, D 2019, '"Not time yet" for Australia's inclusion in Malabar naval games', *The Hindu*, 21 January, viewed 27 August 2019, www.thehindu.com/news/na tional/not-time-yet-for-australias-inclusion-in-malabar-naval-games/article26058080.ece.

Hamilton, C 2018, *Silent Invasion: China's Influence in Australia*, Sydney, Hardie Grant Books.

Higgott, R 2012, 'The theory and practice of global economic governance in the early twenty-first century: the limits of multilateralism', in W Grant and G Wilson (eds), *The Consequences of the Global Financial Crisis: The Rhetoric of Reform and Regulation*, Oxford, Oxford University Press, pp. 16–33.

Hodge, A 2018, 'China warns of "military race" over India's islands deal', *The Australian*, 1 June, viewed 27 August 2019, www.theaustralian.com.au/news/world/china-warns-of-m ilitary-race-over-indias-islands-deal/news-story/a3b535d1f946d4c0ecb7a2735668b8df.

Ji, Y 2016, 'China's emerging Indo-Pacific naval strategy', *Asia Policy*, vol. 22, pp. 11–19.

Lang, D 2015, 'The not-quite-quadrilateral: Australia, Japan and India', *Strategic Insights*, Canberra, Australian Strategic Policy Institute.

Le Thu, H 2018, 'Southeast Asian perceptions of the Quadrilateral Security Dialogue: survey findings', *ASPI Special Report*, October, viewed 27 August 2019, https://www.aspi.org. au/report/southeast-asian-perceptions-quadrilateral-security-dialogue.

Lee, L 2016, 'Abe's democratic security diamond and new quadrilateral initiative: an Australian perspective', *Journal of East Asian Affairs*, vol. 30, no. 2, pp. 1–41.

Lee-Brown, T 2018, 'Asia's security triangles: maritime minilateralism in the Indo-Pacific', *East Asia*, vol. 35, no. 3, pp. 163–176.

Malik, M 2016, 'Balancing act: the China-India-U.S. Triangle', *World Affairs*, vol. 179, no. 1, pp. 46–57.

Manicom, J and O'Neil, A 2010, 'Accommodation, realignment or business as usual? Australia's response to a rising China', *Pacific Review*, vol. 23, no. 1, pp. 23–44.

Mattis, J 2018, *Summary of the 2018 National Defense Strategy of the United States of America: Sharpening the American Military's Competitive Edge*, viewed 27 August 2019, https://dod. defense.gov/Portals/1/Documents/pubs/2018-National-Defense-Strategy-Summary.pdf.

Medcalf, R 2015, 'Reimagining Asia: from Asia-Pacific to Indo-Pacific', *Asan Forum*, 26 June, viewed 27 August 2019, www.theasanforum.org/reimagining-asia-from-asia-pa cific-to-indo-pacific/.

Ministry of External Affairs, Government of India 2018, 'Prime Minister's keynote address at Shangri-La Dialogue', 1 June, viewed 27 August 2019, www.mea.gov.in/Speeches-Sta tements.htm?dtl/29943/Prime+Ministers+Keynote+Address+at+Shangri+La+Dialogue+ June+01+2018.

Ministry of Foreign Affairs of Japan 2007, 'Speech by HE MR Shinzo Abe at the Parliament of the Republic of India, "Confluence of the two seas"', 22 August, viewed 27 August 2019, www.mofa.go.jp/region/asia-paci/pmv0708/speech-2.html.

Moret, E 2016, 'Effective minilateralism for the EU: what, when and how', *European Union Institute for Security Studies Brief*, June, viewed 27 August 2019, www.iss.europa.eu/sites/ default/files/EUISSFiles/Brief_17_Minilateralism.pdf.

Murray, L 2018, 'Labor comes full circle on the quadrilateral security dialogue', *Australian Financial Review*, 15 March, viewed 27 August 2019, www.afr.com/news/world/la bor-comes-full-circle-on-the-quadrilateral-security-dialogue-20180315-h0xi2v.

Nilsson-Wright, J 2017, *Creative Minilateralism in a Changing Asia: Opportunities for Security Convergence and Cooperation between Australia, India and Japan*, Chatham House Research Paper, July.

Padmanabhat, M 2018, 'We are very interested in joining exercise Malabar: Australian Foreign Minister Julie Bishop', *The Hindu*, 23 May, viewed 27 August 2019, www.the hindu.com/opinion/interview/we-are-very-interested-in-joining-exercise-malabar/article 23962368.ece.

Panda, A 2018, 'US, Japan, India and Australia hold senior official-level quadrilateral meet- ing in Singapore', *The Diplomat*, 8 June, viewed 27 August 2019, https://thediplomat. com/2018/06/us-japan-india-and-australia-hold-senior-official-level-quadrilateral-meetin g-in-singapore/.

Prakash, A 2018, 'The Asia-Africa Growth Corridor: bringing together old partnerships and new initiatives', *ORF Issue Brief*, no. 239, April, viewed 27 August 2019, www.orfonline. org/wp-content/uploads/2018/04/ORF_Issue_Brief_Asia_AfricaGrowth_Corridor.pdf.

Roy-Chaudhury, R and Sullivan de Estrada, K 2018, 'India, the Indo-Pacific and the Quad', *Survival*, vol. 60, no. 3, pp. 181–194.

Satake, T and Hemmings, J 2018, 'Japan-Australia security cooperation in the bilateral and multilateral contexts', *International Affairs*, vol. 94, no. 4, pp. 815–834.

Sharma, A 2010, 'The quadrilateral initiative: an evaluation', *South Asian Survey*, vol. 17, no. 2, pp. 237–253.

Silove, N 2016, 'The pivot before the pivot: US strategy to preserve the power balance in Asia', *International Security*, vol. 40, no. 4, pp. 45–88.

Smith, J 2019, 'India and the Quad: weak link or keystone?' *ASPI The Strategist*, 15 January, viewed 27 August 2019, www.aspistrategist.org.au/india-and-the-quad-weak-link-or-key stone/.

Tarapore, A 2018, 'The geopolitics of the Quad', *National Bureau of Asian Research Commentary*, 16 November, viewed 27 August 2019, www.nbr.org/publication/the-geopoli tics-of-the-quad/.

Thankachan, S 2017, 'Japan's "free and open Indo-Pacific strategy": reality before the rhetoric?' *Maritime Affairs*, vol. 13, no. 2, pp. 84–91.

Times of India 2018, 'India, China, forging close economic ties: Chinese media', *Times of India*, 27 April, viewed 27 August 2019, https://timesofindia.indiatimes.com/india/india -china-forging-close-economic-ties-chinese-media/articleshow/63942134.cms

Tow, W 2018, 'Minilateral security's relevance to US strategy in the Indo-Pacific: challenges and prospects', *Pacific Review*, vol. 32, no. 2, pp. 232–244.

US Department of Defense 2018, 'Transcript of remarks by Secretary Mattis at plenary session of the 2018 Shangri-la Dialogue', 2 June, viewed 27 August 2019, https://dod.defense. gov/News/Transcripts/Transcript-View/Article/1538599/remarks-by-secretary-mattis-at -plenary-session-of-the-2018-shangri-la-dialogue/.

Wilson, JD 2018, 'Rescaling to the Indo-Pacific: from economic to security-driven regionalism in Asia', *East Asia*, vol. 35, no. 2, pp. 177–196.

Wuthnow, J 2018, 'US "minilateralism" in Asia and China's responses: a new security dilemma?' *Journal of Contemporary China*, vol. 28, no. 115, pp. 133–150.

Yadav, D 2016, '"Look East" to "Act East": India's policy shift or "old wine"?' in GS Khurana and AG Singh (eds), *India and China: Constructing a Peaceful Order in the Indo-Pacific*, New Delhi, National Maritime Foundation, pp. 50–64.

Yang, S 2016, 'Strategic scenario in the Indo-Pacific region: a Chinese perspective', in GS Khurana and AG Singh (eds), *India and China: Constructing A Peaceful Order in the Indo-Pacific*, New Delhi, National Maritime Foundation, pp. 1–10.

3

THE FUTURE OF THE QUADRILATERAL SECURITY DIALOGUE

Possibilities and challenges[1]

Tomohiko Satake

The revival of the Quadrilateral Security Dialogue

As Chinese power and influence have rapidly increased, growing attention has been paid to the possibility of quadrilateral security cooperation between the United States, Japan, Australia and India. The framework, known as the Quadrilateral Security Dialogue (QSD) or Quad, was first taken up for discussion when these four countries worked closely together as members of a core group following the Indian Ocean tsunami disaster in 2004. At that time, the QSD idea had strong support from US officials who understood the geostrategic implications of the grouping owing to its humanitarian efforts (Satake and Hemmings 2018, p. 827). Possibly encouraged by discussions with these US officials, Japanese politician Shinzo Abe (2006, p. 160) proposed the idea during his election campaign for the leadership of the Liberal Democratic Party of Japan. After Abe became prime minister in September 2006, an informal high-level officials' meeting of the four countries was held in May 2007. Additionally, in September of that same year, Japan and Australia took part for the first time in the US-India joint naval exercise Malabar conducted in the Bay of Bengal.

However, the idea faded away after the Australian government led by Kevin Rudd withdrew suddenly from the QSD proposal. In a joint press conference with the Chinese minister of foreign affairs, Stephen Smith declared that Australia would not join the second round of QSD meetings (The Hon Stephen Smith MP 2008). While Prime Minister Rudd was not necessarily 'pro-China', and thus supported US-Japan-Australia security cooperation, he had clear reservations about 'any future expansion of that [trilateral cooperation] which would unnecessarily exacerbate unresolved strategic tensions between the US and China in particular'

(Hartcher 2007). Indeed, a Chinese diplomat expressed concerns that the United States, Japan, India and Australia would try to develop a 'little NATO [North Atlantic Treaty Organization]' in order to contain China (Nicholson 2007). Even Japanese Prime Minister Yasuo Fukuda, who succeeded Prime Minister Abe in September 2007, paid less attention to the QSD and made maximum efforts to enhance cooperation with China.

Abe, however, never gave up on the QSD. In his speech at the Japan-Australia symposium in June 2009, Abe (2009) said:

> Because of our common values, it is very important to expand the US-Japan-Australia cooperation by adding India to this framework. Expanding cooperation of Japan, Australia and India—'Asia's democratic three'—with the United States leads to the expansion of ideas and values shared by these four countries to the Asian region. This will certainly benefit the people who live in this region. As the first step, our four countries should hold a high-level officials' meeting. Then we should continue to seek the possibility of foreign ministerial or summit level meetings.

It was no surprise, therefore, that Abe reintroduced the idea of the QSD after taking office as prime minister for the second time in December 2012. In an article entitled 'Asia's democratic security diamond', Abe (2012) proposed that Australia, India, Japan and the United States 'form a diamond to safeguard the maritime commons stretching from the Indian Ocean region to the western Pacific'. Consequently, Abe strengthened Japan's bilateral defence and security relations with Australia and India by upgrading them to a 'special strategic (and global) partnership' in 2014. Abe also reinvigorated the Trilateral Strategic Dialogue (TSD) with the United States and Australia, which had not been held at ministerial level since 2009, and launched the Japan-Australia-India high-level officials' meeting in 2015.

The idea of the QSD was officially revived when Japanese Minister for Foreign Affairs Taro Kono revealed his intention to seek the possibility of a strategic dialogue at foreign minister and summit level between Japan, the United States, Australia and India in October 2017. Two days later, a US official endorsed Kono's proposal as it was 'a natural stepping stone from the very productive trilateral conversations, exercises, and cooperation that we've seen between India, Japan, and the United States' (US Department of State 2017). Following this announcement, senior officials from the four countries met in November 2017, and June and November 2018. The most senior-ranking naval officials from each country also met and exchanged opinions about regional security in India in January 2018. Following these developments, the QSD has come to be recognised as a symbol of the 'Free and Open Indo-Pacific' (FOIP), a vision announced by both Abe and US President Donald Trump in August 2016 and November 2017, respectively (Ministry of Foreign Affairs of Japan 2016; The White House 2017).

Why is the QSD relevant now?

As discussed above, the resurrection of the QSD was mainly triggered by the return of Abe, who is a strong supporter of the QSD. Abe's popularity and, in contrast with his first appointment between 2007 and 2008, unusually long-term and stable tenure as prime minister, also contributed to the revival of the QSD. That said, the sudden resurrection of the QSD cannot be explained simply by the politician's personal character. In particular, international structural changes mostly driven by the rise of China and the continuous 'power shift' in the region since around 2008 has contributed greatly to growing momentum for the revival of the QSD not only in Japan and the United States but also in Australia and, to some extent, India.

Since the financial crisis and the 'Great Recession' of 2008, the Chinese economy has slowed from an average of 10 per cent in the decade prior to 2008, to a range between 6 and 7 per cent in 2015 and 2016. While Chinese economic growth has declined by approximately one-third from pre-crisis levels, however, global economic growth has decreased by nearly 50 per cent (Allison 2017, p. 12). China's gross domestic product (GDP) reached nearly two-thirds of that of the United States in 2017, and its GDP on a purchasing-power parity basis has already become four times bigger than that of Japan, even exceeding the United States (World Bank 2018).

China's military spending has continued to increase in tandem with this strong economic growth. In 2015, the Chinese defence budget had more than doubled since 2008 (Caffrey 2015). In March 2016, China announced that it would raise the fiscal 2016 defence budget by RMB 954 billion (US$ 135 billion), an increase of 7.6 per cent compared to the previous year. This was about three times greater than Japan's military budget for the fiscal year 2016 (US$ 45 billion), and more than 40 per cent of the total military budget of Asia, including Oceania (National Institute for Defense Studies 2017, p. 238). China injected this massive investment into the modernisation of its military might, greatly enhancing its nuclear capability and its anti-ship ballistic and cruise missile capabilities in particular. China also strengthened its capabilities in space, cyberspace and electronic warfare and is continuing to challenge the supremacy of the United States in these new fields of military technology (Office of the Secretary of Defense 2016, pp. 63–5).

Beijing continued to assert its claims over territories and sovereignty in both the East China Sea and the South China Sea, while gradually stepping up its 'grey zone' activities in air and sea in these areas. Since around 2015, for example, People's Liberation Army navy ships and submarines have occasionally approached or even entered the contiguous zone around the Senkaku Islands of Japan. The number of scrambles launched against Chinese aircraft by the Japanese Air Self-Defense Forces (SDF) has consistently increased, reaching a record high (851 times) in 2016. China has also continued the construction of military facilities and the deployment of military assets in both the Spratly and Paracel Islands, even after an arbitration tribunal constituted under Annex VII of the United Nations Convention on the Law of the Sea ruled in July 2016 against China's maritime claims made on the basis of a 'nine-dash line' in the South China Sea. The People's Liberation Army of China also entered the Doklam area of Bhutan in June 2017, which resulted in a military stand-off with the Indian Army.

Meanwhile, China has been rapidly increasing its foreign direct investment through the Belt and Road Initiative (BRI). Although China's BRI could potentially contribute to the development of several Indo-Pacific countries, there have been growing concerns over the openness, economic efficiency, soundness and transparency of BRI projects. Indeed, the BRI has already caused many frictions and sparked public opposition over issues such as labour policies, performance delays and concerns over national security and the environment (*Financial Times* 2018). In turn, this resulted in the suspension or termination of some of its infrastructure construction projects in many countries. As Friedberg (2018) argues, 'China's dubious financial dealings with some of the nations along the Belt and Road are raising questions about its intentions, and ironically risk casting it in the role of a twenty-first-century neo-imperialist power'.

There has also been growing international concern over China's 'political interference' in some democratic countries. Some observers believe that Beijing has tried to influence the perceptions and policies of people and governments of industrial democracies, while suppressing information and discouraging the expression of opinions perceived as threatening to the Chinese Communist Party (Friedberg 2018, p. 9). Others have warned that China has used its political and economic influence against weaker states to forcefully change their policy preferences rather than to simply engage in foreign influence activities (Mahnken *et al.* 2018). Beijing's retaliation against the election of Tsai Ing-wen as president of Taiwan in 2016 and Seoul's introduction of the Terminal High Altitude Air Defense missile defence system in 2017 are two examples of China exercising such coercive measures against regional democracies (Harrell *et al.* 2018, pp. 5–6).

Abe's announcement of the FOIP to a large extent reflects these new geopolitical realities which have developed since 2010. In particular, enhancing Japan's strategic cooperation with India, as well as Australia, to encourage India's greater role in counterbalancing China has apparently been the central element of the FOIP. Behind such a strategy is the very geopolitical (and geo-economic) thinking of Japanese central policymakers, one of them being Deputy Secretary General of National Security Secretariat Nobukatsu Kanehara, who has highly evaluated the importance of India in order to offset Chinese growing power and influence (Suzuki 2017, especially Chapter 4). Engaging India eastwards could also force Beijing to divert some of its resources and attention to the Indian Ocean away from the East and South China Seas (Chanlett-Avery 2018). The QSD, as a regional minilateral grouping, is a measure to involve India in the twenty-first-century's great power politics in Asia, by creating a 'coalition of democracies' against the rising revisionist power.

In a reversal of attitudes held ten years ago both Tokyo and Washington, as well as Canberra, have demonstrated bipartisan support for the QSD. Former Minister of Foreign Affairs, Julie Bishop, stated that Australia would 'welcome' the development of senior officials' meetings between the four countries one week after Kono's announcement (Wroe 2017). Bishop also said that the QSD is a 'natural extension of these mini-lateral relationships', such as the TSD, and that Australia has a 'bipartisan approach toward the Quadrilateral' (Padmanabhan 2018). In fact, Labor's shadow foreign and defence ministers declared their support for the QSD in the *Australian Financial Review* (Wong and Marles 2018). The Joint Statement of the Australia–US Ministerial Consultations in July 2018 also made reference to the fact that both the United States and Australia 'welcomed' the senior officials' meetings of the four countries (US Embassy and Consulates in Australia 2018).

By contrast, India maintained a cautious attitude towards the QSD. In April 2018, it was reported that India had repudiated Australia's wish to join the US–India–Japan joint naval exercise Malabar. Indeed, this was the fourth year in a row that India had refused to allow Australia to participate in the exercise (Grossman 2018). In his keynote address at the Shangri-La Dialogue in June 2018, Indian Prime Minister Narendra Modi implicitly denied that India was fully committed to the QSD by stating that 'India does not see the Indo-Pacific Region as a strategy or as a club of limited members', nor 'as a grouping that seeks to dominate' (Ministry of External Affairs of India 2018). India also decided not to join an initiative launched by the United States, Japan and Australia to fund infrastructure projects intended to counterbalance China's BRI in the Indo-Pacific region. The decision disappointed many Japanese, who recognised the QSD as one of the key elements that would promote Japan's FOIP strategy in both its geopolitical and geo-economic contexts (Okada 2018).

Nevertheless, New Delhi has gradually enhanced its bilateral security cooperation with each member country of the QSD. In addition to the first 2+2 dialogue with the United States held in September 2018, India began to hold regular military exercises and signed a logistics supply agreement as well as a communications agreement with the United States (Jaishankar 2018). India held staff talks with three services and upgraded its strategic dialogue to the ministerial level with Japan. Both the Indian Army and Air Force for the first time conducted bilateral training with the Japanese Ground SDF and Air SDF in 2018. The first 2+2 dialogue between India and Japan was held in November 2019.

Furthermore, India has recently moved to enhance its strategic relationship with Australia, the 'weakest link' of the QSD. India and Australia established an annual maritime dialogue in 2015 and a 2+2 meeting in 2017. Both countries' militaries have increasingly interacted, as demonstrated by the Indian Air Force's participation in Australia's Pitch Black exercise and the Royal Australian Navy's participation in India's multilateral naval exercise MILAN, both of which took place in 2018 (Jaishankar 2018). Although the QSD itself is not yet fully developed, all four countries have increasingly enhanced information sharing and interoperability through bilateral and trilateral settings. These could be the basis for a more meaningful level of cooperation or collaboration within the QSD in future.

Will the QSD weaken or strengthen the existing order?

If the United States, Japan, India and Australia can effectively coordinate their military and economic policies through close consultation, information sharing or military exercises, it can significantly help to deter and dissuade Chinese hegemonic intentions. This will certainly contribute to the creation of a more stable power balance in the region. The QSD will also contribute to the establishment of a FOIP, envisioned by all four powers, by providing a foundation of such an order from its base. By creating such equilibrium, all regional powers, including Japan, Australia and India, could maintain constructive relations with China without fearing exploitation by or excessive dependency on this regional giant. While the United States has up until now played a major role as a regional balancer, Japan, India and Australia are expected to play an increasingly important role in maintaining a stable power balance in the region.

Creating a more stable power balance has become extremely important as US–Sino competition rapidly escalates. As power transition theory suggests, conflicts are most likely to occur when the power gap between a rising power and the existing hegemon narrows (Gilpin 1981; Kugler and Lemke 1996; Organski and Kugler 1980; Tammen *et al.* 2000). International tensions are expected to increase as the existing hegemon is likely to try to prevent the rising power from replacing its position through all necessary measures—often referred to as the 'Thucydides' Trap' (Allison 2017). Indeed, recent US policies towards China, including the imposition of high tariffs on imported goods or the direction of harsh criticism against Chinese foreign and domestic behaviour, appear to endorse such a pessimistic school of thought. To avoid a hegemonic war, and to escape from the 'Thucydides' Trap', one must find a broader space that can accommodate both the rising power and the declining hegemon.

Expanding the geopolitical concept from 'Asia Pacific' to 'Indo-Pacific' can be understood as an attempt to find and create such a broader strategic space in the region. Unlike the Asia Pacific where the United States was a dominant power both economically and militarily, the Indo-Pacific has more diverse actors including China, India and some of the Southeast Asian countries. One consequence is that, while the United States and China may continue to be major players, other regional powers, including Japan, India, Australia and member countries of the Association of Southeast Asian Nations (ASEAN), and even extra-regional powers such as the United Kingdom and France, will play a greater role in maintaining a stable and multiple power balance in the region.

This does not necessarily imply that the United States and regional powers would try to 'exclude' or 'contain' China. Instead, as suggested above, regional actors can build constructive relations with China without 'choosing' between the United States and China. The fundamental objective of the FOIP is therefore how to co-exist with China by creating an 'open, inclusive and rules-based' order, rather than to exclude or contain it (Ministry of Foreign Affairs of Japan 2018). China is welcome to join the FOIP vision so long as it respects basic principles such as sovereignty, international law, freedom of navigation and overflight, and sustainable development. The QSD could provide an important foundation to create such parity which is necessary to maintain stable relations between China and regional powers.

Challenges for the QSD

Although the strategic interests of the four countries have increasingly converged, some significant differences seem to remain. These differences exist in each country's strategic priorities, relationship with China, and visions for the future regional order. Furthermore, the intensification of Sino-US strategic rivalry could discourage, rather than encourage, the development of QSD cooperation.

Different strategic priorities

First, Japan, India and Australia have different strategic priorities, despite a broader consensus over the FOIP policy. Although Japan has expanded both its economic and military engagement with Indo-Pacific countries under the FOIP banner, many of those initiatives involve low-key cooperation in areas such as defence exchanges, soft and hard infrastructure development, capacity building, norm setting, or rule making (Ministry of Defense of Japan 2016). Japan's primary security and strategic interests remain in Northeast Asia or in the defence of the Japanese homeland, rather than in the Indo-Pacific (or the even narrower Asia Pacific). Indeed, some Japanese experts argue that Japan should concentrate its available resources to its 'core interests', most notably addressing the threats and challenges regarding the Senkaku Islands in the East China Sea, China's anti-access/area-denial strategy close to Japan's own shore, and North Korea's nuclear and ballistic missile threats (Tsuruoka 2018). Such demand for 'Japan first' may grow even bigger as Japanese security resources become increasingly constrained by both the country's burgeoning financial deficit and an ageing society.

Like Japan, India's primary security interests lie in continental, rather than regional or maritime security issues. In particular, New Delhi's chief concern is how to cope with local threats from Pakistan and China on its northern land borders, and this is why India is continually expanding its ground forces rather than rationalising and modernising them (Tarapore 2017). While India has rapid naval build-up capabilities, its ability to project naval power to the broader Indo-Pacific remains limited (Tarapore 2017, pp. 166–7). In fact, there is a significant mismatch between what the Indian Navy needs and what it will possess in the future (Liu 2018). The Indian Navy also suffers from the ageing of vessels, as well as delays in weapons delivery and research and development. Such a 'continental mindset' and shortage of naval power may limit its maritime presence beyond the Indian Ocean (Roy-Chaudhury and Sullivan de Estrada 2018).

While Australia has also broadened its strategic scope to the Indo-Pacific, its primary focus beyond homeland defence lies in 'maritime South East Asia and the

South Pacific', not Northeast Asia or the Indian Ocean (Department of Defence, Australian Government 2016, p. 17). This 'tyranny of distance', as well as its concerns with the provocations of China, have prevented Australia from concluding a formal alliance with Japan or strengthening its strategic outreach to the Indian Ocean region (Satake 2018; Satake and Hemmings 2018). Some sceptics contend that for a middle-sized power like Australia it is too ambitious to attempt to encompass an area as huge as the Indo-Pacific (Wilkins 2018). While Australia has implemented the largest-ever naval build-up project, including doubling the number of submarines and constructing nine new frigates, the successful implementation of such a policy has been already under scrutiny due to increasing costs and delays in the planned schedule (Australian National Audit Office 2018; Maley 2018). Fully conscious of these limitations, Australia's strategic thinkers, such as the former Secretary for Foreign Affairs, Peter Varghese (2018, p. 379), have rejected the idea of treating the Indian and Pacific Oceans as a 'single strategic system'. Opposing views of the Indo-Pacific due to different strategic priorities could make it difficult for Australia to closely engage with QSD cooperation in areas beyond Australia's strategic focus, such as Northeast Asia or the western Indian Ocean.

Relations with China

Another challenge is QSD members' relations with China. As already mentioned, the fundamental aim of the Indo-Pacific strategy is to establish an open, inclusive and rules-based regional order that is reliant upon a stable power balance. China in this context is positioned as one of the most important players of the Indo-Pacific, rather than excluded from it. Whether China understands or shares such a vision for order is, however, a different matter. For some observers, the idea behind the Indo-Pacific is 'to keep the United States in, lift India up and keep China out of the Indian Ocean' (Bisley 2012). In fact, Chinese scholars and state-owned media have repeatedly accused the QSD's Indo-Pacific strategy of being 'an attempt to divide the Asia-Pacific along Cold War fault lines' (Yang 2017).

This raises a question for all QSD members, especially Japan, India and Australia. While these countries have become increasingly concerned about China's growing power and influence, especially in their surrounding regions, they are at the same time all economically dependent on China. Furthermore, none of them has the capacity to cope with Chinese assertiveness independently. It is for this reason that Tokyo, New Delhi and Canberra have attempted to improve or restore their political and economic relations with Beijing, despite the Trump administration's increasingly tough stance towards China. For example, in October 2018 Abe became the first Japanese prime minister in seven years to visit Beijing. Abe and Chinese President Xi Jinping reportedly agreed on 'three principles'—shifting from 'competition to collaboration', working together as partners who will not threaten each other, and developing a free and fair trading system (Kobara 2018). Modi has also tried to improve India's relationship with China, which had deteriorated after the Doklam stand-off in 2017 (Aires 2018). Finally, Australia's former Prime

Minister Malcolm Turnbull proposed to 'reset' Australia's relations with China, and new Prime Minister Scott Morrison stressed, like his predecessors, that Australia does not have to 'choose' between the United States and China (Coorey 2018a, 2018b).

As already mentioned, it is vital for all these powers, especially Japan and Australia, to maintain a stable balance in order to safeguard constructive relations with China. While the QSD could potentially help to establish such an equilibrium, tensions could escalate were China to interpret such actions as an attempt to 'contain' or 'exclude' it. Alternatively, if China really is seeking to establish a so-called China-centric regional order, as some observers have argued, then the Indo-Pacific concept, which assumes the presence of multiple actors rather than a single hegemon, is entirely inconsistent with its vision. Indeed, maintaining good relations with China while simultaneously enhancing QSD cooperation would require considerable skill on the part of Tokyo, New Delhi and Canberra.

Different visions for regional order

While all members of the QSD broadly agree that there is a need to establish an open, inclusive and rules-based Indo-Pacific order, they appear to have different visions over who leads such an order and what kind of values or norms legitimise it. Such differences are particularly prominent between TSD member states (the United States, Japan and Australia) and India. Since the ending of the Cold War, the United States, Japan and Australia have collectively or individually pursued the US-led 'liberal international order', based on democracy, human rights and the rule of law (at least until late 2016 when Trump was elected as president of the United States). Japan and Australia have also worked hard to sustain US leadership by supporting the strong US military presence in the region.

This is the reason why both Tokyo and Canberra actively contributed to the US-led global 'war on terror' following the terrorist attacks on the US mainland perpetrated on 11 September 2001. While terrorism has remained a major concern for both Japan and especially Australia, their primary concerns are to maintain a strong US military presence in the region by supporting or supplementing US global roles and by avoiding the isolationist turn of the US foreign posture (Satake 2012). For the same reason, these two allies also became major players in regional security issues, such as peacekeeping or peace-building activities in East Timor or offering humanitarian assistance and disaster relief (HADR) following the Sumatra earthquake in 2004. By supporting and supplementing the United States in the region and across the globe, Japan and Australia have tried to reduce the US burden so that it can continue to engage in the Asia Pacific region.

Japan's announcement of the FOIP was also intended to bolster a strong US regional engagement by expanding the scope of the US-Japan alliance from the Asia Pacific to the Indo-Pacific. Trump's announcement to implement the FOIP in November 2017 was therefore a clear diplomatic victory for Japan (The White House 2017). In fact, over the past few years Japan has increased its level of cooperation with the United States in the wider Indo-Pacific region, in matters such as capacity building, military exercises and training, and investment in infra-structure (Satake 2018, pp. 233–6). Similarly, the formulation of the QSD is an important measure for Japan to sustain the US-led regional order with the coordination and participation of other regional democracies (Chanlett-Avery 2018).

By contrast, India has always hesitated to endorse the US-led order—as demonstrated by its opposition to US military action in Iraq. Instead of supporting US primacy, India has pursued the 'multipolarisation' of the world and has aspired to become one of its 'poles'. This was evident in Modi's speech at the World Economic Forum in January 2018, in which he stated that 'today we believe in a multicultural world—and a multipolar world order' (Babones 2018). This concept of the multipolarisation of the world also reappeared in Modi's subsequent meet-ings with the Chinese and Russian leaders. In a keynote speech given at the Shangri-La Dialogue in June 2018, Modi recalled an occasion during which he and Russian President Vladimir Putin shared their views on 'the need for a strong multi-polar world order'. While Modi mentioned cooperation with Japan, the United States and Australia, respectively, and although he stressed the importance of a 'rules-based order', he did not refer to the FOIP advocated by Japan and the United States (Ministry of External Affairs of India 2018).

An acclaimed report entitled *Nonalignment 2.0* (Khilnani *et al.* 2012) also endorsed India's preference for a multipolar world order. Although the report was not written by Indian policymakers, some of its authors were members of the National Security Council of India. According to the report, India would never 'define its national interest or approach to world politics in terms of ideologies and goals that had been set elsewhere' and retains 'maximum strategic autonomy to pursue its own developmental goals', while aspiring to create 'a more just and equitable global order' (ibid., p. 8). Such a strategy of India reflects the reality of an international society in which 'power itself is becoming far more diffused and fragmented—less a once-and-for-all achievement, and more a constant wary game to stay a few moves ahead of competitors and opponents' (ibid., p. 9). While the report recognises that the United States and China are both superpowers, it argues that these two powers cannot exercise a 'full-spectrum global dominance'—unlike in the Cold War era—and recommends that India should conduct more complex and skilful diplomacy in an essentially unstable and volatile environment (ibid.).

This strategy is designed to maximise India's national interests by engaging with various countries rather than making a clear friend or enemy, given the multi-polarisation and fluidisation of the international order. In such a strategy, it is not acceptable to join a collective mechanism fixed by an ideology such as a 'coalition of democracies' or a 'democratic security diamond'. Indeed, the *Nonalignment 2.0* report suggests that India should play a bridging role between countries that have different values. There is also no sense in distinguishing between a 'guardian' (or a status quo power) and a 'challenger' (or a revisionist power), which is often dis-cussed in the context of the US-led liberal international order. It is essentially a value-free worldview, which puts more weight on pragmatism or material power than it does on values or norms. This is why India, while hedging against the rise of China by strengthening its relations with the United States, Japan and ASEAN member countries, has at the same time enhanced its cooperation with China and Russia through its 'multi-directional foreign policy' (Mohan 2017).

Intensification of US-Sino competition

Meanwhile, the Sino–US rivalry has rapidly escalated in the region. The Trump administration has already taken several steps to enhance its competitive strategy with China, which increased tensions between the two countries. To some extent, the Trump administration's tough stance towards China is desirable for regional powers like Japan and Australia, as it enhances US strategic presence in some critical areas such as the East or South China Seas. At the same time, however, these regional allies are also concerned about the serious effects caused by US–Sino long-term competition over trade policy (Shimomura 2018). It is also very unlikely that New Delhi would support Washington's highly ideological approach to Beijing.

Should the US–Sino rivalry continue and escalate to the extent that it becomes what some call a 'hegemonic war', regional allies and partners of the United States may ultimately be forced to 'choose' between the United States and China. In such a case, the Indo-Pacific order characterised by diversity and inclusiveness would collapse and be replaced by a more polarised and exclusive new Cold War order. It goes without saying that neither Japan, nor Australia or India, want that to happen. While the QSD has basically been developed to avoid such a worst-case scenario, it could also potentially invite it if it simply becomes a means of promoting a US-led 'containment' posture against China.

Towards the future of the QSD

As discussed earlier in the chapter, the fundamental reason for reviving the QSD is the continuous shift in the balance of regional power due to the rise of China. Faced with China's growing power and influence, as well as foreign interference and political and economic forms of coercion, not only the United States and Japan, but to some extent even Australia and India, have supported the development of the QSD. If successfully managed, the QSD can create a more stable power balance that supports a free, open and inclusive Indo-Pacific order. Nevertheless, the QSD is facing many challenges, including the different strategic priorities of member states and their relations with China, as well as the lack of consensus over a desirable international order between US allies and India. The rapid and continuous intensification of the Sino–US strategic rivalry could also widen the gap between QSD members over their policies and priorities.

If the four countries wish to advance QSD cooperation, therefore, they should fully acknowledge these difficulties and consider how to narrow the gaps. In particular, both Japan and Australia may need to accept the reality that they can no longer expect as much support from the United States in maintaining the FOIP policy under the current Trump administration. Instead, Tokyo and Canberra could endeavour to play more autonomous roles in creating an open, inclusive and rules-based Indo-Pacific beyond the previous paradigm of merely supporting the US-led order. Japan needs to enhance and upgrade its defence and security policy by accelerating its security reform, including the amendment of the pacifist Constitution, as well as continuously increasing its defence budget. Australia needs to consistently implement its planned defence build-up project, while enhancing its regional engagement policy. Their active cooperation in 'middle-power coalitions', including Japan-Australia-India trilateral arrangements, could be further accelerated (Medcalf and Mohan 2014).

India could also strengthen its commitment to promoting the FOIP policy by acknowledging that its continuous development largely depends on the longevity of a free, open and rules-based international order. While New Delhi has benefited greatly from such an order, for many years it has been indifferent to the provision of international public goods, such as free trade or multilateral institutions. Nevertheless, under Modi the tide seems to be turning towards greater commitment to an open, rules-based and inclusive regional order. While maintaining its traditional non-alignment posture, India has enhanced its regional engagement, mostly with ASEAN, to support that organisation's unity and centrality. By accelerating such efforts, India could gain more opportunities to collaborate with regional partners, including Japan and Australia, in capacity building, counter-terrorism, HADR or other activities in Southeast Asia and beyond.

Finally, Japan, India and Australia need to keep stressing that cooperation among QSD members does not seek to contain or exclude China from the Indo-Pacific. While the QSD itself is an exclusive grouping of regional democracies, its aim is to create and maintain a multiple power balance against or with China so that the region can enjoy a more stable and inclusive order compared to one shaped by US-Sino bipolarity. This in turn not only benefits regional democracies, but all regional countries including China—unless it pursues regional hegemony. The future of the Indo-Pacific therefore hugely depends on how regional middle-power democracies, especially Japan, India and Australia, can create an order that encompasses various countries into a common cooperative, as well as competitive, framework. If successfully managed, the QSD can play a key role in the establishment of such an open, inclusive and more pluralistic order in the Indo-Pacific.

Note

1   Views expressed in this paper are the author's own and do not represent the official viewpoints of the National Institute for Defense Studies or the Ministry of Defense of Japan.

References

Abe, S 2006, *Utsukushii kuni-e* [*Towards a Beautiful Country*], Tokyo, Bungeishunjyu.

Abe, S 2009, 'Nichigo Shimpojium Kicho Koen' [Keynote speech at Japan-Australia Symposium], 4 June, www.s-abe.or.jp/wp-content/uploads/200901.pdf.

Abe, S 2012, 'Asia's democratic security diamond', *Project Syndicate*, 27 December.

Aires, B 2018, 'Perceptible improvement in India–China relations, say Modi and Xi on G20 sidelines', *India Today*, 1 December.

Allison, G 2017, *Destined for War: Can America and China Escape Thucydides's Trap?* New York, Houghton Mifflin Harcourt.

Australian National Audit Office 2018, 'Naval construction programs: mobilisation', 14 May, www.anao.gov.au/work/performance-audit/naval-construction-programs-mobilisation.

Babones, S 2018, 'Modi at Davos: "Today we believe in a multicultural world and a multipolar world order"', *Forbes*, 23 January.

Bagshaw, E 2018, 'Donald Trump's trade war will cost Australia's economy at least $36 billion', *Sydney Morning Herald*, 7 September.

Bisley, N 2012, 'The Indo-Pacific: what does it actually mean?' *East Asia Forum*, 6 October.

Bruni, J 2012, 'Australia's proposed "Indo-Pacific" Strategy: A case of biting off more than it can chew?' *SAGE International*.

Caffrey, C 2015, 'China's defence budget more than doubles since 2008', *Jane's 360*, 5 March, www.janes.com/article/49742/china-s-defence-budget-more-than-doubles-since-2008.

Chanlett-Avery, E 2018, 'Japan, the Indo-Pacific, and the "Quad"', *Chicago Council on Global Affairs*, 14 February, www.thechicagocouncil.org/publication/japan-indo-pacific-and-quad.

Coorey, P 2018a, 'Malcolm Turnbull hits reset button over China', *Australian Financial Review*, 7 August.

Coorey, P 2018b, 'We could work with China in region: PM', *Australian Financial Review*, 13 November.

Department of Defence, Australian Government 2016, *Deence White Paper 2016*, Canberra, Commonwealth of Australia.

Financial Times 2018, 'China's Belt and Road Initiative is falling short', 29 July, www.ft.com/content/47d63fec-9185-11e8-b639-7680cedcc421.

Friedberg, A 2018, 'Competing with China', *Survival*, vol. 60, no. 3, pp. 7–64.

Gilpin, R 1981, *War and Change in World Politics*, Cambridge, Cambridge University Press.

Grossman, D 2018, 'India is the weakest link in the Quad', *Foreign Policy*, 23 July, https://foreignpolicy.com/2018/07/23/india-is-the-weakest-link-in-the-quad/.

Harrell, P, Rosenberg, E and Saravalle, E 2018, *China's Use of Coercive Economic Measures*, Washington, DC, Center for a New American Century.

Hartcher, P 2007, 'Rudd looks to alliance in Asia-Pacific', *Sydney Morning Herald*, 24 August.

Jaishankar, D 2018, 'The real significance of the Quad', *ASPI The Strategist*, 24 October, www.aspistrategist.org.au/the-real-significance-of-the-quad/.

Japan Ministry of Defense 2016, 'Vientiane Vision: Japan's defense cooperation initiative with ASEAN', www.mod.go.jp/e/d_act/exc/vientianevision/.

Khilnani, S, Kumar, R, Mehta, PB, Menon, P, Nilekani, N, Raghavan, S, Saran, S and Varadarajan, S 2012, *Nonalignment 2.0: A Foreign and Strategic Policy for India in the 21st century*, New Delhi, Center for Policy Research.

Kobara, J 2018, 'Japan and China see Abe's "3 principles" slightly differently', *Nikkei Asian Review*, 30 October, https://asia.nikkei.com/Politics/International-Relations/Japan-and-China-see-Abe-s-3-principles-slightly-differently.

Kugler, J and Lemke, D (eds) 1996, *Parity and War: Evaluations and Extensions of 'The War Ledger'*, Ann Arbor, University of Michigan Press.

Liu, R 2018, 'Act East in the Indo-Pacific: India and Quad 2.0', *Prospect Journal*, no. 19, pp. 53–71.

Mahnken, TG, Babbage, R and Yoshihara, T 2018, *Countering Comprehensive Coercion: Competitive Strategies against Authoritarian Political Warfare*, Washington, DC, Center for Strategic and Budgetary Assessments.

Maley, P 2018, 'Collins-class subs poised to fill the gap left by construction delays', *The Australian*, 1 October.

Medcalf, R and Mohan, CR 2014, *Responding to Indo-Pacific Rivalry: Australia, India and Middle Power Coalitions*, Sydney, Lowy Institute.

Ministry of External Affairs, Government of India 2018, 'Prime Minister's keynote address at Shangri La Dialogue', 1 June, https://mea.gov.in/Speeches-Statements.htm?dtl/29943/.

Ministry of Foreign Affairs of Japan 2016, 'Address by Prime Minister Shinzo Abe at the opening session of the sixth Tokyo International Conference on African Development (TICAD VI)', 27 August, www.mofa.go.jp/afr/af2/page4e_000496.html.

Ministry of Foreign Affairs of Japan 2018, 'Jiyu de Hirakareta Indo-Taiheiyo ni Mukete [Toward a Free and Open Indo-Pacific]', September, www.mofa.go.jp/mofaj/files/000407642.pdf.

Mohan, CR 2017, 'Raja Mandala: India's diplomacy, beyond the canon', *Carnegie India*, 12 December.

National Institute for Defense Studies 2017, East Asian Strategic Review 2017, Tokyo, National Institute for Defense Studies.

Nicholson, B 2007, 'China bans Canberra on security pact', *The Age*, 15 June.

Office of the Secretary of Defense, Government of PRC 2016, *Annual Report to Congress: Military and Security Developments Involving the People's Republic of China*, https://dod.defen se.gov/Portals/1/Documents/pubs/2016%20China%20Military%20Power%20Report.pdf.

Okada, M 2018, 'Kino fuzan in ochiiru Abe "Indo Taiheiyou" Senryaku [Abe's Indo-Pacific Strategy falls into dysfunction]', *Business Insider Japan*, 21 August.

Organski, AFK and Kugler, J 1980, *The War Ledger*, Chicago, University of Chicago Press.

Padmanabhan, M 2018, 'We are very interested in joining exercise Malabar: Australian foreign minister Julie Bishop', *The Hindu*, 23 May, www.thehindu.com/opinion/interview/we-are-very-interested-in-joining-exercise-malabar/article23962368.ece.

Roy-Chaudhury, R and Sullivan de Estrada, K 2018, 'India, the Indo-Pacific and the Quad', *Survival*, vol. 60, no. 3, pp. 181–194.

Satake, T 2012, 'Japan, Australia and international security burden-sharing with the United States', in WT Tow and R Kersten (eds), *Bilateral Perspectives on Regional Security: Australia, Japan and Asia-Pacific Region*, London, Palgrave Macmillan, pp. 183–199.

Satake, T 2018, 'Chapter 7 Japan US-Japan alliance amid uncertainty', *East Asian Strategic Review*, Tokyo, National Institute for Defense Studies, pp. 215–242.

Satake, T and Hemmings, J 2018, 'Japan-Australia security cooperation in the bilateral and multilateral context', *International Affairs*, vol. 94, no. 4, pp. 815–834.

Shimomura, R 2018, 'Trade war squeezes corporate earnings in Japan and China', *Nikkei Asian Review*, 5 November.

Suzuki, Y 2017, *Nihon no senryaku gaiko [Japan's Strategic Diplomacy]*, Tokyo, Chikuma Syobo.

Tammen, RL, Kugler, J, Lemke, D, Stam III, AC, Alsharabati, C, Abdollahian, MA, Efird, B and Organski, AFK 2000, *Power Transitions: Strategies for the 21st Century*, New York and London, Chatham House.

Tarapore, A 2017, 'India's slow emergence as a regional security actor', *Washington Quarterly*, vol. 40, no. 2, pp. 163–178.

The Hon Stephen Smith MP (Australian Minister for Foreign Affairs and Trade) 2008, 'Joint press conference with Chinese Foreign Minister', 5 February, viewed 28 November 2018, https://webarchive.nla.gov.au/wayback/20190808194813/https://foreignminister.gov.au/transcripts/2008/080205_jpc.html.

The White House 2017, 'Remarks by President Trump at APEC CEO Summit', 10 November, www.whitehouse.gov/briefings-statements/remarks-president-trump-apec-ceo-summit-da-nang-vietnam/.

Tsuruoka, M 2018, 'Japan first versus global Japan', *National Interest*, 14 January.

US Department of State 2017, 'Briefing by Acting Assistant Secretary for South and Central Asian Affairs and Acting Special Representative for Afghanistan and Pakistan Alice G. Wells', 27 October, www.state.gov/briefing-by-acting-assistant-secretary-for-south-and-central-asian-affairs-and-acting-special-representative-for-afghanistan-and-pakistan-alice-g-wells/.

US Embassy and Consulates in Australia 2018, 'Joint Statement: Australia-U.S. Ministerial Consultations 2018', 25 July, https://au.usembassy.gov/joint-statement-australia-u-s-ministerial-consultations-2018/.

Varghese, P 2018, *An India Economic Strategy to 2035: Navigating from Potential to Delivery*, Canberra, Department of Foreign Affairs and Trade.

Wilkins, TS 2018, 'Australia and the Indo-Pacific: a region in search of a strategy, or a strategy in search of a region?' *Italian Institute for International Political Studies*, 4 June, www.ispionline.it/en/pubblicazione/australia-and-indo-pacific-region-search-strategy-or-strategy-search-region-20694.

Wong, P and Marles, R 2018, 'Why Labor believes the Quad is a vital complement to ASEAN', *Australian Financial Review*, 16 March.

World Bank 2018, International comparison program database, https://data.worldbank.org/indicator/NY.GDP.MKTP.CD.

Wroe, D 2017, 'Australia weighing closer democratic ties in region in rebuff to China', *Sydney Morning Herald*, 31 October.

Yang, L 2017, 'Australia rejoining Quad will not advance regional prosperity, unity', *Global Times*, 15 November.

4

LANCANG-MEKONG COOPERATION

Minilateralism in institutional building and its implications

Xue Gong

Introduction

Since the inception of the Belt and Road Initiative (BRI) and the Asian Infrastructure Investment Bank, China has adopted various multilateral and bilateral approaches in order to expand its influence. As well as participating in multilateral mechanisms centred on the Association of Southeast Asian Nations (ASEAN), such as the East Asia Summit and the ASEAN Regional Forum (ARF), China also has quickened its pace to strengthen its regional leadership through various forms of proactive economic engagement. In a move to extend its influence across all the mainland Southeast Asian countries, China established the Lancang-Mekong Cooperation (LMC) mechanism at the sub-regional level. China's multilateral and bilateral approaches have a common feature: Beijing's growing interest in establishing different levels of mechanisms to promote its interests in Southeast Asia.

In comparison to the BRI that has fuelled the debate over the impact of China's 'institutional statecraft' (Ikenberry and Lim 2017), the LMC initiative has received less attention. The LMC is a China-led mechanism that includes all the mainland Southeast Asian countries, namely Cambodia, Laos, Myanmar, Thailand and Vietnam. According to the Chinese government, the LMC focuses on three pillars of cooperation: political-security issues; economic affairs and sustainable development; as well as social affairs and people-to-people exchanges. It prioritises regional connectivity, industrial cooperation, cross-border economic cooperation, water resources management and agricultural cooperation, and poverty reduction. The three pillars combined with these five priorities have been labelled the '3+5 cooperative framework' (Ministry of Foreign Affairs of the People's Republic of China 2017b).

Many experts have questioned China's reasons for establishing the LMC (Biba 2018), given the fifteen mechanisms already in existence that were initiated either by Mekong countries or by external players (Le 2018). Some scholars argue that the establishment of the LMC is consistent with China's geostrategic goal of drawing mainland Southeast Asian countries into its sphere of influence (Goh 2007; Kurlantzick 2006). Indeed, China has been attempting to influence Mekong countries primarily through economic statecraft. Some argue that the LMC serves China's ambition of shaping regional governance structures related to water resources management. Many experts see the LMC as a rival organisation to the long-standing Mekong River Commission (MRC), of which China is still not a full member. The LMC's establishment shows China's strategic water diplomacy—although it is not different from its previous water policy, it would legitimise China's monopoly of the river water (Biba 2018).

Prior to the launch of the LMC, Beijing had already attained the status of an upstream hegemon and the role of system-maker in the Mekong (Vu 2014). China also claimed that it had established the Indo-China Peninsular Economic Corridor as one of the BRI flagship initiatives. As many experts have suggested, China has gradually proved its leadership capabilities through existing mechanisms such as the Greater Mekong Subregion (GMS) Economic Cooperation (Lu 2016). A fundamental question has emerged: why is China still interested in establishing the LMC given that its influence is already dominant in the region?

While these schools of thought contain some elements of truth, analysis is lacking in several areas. First, the current literature cannot explain the timing issue: why did China choose to launch the LMC only at the stage when it has apparently already established its influence through its economic, political and geographical advantages over the Mekong countries? Second, these studies barely account for the inclusion of political-security factors in the LMC agenda and they do not analyse the rationale for including political and security cooperation. Third, the current literature cannot answer whether other Mekong countries endorse China's leadership and it also overlooks complex dynamics between different players within the LMC mechanism. The analysis of responses from the sub-regional countries is important if we are to understand the effects of China's institutional statecraft.

This chapter joins the debate by using minilateralism theory to argue that China has intentionally improved its relationship with Mekong countries by selectively embracing water resources management cooperation in order to shape regional security governance. It uses minilateralism as a cover to exclude other external players by highlighting identity, selectively setting the agenda and providing regional public goods. Although this minilateral initiative lacks multilateral substance, it complements China's bilateral approach and enhances its dominance in the region. Lower Mekong countries are motivated to participate in the LMC because minilateralism addresses urgent issues on economic development and water governance. Therefore, the inherent exclusiveness of minilateralism will inevitably have a significant impact on regional architecture.

This chapter consists of three parts. It begins with a geopolitical and geo-economic analysis of the LMC before presenting the concept of minilateralism in the LMC. It is followed by a discussion of the impact of the LMC on the regional architecture before making some concluding remarks.

Geopolitics and geo-economics in understanding the LMC

Flowing from the same water source that rises in Tibet, the transboundary water-way (called the Lancang River [*jiang*] in China, and the Mekong River in continental Southeast Asia) provides the hydropower, agriculture, navigation and aquaculture needed to sustain livelihoods along the Mekong. For a long time, China has pursued three major goals in the Mekong sub-region: advancing economic development for its western region; increasing China's strategic influence; and improving its political and security environment (Li 2015). To achieve these goals, China has wooed the region by providing economic incentives for the region. Not only have these economic incentives enhanced China's economy, they have also increased its regional influence (Kurlantzick 2006). As China's power has increased, so too has its ability and ambition to lead the regional architecture.

Nonetheless, Beijing's push for regional integration is hindered by the lack of trust in its political and security initiatives. There are ongoing conflicts between countries in the region, such as the South China Sea dispute and the border dispute between Thailand and Cambodia. One of the biggest problems in the sub-region is poor water resources management. After China began its hydropower activities in the 1980s, concerns and tensions in the region increased. For example, as a Lower Mekong country, Vietnam has become seriously concerned about China's upstream activities. Given that the Mekong Delta in Vietnam alone produces 40 per cent of the rice and protein of the basin, some observers believe that China could use water issues to increase its political leverage in Vietnam's South China Sea policy (Brennan 2018). Others claim that after the South China Sea dispute, potential water resource conflicts could prove to be one of the biggest flashpoints between China and ASEAN (Zhang and Li 2018, p. 5). Because of this, some have warned that China's control of both the South China Sea and the Mekong River will strategically sandwich the Mekong countries (Brennan 2018). China's refusal to participate in the MRC has sparked deeper concerns among the international media, activists and even Mekong government officials over hydropower projects (Qin 2010). China's long-standing 'uncooperative water hegemon' stance on water disputes have limited the success of its appeal for cooperation in the sub-region. This can be seen in recent anti–Chinese investment sentiments at the societal level in Myanmar, Cambodia, and Vietnam (Chen 2014).

Geopolitical tensions and competition with other major powers have triggered a change in the Chinese leadership's approach to neighbourhood diplomacy. Many Chinese sources suggest that China's security environment has deteriorated after Washington's pivot to Asia (Liu and Liu 2019). The escalating territorial disputes between China and its neighbours in the East and South China Seas have led to a strategic realignment between the United States and other regional countries. China considers the US-led security cooperation architecture in the region to be a threat to its own security. Through a broad spectrum of cooperation, the United States has not only built closer military ties with its allies and partners but it has also improved its political relationship with Myanmar, Cambodia and Vietnam (Capie

2015). At the sub-regional level, Washington has strengthened its ties in the Mekong region, a move which China considers a countervailing influence (Dai and Zeng 2017). Closer defence cooperation between Washington and Hanoi on the South China Sea issue has clearly been detrimental to China's security interests.

Thus, the Mekong sub-region has been included as one of the most important targets for China's peripheral diplomacy. For the first time in China's diplomatic history, the Chinese government organised a Peripheral Diplomacy Working Group in October 2013. Complementary to its peripheral diplomacy, China also called for a new security structure—an Asian Security Concept—highlighting that 'multi-polarity is becoming a global trend, [and] regional security affairs should be decided by all the countries in the region through equal participation' (Ministry of Foreign Affairs of the People's Republic of China 2017a).

In the context of China's implementation of the BRI in the strategically important Mekong sub-region, China requires an institution that can reduce threats and strengthen the legitimacy of its leadership. Moreover, China has realised that the use of water resources has affected the stability of relations among countries in the Mekong. China also understands the importance of discursive power in regional governance (Biba 2018). Thus, China is keen to establish an institution that can strengthen its discursive power and improve its security situation. China embraced the opportunities presented by Thailand's launch of a sustainable development initiative in the Mekong sub-region by incorporating political-security, economic, socio-cultural and sustainable development in the LMC.

By including political and security cooperation, the LMC's objectives are not merely driven by economics; in fact, they are part of China's broader strategy (Luo and Su 2019). Although the security and political cooperation are narrowly confined to the non-traditional security arena (Lancang-Mekong Cooperation China Secretariat 2018), this chapter argues that China is pursuing a more comprehensive and committed role in its political and security cooperation with the Mekong sub-region in order to gradually shape regional security norms and institutions in the future. To achieve this, some Chinese scholars have called for bilateral and mini-lateral cooperation to promote political and security cooperation that can facilitate the construction of a regional security architecture that regional states can 'equally participate' in (Wei 2013).

Conceptualising minilateralism in the LMC

Minilateralism was originally introduced when sub-groups of actors typically sought to set ambitious goals beyond multilateral agreements. It is generally understood as a functional approach to address major multilateral issues based on the flexibility of institutional arrangements. The purpose of minilateralism is to use the least number of actors (known as the 'magic number') to achieve the greatest impact on problem solving in the group formation (Nilsson-Wright 2017; Tow 2018). By definition, minilateralism complements multilateralism even though it is informally formed to address contingency issues with fewer states. Eventually, minilateralism can overcome barriers to solve collective action problems by insisting on 'magic numbers' and, more importantly, on a narrower convergence of interests (Lee-Brown 2018). In sum, minilateralism reflects the functionality and flexibility that can overcome the inadequacy of existing formal international and regional institutions to address challenges in world politics.

Borrowing concepts of minilateralism, I will explain in this chapter why China is interested in adopting minilateralism by forming the LMC and how China's approach deviates from the common understanding of minilateralism. First, in minilateralism, the group of players need to have a common or converged interest to join the club. In the Mekong region, China tries to cater to the Mekong countries' demand for development and fulfil these countries' expectations for its role in water governance.

China's LMC minilateralism can fill the gaps left by the established economic institutions. The growing number of mechanisms and institutions shows a trend towards overcapacity in institutionalising cooperation (see Table 4.1). The overlapping yet uncoordinated institutional set-ups by different players have led to institutional congestion in the region (Bi 2008). This institutional congestion has hindered project implementation and resource allocation. The projects under the Ayeyawady-Chao Phraya-Mekong Economic Cooperation Strategy (ACMECS) led by Thailand, which were intended to complement ASEAN's vision for development, do not necessarily translate into economic and social progress (Prachason 2008). Owing to limited funding, not all of the Mekong basin countries' priorities can be met. For example, Yangon, Nay Pyi Taw and Vientiane are not included in any economic corridors in sub-regional cooperation (Asian Development Bank 2018).

Moreover, none of these existing mechanisms has enabled China to cooperate with Mekong countries on water resources management. In the region, there is an urgent need for effective management and proper development of water resources. In 2012, Thailand initiated the International Conference on Sustainable Development, which was designed to engage with China to address water issues. China has realised that institutionalisation of comprehensive cooperation would not be possible without bringing water issues to the negotiating table because Thailand and Vietnam had always requested their inclusion in any negotiations (Le 2018). China considers securitisation of the water disputes by external countries as an impediment to its cooperation with Mekong riparian countries (Luo and Su 2019). China's willingness to incorporate water resource issues into the agenda appears to be a tactic to involve other Mekong countries in the mechanism. Thus, China expects less resistance to its leadership as it shows compromise on water cooperation. Without China's compromise on water cooperation, it is difficult to form such a convergent interest.

Mekong countries appear to be supportive of the LMC because the initiative matches their economic and sustainable development needs while partially addressing transboundary water issues. Having experienced conflict and poverty, the Mekong riparian countries believe that economic development is the best way to

TABLE 4.1 Institutional arrangements by Mekong countries

Member countries	GMS	AMBDC	MRC	FCDI	QEC	AEM-METI	ACMECS	Emerald Triangle	CLVDT	GQEC
Cambodia	x	x	x	x		x	x	x	x	x
Laos	x	x	x	x	x	x	x	x	x	x
Myanmar	x	x			x	x	x			
Thailand	x	x	x		x		x	x		x
Vietnam	x	x	x	x		x	x		x	x
China	x	x			x					

Source: Author's compilation.

Notes: GMS (Greater Mekong Subregion); AMBDC (ASEAN Mekong Basin Development Cooperation); MRC (Mekong River Commission); FCDI (Forum for the Comprehensive Development of Indo-China); QEC (Quadripartite Economic Cooperation: China–Yunnan, Laos, Myanmar and Thailand); AEM-METI Working Group on Economic Cooperation in Cambodia, Laos and Myanmar; ACMECS (Ayeyawady-Chao Phraya–Mekong Economic Cooperation Strategy); Emerald Triangle (Cambodia, Laos and Thailand); CLVDT (Cambodia-Laos-Vietnam development triangle); GQEC (Golden Quadrangle Economic Cooperation).

avoid future strife and to ensure regional and regime stability. Mekong countries tend to share a common vision for economic development with China while downplaying the difficult issues that confront them.

In water resources management where differences and conflicts of interests along the Mekong River undermine regional cooperation, China has expressed its willingness to share more data on water quantity and quality through the LMC, particularly during the dry season. In order to demonstrate that it is a responsible upstream country, China decided to channel water from the Jinghong hydropower station in April 2016 to the Mekong River to help downstream countries to mitigate severe droughts. Moreover, LMC countries face common non-traditional security issues (such as international money laundering, human trafficking and drugs and arms smuggling) that have a severe security impact on societal and economic activities.

Second, the formation of 'magic numbers' in minilateralism implies exclusiveness. The membership size is necessary for forming a grouping with the most significant impact. The purpose of exclusiveness is to reduce the potential barriers to cooperation. These include agenda setting, means, purposes and membership. The exclusiveness in membership provides opportunities for the powerful group to include norms, promote concepts and to enhance its influence through the provision of public goods.

Tapping into the appeal of Thailand, China tactically chooses to unite the region with the shared water issue. The geographical label 'Lancang-Mekong' is used in the framework's name to limit membership to countries in the region. It is an effective way for China to exclude the involvement of the United States and Japan. Using different levels of official statements, the Chinese leadership has highlighted not only shared water issues but also the importance of the regional countries' historical, geographical and cultural ties with China. In a joint communiqué released by the LMC, it stated that the six countries 'along the Lancang-Mekong River are closely linked geographically, socially and culturally' (Lancang-Mekong Cooperation China Secretariat 2015). In Chinese Premier Li Keqiang's words, 'our security and development interests are closely inter-connected' (ibid. 2016a). In establishing the mechanism, China also sought to strengthen a common identity by ensuring that the future of the Lancang-Mekong countries is intrinsically linked to that of China. In highlighting the concept of a shared identity, China is implying that it has a share in the future development of the Mekong sub-region.

As the most powerful country in the initiative, the membership criteria of the LMC allows China to assume a leading position and to exert influence by setting norms, promoting new concepts and redefining sub-regional cooperation. By highlighting the LMC's functionality, China has emphasised its ability to provide public goods and showcased its capacity for greater regional governance. Understanding that Mekong riparian countries prefer short-term projects that effectively support livelihoods, Beijing highlighted the benefits of its task-oriented approach to the sub-region (Zhou 2018). According to Li, the 'LMC is not an empty talk shop but a pragmatic actor' (Ministry of Foreign Affairs of the People's Republic of

China 2018). Many Chinese sources have also suggested that the LMC will over-take existing mechanisms such as the GMS because these mechanisms have been unable to meet the demands of regional cooperation and have become 'ineffective' in public goods provision and in regional cooperation (F Luo 2018).

At the first LMC Leaders' Meeting in March 2016, China demonstrated its capability by committing RMB 10 billion (US$ 1 billion) in preferential loans and a credit limit of US$ 10 billion (US$ 5 billion for special loans for capacity coop-eration and US$ 5 billion for preferential export buyer credit) to support infra-structure and production capacity projects of the Mekong countries. China also promised to provide support for projects in support of poverty reduction, the promotion of small and medium-sized enterprises, agriculture, training in water resource use and education. The Chinese media claimed that all 45 Early Harvest Projects identified at the first Leaders' Meeting were executed as planned. The proposed US$ 5 billion special loans for production capacity cooperation even exceeded the original target. Furthermore, the China-sponsored special fund for the first 132 cooperative projects has now been fully launched (Y Luo 2018). By leading the LMC, China can secure a high level of cooperation as well as assure regional partners of the benefits of Chinese projects. For example, China's invest-ment in 2017 grew by more than 20 per cent from the previous year. Following the First Leaders' Meeting, more than 330 new flight routes between China and five countries were opened, and about 30 million person-to-person exchanges were reported in 2017 (Ministry of Foreign Affairs of the People's Republic of China 2018).

Third, minilateralism fits China's preferred functional and flexible approach in tackling water governance issues. Generally, China has been suspicious of joining multilateral institutions such as the United Nations Convention on the Law of Non-Navigational Uses of International Watercourses (Biba 2014). Unlike the MRC, the LMC's founding documents do not mandate any prior consultation and makes no mention of disputes or resolutions, thus setting few, if any, restrictions on its future hydropower activities. Instead, the LMC's approach is based on consensus, mutual benefits, coordination and implementation (Guan and Wu 2018).

The launch of the LMC shows that China has transformed its tactics towards the institutionalisation of the water issue. China recognises that the exclusive nature and functional role of minilateralism do not necessarily undermine its interests. In fact, minilateralism complements its preferred bilateralism. China has reiterated that the LMC's establishment is an innovative way of exploring bilateral and multilateral relations (Y Luo 2018). In practice, China has set up bilateral water cooperation with Cambodia and Laos. Memorandums of Understandings (MoUs) were signed between the water authorities of China and these two countries. In this regard, the multilateral package lacks substance but facilitates greater collaboration at the bilateral level.

To assuage growing concerns about its impact, the Chinese government defines the relationship between the LMC and existing mechanisms as 'complementary and coordinative' during the preparation period (Lu and Luo 2018). For example, at the LMC's first Leaders' Meeting, Li Keqiang stated that the LMC would be a beneficial, complementary and upgraded version of the bilateral cooperation between China and ASEAN (Lancang-Mekong Cooperation China Secretariat 2016b). At the second Leaders' Meeting, Li highlighted that the 'LMC will not replace other cooperative mechanisms … and it will mutually reinforce the progress and development of the existing mechanism such as GMS' (Ministry of Foreign Affairs of the People's Republic of China 2018). In order to further reassure the members of ASEAN, Li reiterated that the three pillars of the LMC were highly compatible with the ASEAN Community, and that the reduction of the development gap between ASEAN members would enhance the further integration of ASEAN (ibid.).

China also embraces multilateral elements selectively through marginal compromises on water issues. To achieve this, China has been selective in extending support in water cooperation. China uses its leadership role to decide which issues should be prioritised and which can be dealt with at a later date. China's call for water governance cooperation is done mainly through Track II exchanges, as well as technological, education and human resources training. For instance, in March 2017, the Lancang-Mekong Water Resources Cooperation, sponsored by China's Ministry of Water Resources, organised a number of activities that were intended to improve communication, capacity building and interaction with Lower Mekong countries (Global Water Partnership 2017). China also set up the Lancang-Mekong Water Resource Cooperation Centre and the Global Centre for Mekong River Studies. Beijing started to engage with other existing institutions such as the MRC by signing the Agreement on the Provision of Hydrological Information on the Lancang-Mekong River (which is conditional upon providing water data) and by engaging in the Global Water Partnership (Mekong River Commission 2017).

Moreover, the LMC has provided the Lower Mekong countries with opportunities to influence China with regard to transboundary water cooperation. In cooperation theory, the weaker states cooperate through institutions in order to attain 'voice opportunities' vis-à-vis their stronger partners. Meanwhile, the powerful group legitimises its leadership and power through constructing a framework that may require the relinquishment of some degree of leadership or some benefits to the weaker group (Goh 2011).

China's agreement to the inclusion of the water issue has demonstrated the 'voice' effect of the Mekong countries. To encourage participation of Mekong riparian countries, China highlighted discourse power in the institution and 'consultation on equal footing' (Ministry of Foreign Affairs of the People's Republic of China 2018). On several occasions, China reiterated that Mekong countries should not view China merely as a partner for dialogue or development but as an equal partner in co-managing the Mekong River (Lancang-Mekong Cooperation China Secretariat 2017). The consensus-based agreement on the LMC shows that the Mekong countries can propose or object to agendas based on their interest calculation.

The common interests, exclusiveness, functionality and flexibility of mini-lateralism helps China to align the preference of Mekong countries to its interests and to expand its influence under the cover of small-scale multilateralism. Through membership, agenda setting and institutional incentives that have empowered the 'voices' of the Mekong countries, China has tactfully changed the course of regional governance.

Impact on the regional architecture

The LMC holds a very different meaning and rethinking of the regional architecture. The exclusive nature of the LMC suggests that the emergence of China-led regionalism is taking place in the Mekong sub-region, and is manifested through closer political-security cooperation, China-shaped regional governance and strengthened multipolar structure.

The LMC showcases the way China approaches the Mekong with interests in economic cooperation and in potential political and security cooperation. In the 1990s, law enforcement cooperation between China and Mekong countries was small scale and sporadic. It was only in 2011, after the murder of Chinese merchants on the Mekong River provided China with an opportunity to strengthen its leadership in law enforcement and security cooperation, that China, Laos, Myanmar and Thailand issued the Joint Declaration on Law Enforcement and Security Cooperation on the Mekong and signed the Joint Declaration on Joint Law Enforcement Ministerial Level Meeting to conduct joint patrols (The Central People's Government of the People's Republic of China 2011). Through the LMC, China has become successful in expanding the economic cooperation agenda to further consolidate political and security cooperation, elevating the quadrilateral cooperation to sub-regional cooperation. Eventually, China set up the Lancang-Mekong Integrated Law Enforcement and Security Cooperation Centre in Kunming in December 2017.

Moreover, China's attempt to expand political and security cooperation from the Mekong sub-region to ASEAN has been consistent. As early as 2002, China proposed the Joint Declaration on Cooperation in the Field of Non-traditional Security Issues at the ARF and signed the MoU on Non-traditional Security Cooperation with ASEAN in 2004. China's participation in non-traditional security cooperation during this period was multilateral under ASEAN and mostly issue-based. However, China highlighted that security cooperation is needed to assist the smooth implementation of the BRI (ASEAN 2017). In October 2015, China hosted not only the Ministerial Meeting on Law Enforcement and Security Cooperation along the Mekong River, but also the China-ASEAN Ministerial Dialogue on Law Enforcement and Security Cooperation with the theme 'Security for Prosperity'. To prove its capability for regional governance, China provided public security goods such as funding, technology and capacity building for law enforcement officers.

China has also been keen to instigate bilateral security and political cooperation while using minilateral settings to garner regional support. For example, since 2018

China has conducted the annual Sino-Cambodian humanitarian assistance and disaster relief exercise (known as Dragon Gold). It was interpreted as Cambodia's intention of distancing itself from the United States after Phnom Penh suspended the Angkor Sentinel exercise (an annual bilateral military exercise) with the United States in 2017. Cambodia also postponed indefinitely the humanitarian mission provided by the US Seabees (Congressional Research Service 2019). Interestingly, China's military engagement with Thailand, a US ally, also increased following the Thai *coup d'état* in 2014. In 2016, Chinese arms sales to Thailand overtook those from the United States by US\$ 30 million (US-China Economic and Security Review Commission 2017, p. 313). Both sides also expanded their naval drill bilateral exercises to include joint air force exercises (Crispin 2016).

The LMC also has significant implications for Mekong River governance as the features of the institutional setting are designed to shape regional governance according to China's preference. The LMC is expected to sideline existing mechanisms such as the MRC and the ASEAN Mekong Basin Development Cooperation as China aspires to play an important role in regional and global governance. The absence of an effective forum for monitoring hydropower activities on the Mekong limits the ability of the MRC to oversee the member and dialogue states (China and Myanmar). While China is seen as cooperating with the MRC, if a joint organisation comes to fruition, the principles and rules remain questionable (Middleton 2018).

Regarding ASEAN's role, it is perceived to be less interested than the LMC in the Mekong sub-region. For example, in terms of scale and size, the ASEAN-Mekong Basin Development Cooperation has invested and achieved much less than the newly established LMC (Ho and Pitakdumrongkit 2019). It appears that the LMC is likely to alleviate sub-regional poverty, and improve industrial cooperation and many other economic-centred agendas. However, as China exerts enormous capital and political influence on the weaker Mekong countries, Southeast Asian countries could become further divided on regional issues. China's ability to get Mekong countries to acknowledge its global interests is becoming a reality. Cambodia, for example, repeatedly blocked ASEAN from issuing critical statements about China's activities in the disputed South China Sea in 2012 and 2016. China's close relationship with Cambodia has undercut ASEAN's ability to promote freedom of navigation in the South China Sea. Therefore, a minilateralised LMC has the potential to challenge the centrality of ASEAN in regional issues.

This region will gradually witness a more complex multipolar regional order. In the three decades following the ending of the Cold War, the regional architecture in Asia has been dominated by the 'hub-and-spokes' US-led bilateral alliance system and ASEAN-led multilateral institutions. The LMC's emergence could be the first of many minilateral initiatives that may change the landscape of the regional architecture.

Yet despite the erosion of Washington's role, regional players are not seen as bandwagoning with China. Instead, minilateralism in the Mekong region has gained more traction owing to concerns over China's rising political and economic clout. Lower Mekong countries, together with external powers, have responded to the China-led LMC by resisting the potential dominance of China. For example, Thailand's concerns about China were reflected in the revival of ACMECS. This sub-regional initiative was launched by former Thai Prime Minister Thaksin Shinawatra, who was ousted by the Thai military regime. Its revival implied the growing concerns of the Thai military regime about China's leadership in the LMC where China has been supplying all the necessary resources to the sub-region (*The Nation* 2018). At the fourth ACMECS Mekong Ministerial Meeting in 2018, Thailand invited Japan, India, South Korea and the United States to be development partners in ACMECS, but excluded China (Ministry of Foreign Affairs of the Kingdom of Thailand 2018). Vietnam also sees the LMC as facilitating China's growing influence on regional foreign policy and security. Hence, Vietnam has been taking advantage of its leadership position under the Cambodia-Laos-Vietnam Development Triangle (CLVDT) supported by Japan (Chheang 2018). Vietnam's leadership in the CLVDT is considered to be geopolitically driven because it is aimed at weakening China's influence and increasing its sub-regional influence (Ariffin 2018). All these developments demonstrate that rather than bandwagoning with China, regional powers are more likely to balance it.

Since the United States has pulled back from previous commitments to move towards institutionalised regional and global engagement, China has taken the opportunity to capitalise on this change in stance. China appears to have committed more resources to the LMC than the United States has committed to the Lower Mekong Initiative (LMI) (Thongnoi 2019). For example, the amount of funding for the LMI dropped from US$ 11.5 million in 2015 to US$ 3 million in 2016—a 74 per cent decline (US-China Economic and Security Review Commission 2017, pp. 292–3).

Despite the limited commitment of Washington, concerns about China's potential institutional dominance in the LMC is driving other regional players to strengthen their relationship with Mekong countries and even the whole region. Among these players, Japan is emerging as a major regional power. Recently, China's strong push into the financing and development of the Mekong region's infrastructure has spurred Japan to become more active. Tokyo has thus proposed its own policy platform to engage the Mekong sub-region, hoping to draw regional states away from too much Chinese influence. For example, Japan issued the New Tokyo Strategy 2015 for Mekong-Japan Cooperation to promote hard and soft connectivity within the Mekong region.

Australia has also made attempts to stay relevant by initiating the Greater Mekong Water Resources Program (Australian Mission to ASEAN n.d.). Since 2005, Canberra has committed over A$ 560 million (US$ 384 million) to regional programmes in Southeast Asia and launched the Mekong Business Initiative and the Greater Mekong Subregion Trade and Transport Facilitation Program in response to China's BRI. India has also promoted its conceptions of regional order through initiatives such as Project Mausam (Pillalamarri 2014).

Although observers may argue that Australia and India will be unable to match the number of economic packages provided by China, these initiatives geared at the Southeast Asian countries can mitigate China's influence to a certain extent (Gong 2019). In fact, concerns about China's dominance in the region is driving the Mekong Basin countries to deepen their strategy of hedging with other major powers. In the Tokyo Strategy of 2018, the Mekong Basin countries expressed their common position and support for the Japan-initiated Free and Open Indo-Pacific strategy (Ministry of Foreign Affairs of Japan 2018). Meanwhile, Vietnam, which waged a ferocious war against the United States in the 1960s, has increased its bilateral defence cooperation with the United States.

In addition, the proliferation of emerging minilateral or trilateral initiatives in recent years is also evidence of attempts by regional powers to develop a regional order. These attempts include the signing of a trilateral cooperation agreement between India, Japan and Vietnam in December 2014 (Panda 2019). In 2016, Japan and India also agreed to develop an Asia-Africa Growth Corridor that will connect Mekong with the Indian subcontinent.

Such developments indicate that it will not be easy for China to dominate the region even though the United States lacks commitment to the region. This region is expected to see a multipolar trend with different players affecting the regional order. At least for now, rather than bandwagoning with China, regional powers are more likely to continue to balance China's expanding presence (Bajpaee 2017).

Conclusion

In response to geopolitical tensions and geo-economic competition with the United States and other major powers in the region, the Chinese leadership has sought to create an institution that could help to strengthen its leadership, improve its global image on matters relating to water governance and enhance its security environment. To achieve this, China has employed the tactic of using minilateralism's functionality, flexibility and exclusiveness of membership to institutionalise cooperation.

All the Mekong riparian countries agree with China that economic development is imperative for sustaining stability and security. Nevertheless, none of the existing mechanisms has enabled China to cooperate with the Mekong countries on water resources management. China is using minilateralism as a cover to exclude other external players by highlighting identity, selectively setting an agenda that interests the other members, and providing regional public goods. Given its important location on the transboundary river, China is able to embrace multilateral elements selectively by making minimal concessions on the water issues without compromising its strategic interests.

The Lower Mekong countries are also motivated by the LMC's functionality and flexibility to collaborate with one another. It appears that LMC economic projects are likely to reduce poverty, enhance industrial cooperation and support many other economic-centred agendas. In this regard, China's minilateral mechanisms on economic development and connectivity are complementary to the vision of ASEAN.

However, this minilateral initiative lacks multilateral substance. Instead, it complements China's bilateral approach towards water governance. China has been able to shape water governance based on its preferences, mainly in bilateral cooperation and in its conditional support for the MRC and other existing mechanisms. Beijing also has strengthened its role in regional political and security cooperation. The centrality of ASEAN and other existing mechanisms have been challenged by China's pursuit of regional governance through political-security cooperation and increased capabilities. Compared to the LMC (and other mechanisms established by external players), ASEAN seems to be less relevant in the development and governance of the Mekong sub-region.

As the United States has moved away from institutionalised regional and global engagement, China is reaping the benefits and taking advantage of the declining US presence. China's ability to get the Mekong countries to acknowledge its global interests is becoming a reality as demonstrated by Cambodia's foreign policy on regional issues. The emergence of the LMC will change the landscape of the regional architecture which is based on the US alliance system and ASEAN-centred multilateralism. However, the Lower Mekong countries, together with other external players such as Japan, Australia and India, will continue to resist the potential dominance of China not just in the Mekong sub-region but also at the regional level. It is probably fair to say that the launch of the LMC will strengthen the trend towards a multipolar Asia in the future.

References

Ariffin, E 2018, 'What is the CLV development triangle area?' *ASEAN Post*, 15 November, viewed 12 November 2018, https://theaseanpost.com/article/what-clv-development-triangle-area.

ASEAN 2017, 'Joint Statement: the Fifth ASEAN Plus China Ministerial Meeting on Transnational Crime (5th AMMTC+China) Consultation', 21 September, viewed 13 January 2019, https://asean.org/joint-statement-the-fifth-asean-plus-china-ministerial-meeting-on-transnational-crime-5th-ammtc-china-consultation/.

Asian Development Bank 2018, *Review of Configuration of the Greater Mekong Subregion Economic Corridors*, viewed 10 October 2018, www.adb.org/sites/default/files/institutional-document/400626/gms-corridors-configuration-review.pdf.

Australian Mission to ASEAN n.d., 'Cooperation programs: Australia's ASEAN and Mekong program', viewed 29 July 2019, https://asean.mission.gov.au/aesn/cooperationprograms2.html.

Bajpaee, C 2017, 'The birth of a multipolar Asia', *The Interpreter*, 22 May, viewed 31 July 2019, www.lowyinstitute.org/the-interpreter/birth-multipolar-asia.

Bi, S 2008, 'Taiguo yu yuenan zai meigonghe diqu de hezuo yu jingzheng' [Cooperation and competition in the Mekong River Basin between Thailand and Vietnam], *Dongnanya yanjiu [Southeast Asian Studies]*, vol. 1, pp. 27–31.

Biba, S 2014, 'Desecuritization in China's behavior towards its transboundary rivers: the Mekong River, the Brahmaputra River, and the Irtysh and Ili Rivers', *Journal of Contemporary China*, vol. 23, no. 85, pp. 21–43.

Biba, S 2018, 'China's "old" and "new" Mekong river politics: the Lancang-Mekong Cooperation from a comparative benefit-sharing perspective', *Water International*, vol. 43, no. 5, pp. 622–641.

Brennan, E 2018, 'China eyes its next prize – the Mekong', *The Interpreter*, 5 June, viewed 30 November 2018, www.lowyinstitute.org/the-interpreter/china-eyes-its-next-prize-mekong.

Capie, D 2015, 'The United States and humanitarian assistance and disaster relief (HADR) in East Asia: connecting coercive and non-coercive uses of military power', *Journal of Strategic Studies*, vol. 38, no. 3, pp. 309–331.

Chen, Q 2014, 'Zhongguo zhoubian waijiao de zhengce tiaozheng yu xinlinian' [The adjustment and new outlook on China's neighbourhood diplomacy], *Dangdaiyatai [Contemporary Asia-Pacific]*, vol. 3, pp. 4–26.

Chheang, V 2018, 'The Cambodia-Laos-Vietnam Development Triangle Area', *Perspective*, no. 30, 6 June.

Congressional Research Service 2019, 'Cambodia: background and U.S. relations', 28 January, viewed 20 May 2019, https://fas.org/sgp/crs/row/R44037.pdf.

Crispin, S 2016, 'Thailand's post-coup foreign policy: omnidirectional or directionless?' *The Diplomat*, 10 June, viewed 13 May 2019, https://thediplomat.com/2016/06/thailands-post-coup-foreign-policy-omnidirectional-or-directionless/.

Dai, Y and Zeng, K 2017, 'Lanmeihezuo jizhi de xianzhuang pingxi: chengxiao, wenti yu duice' [Comment and analysis of Lancang Mekong Cooperation mechanism: effectiveness, problems and solutions], *International Forum*, vol. 19, no. 4, pp. 1–6.

Global Water Partnership 2017, *GWP in Lancang-Mekong Water Resources Cooperation*, viewed 10 October 2018, www.gwp.org/en/GWP-China/about-gwp-china/events-list/2017/gwp-in-lancang-mekong-water-resources-cooperation/.

Goh, E 2007, 'Developing the Mekong: regionalism and regional security in China-Southeast Asian relations', *Adelphi Paper*, no. 387.

Goh, E 2011, 'Institutions and the great power bargain in East Asia: ASEAN's limited "brokerage" role', *International Relations of the Asia-Pacific*, vol. 11, no. 3, pp. 373–401.

Gong, X 2019, 'The Belt & Road Initiative and China's influence in south-east Asia', *Pacific Review*, vol. 32, no. 4, pp. 635–665.

Guan, Z and Wu, Y 2018, 'Lanmei sudu shi ruhe liancheng de?' [How is the speedy efficiency of the LMC ensured?], State Council of the People's Republic of China, 14 January, viewed 28 July 2019, www.gov.cn/xinwen/2018-01/14/content_5256587.htm.

Ho, S and Pitakdumrongkit, K 2019, 'Can ASEAN play a greater role in the Mekong sub-region?' *The Diplomat*, 30 January, viewed 12 May 2019, https://thediplomat.com/2019/01/can-asean-play-a-greater-role-in-the-mekong-subregion/.

Ikenberry, J and Lim, D 2017, *China's Emerging Institutional Statecraft: The Asian Infrastructure Investment Bank and the Prospect for Counter-Hegemony*, Washington, DC, Brookings Institute.

Kurlantzick, J 2006, 'China's charm offensive in Southeast Asia', *Current History*, vol. 105, no. 692, pp. 270–276.

Lancang-Mekong Cooperation China Secretariat 2015, 'Joint Press Communiqué of the First Lancang-Mekong Cooperation Foreign Ministers' Meeting', 12 November, viewed 14 August 2018, www.lmcchina.org/eng/zywj_5/t1514151.htm.

Lancang-Mekong Cooperation China Secretariat 2016a, 'Sanya Declaration of the First Lancang-Mekong Cooperation (LMC) Leaders' Meeting', 23 March, viewed 20 September 2019, www.lmcchina.org/eng/zywj_5/t1513793.htm.

Lancang-Mekong Cooperation China Secretariat 2016b, 'Li Keqiang's address at the 1st Lancang-Mekong Cooperation Leaders' Meeting', 25 March, viewed 14 August 2018, www.lmcchina.org/eng/zywj_5/t1514128.htm.

Lancang-Mekong Cooperation China Secretariat 2017, 'Lanmei hezuo wuge shenme' [Five 'whats' in Lancang-Mekong Cooperation], 10 March, viewed 14 August 2018, www.lmcchina.org/lmwsj/t1517484.htm.

Lancang-Mekong Cooperation China Secretariat 2018, 'Lancangjiang Meigonghe hezo wunian jihua (2018–2022)' [Five-year plan of the Lancang-Mekong Cooperation], 1 November, viewed 18 May 2019, www.lmcchina.org/zywj/t1524906.htm.

Le, HB 2018, 'Cooperation mechanisms in the Mekong region and Vietnam's participation', *Communist Review*, 27 July, viewed 15 December 2018, http://english.tapchicongsan.org. vn/Home/Foreign-Relations-and-International-Intergration/2018/1141/Cooperation-M echanisms-in-the-Mekong-Region-and-Vietnams-participation.aspx.

Lee-Brown, T 2018, 'Asia's security triangles: maritime minilateralism in the Indo-Pacific', *East Asia*, vol. 35, no. 2, pp. 163–176.

Li, M 2015, 'The People's Liberation Army and China's smart power quandary in Southeast Asia', *Journal of Strategic Studies*, vol. 38, no. 3, pp. 359–382.

Liu, F and Liu, R 2019, 'China, the United States and order transition in East Asia: an economy-security nexus approach', *Pacific Review*, viewed 11 September 2019, www.ta ndfonline.com/doi/abs/10.1080/09512748.2018.1526205?journalCode=rpre20.

Lu, G 2016, 'China seeks to improve Mekong sub-regional cooperation: causes and policies', *Policy Report*, February.

Lu, G and Luo H 2018, 'Lanmei hezuo jinru "gaotie shida"' [Lancang Mekong Cooperation enters the era of 'high-speed railway'], Lancang-Mekong Cooperation China Secretariat, 16 January, viewed 30 January 2019, www.lmcchina.org/hzdt/t1526032.htm.

Luo, F 2018, 'Cong dameigonghejizhi dao lanmeihezuo: zhongnanbandao shang de guoji zhidujingzheng' [From Greater-Mekong mechanism to Lancang-Mekong Cooperation: international institutional competition in the Indochina peninsular], *Waijiao pinglun* [*Foreign Affairs*], vol. 6, pp. 119–156.

Luo, S and Su, L 2019, 'Lanmei hezuo yu damei hezuo de bijiao ji qishi' [Comparative studies between Lancang Mekong Cooperation and Greater Mekong Subregion cooperation and lessons], *Heping yu fazhan* [*Peace and Development*], vol. 1, pp. 47–64.

Luo, Y 2018, 'Lanmei hezuo jizhi: jichu deyi wushi, qianjiang gengjia guangkuo' [Lancang-Mekong Cooperation: enhance the foundation for a more promising future], Zhonghua Renmin Gongheguo Zhongyang Renmin Zhengfu [The Central People's Government of the People's Republic of China], 1 October, viewed 30 March 2019, www.gov.cn/ xinwen/2018-01/10/content_5255765.htm.

Mekong River Commission 2017, 'About MRC: upstream partners', viewed 14 August 2018, www.mrcmekong.org/about-mrc/upstream-partners/.

Middleton, C 2018, 'Can Chinese "reciprocity" protect the Mekong?' *China Dialogue*, 12 November, viewed 14 November 2018, www.chinadialogue.net/article/show/single/en/ 10901-Can-Chinese-reciprocity-protect-the-Mekong-.

Ministry of Foreign Affairs of Japan 2018, 'Tokyo strategy 2018 for Mekong-Japan cooperation', 9 October, viewed 15 November 2019, https://www.mofa.go.jp/files/000406731.pdf.

Ministry of Foreign Affairs of the Kingdom of Thailand 2018, 'The Minister of Foreign Affairs of Thailand attended Mekong sub-regional ministerial meetings 2–3 August 2018, Singapore', 10 August, viewed 14 August 2018, www.mfa.go.th/main/en/news3/6886/ 93044-The-Minister-of-Foreign-Affairs-of-Thailand-Attend.html.

Ministry of Foreign Affairs of the People's Republic of China 2017a, 'China's policies on Asia-Pacific security cooperation', 11 January, viewed 14 July 2019, www.fmprc.gov. cn/mfa_eng/zxxx_662805/t1429771.shtml.

Ministry of Foreign Affairs of the People's Republic of China 2017b, 'Wang Yi: Dazao genggao shuipingde zhongguo-dongmeng zhanlve huoban guanxi' [Wang Yi: Building a higher level of ASEAN-China strategic partnership relationship], 6 August, viewed 14 August 2018, www.mfa.gov.cn/chn//pds/wjb/zzjg/yzs/dqzz/dnygjlm/xgxw/t1482789.htm.

Ministry of Foreign Affairs of the People's Republic of China 2018, 'Li Keqiang zai Lan-cangjiang-Meigonghe hezuo dierci lingdaoren huiyi shangde jianghua' [Speech by Prime Minister Li Keqiang at the Second Leaders' Meeting on Lancang-Mekong Cooperation], 11 January, viewed 14 January 2019, www.fmprc.gov.cn/web/zyxw/t1524884.shtml.

Nilsson-Wright, J 2017, *Creative Minilateralism in a Changing Asia: Opportunities for Security Convergence and Cooperation between Australia, India, and Japan*, London, Chatham House.

Panda, J 2019, 'The India-Japan-Vietnam trilateral: an "inclusive" proposition', Italian Institute for International Political Studies, 16 April, viewed 31 July 2019, www.ispion line.it/sites/default/files/pubblicazioni/commentary_panda_16.04.2019.pdf.

Pillalamarri, A 2014, 'Project Mausam: India's answer to China's "Maritime Silk Road"', *The Diplomat*, 18 September, viewed 20 July 2019, https://thediplomat.com/2014/09/p roject-mausam-indias-answer-to-chinas-maritime-silk-road/.

Prachason, S 2008, 'Ayeyawady-Chao Phraya-Mekong Economic Cooperation Strategy (ACMECS): another perspective from Thailand', in AC Chandra and JJ Chavez (eds), *Civil Society Reflection on Southeast Asian Regionalism: ASEAN@40*, Quezon, South East Asian Committee for Advocacy.

Qin, H 2010, 'Meigonghe kushui zhi si' [Thoughts on the drought of the Mekong River], *Jingji Kuancha Wang* [*Economic Affairs Observer*], 13 April, viewed 12 September 2018, http://www.eeo.com.cn/observer/shijiao/2010/04/13/167385.shtml.

The Central People's Government of the People's Republic of China 2011, 'Zhong lao tai mian meigonghe lianhe xunluo zhifa buzhangji huiyi lianhe shengming' [Joint Declaration of Ministers from China, Laos, Myanmar and Thailand on Joint Patrolling and Law Enforcement on the Mekong River], 29 November, viewed 20 June 2019, www.gov.cn/jrzg/2011-11/29/content_2006374.htm.

The Nation 2018, 'A disappointing show from ACMECS', *The Nation*, 18 June, viewed 21 November 2018, www.nationmultimedia.com/detail/opinion/30348079.

Thongnoi, J 2019, 'Too little, too late for US "recommitment" to Mekong countries? China's already there', *South China Morning Post*, 16 June, viewed 31 July 2019, www.sc mp.com/week-asia/politics/article/3014612/too-little-too-late-us-recommitment-mekon g-countries-chinas.

Tow, WT 2018, 'Minilateral security's relevance to US strategy in the Indo-Pacific: challenges and prospects', *Pacific Review*, vol. 32, no. 2, pp. 232–244.

US-China Economic and Security Review Commission 2017, 'China and the world', in *2017 Annual Report*, viewed 18 September 2019, www.uscc.gov/sites/default/files/Annua l_Report/Chapters/Chapter%203%2C%20Section%201%20-%20China%20and%20Conti nental%20Southeast%20Asia.pdf.

Vu, T 2014, 'Between system maker and privileges taker: the role of China in the Greater Mekong Sub-region', *Revista Brasileira de Política Internacional* [*Brazilian Journal of International Politics*], vol. 57, pp. 157–173.

Wei, H 2013, 'The architecture of non-traditional security cooperation mechanisms in south-east Asia and China's strategic thinking', *Southeast Asian Affairs*, vol. 154, no. 2, pp. 1–8.

Zhang, H and Li, M 2018, 'Thirsty China and its transboundary waters', in H Zhang and M Li (eds), *China and Transboundary Water Politics in Asia*, New York, Routledge, pp. 3–24.

Zhou, S 2018, 'Lancangjiang-Meigonghe hezuo jizhi: dongli, tedian he qianjingfenxi' [Lancang-Mekong Cooperation mechanism: motivation, characteristics and prospect analysis], *Crossroads: Southeast Asian Studies*, vol. 1, pp. 70–76.

5

LANCANG-MEKONG COOPERATION

The current state of China's hydro-politics

Shang-su Wu

Introduction

The Lancang-Mekong Cooperation (LMC) mechanism is China's multi-pronged initiative regarding the regional development of the countries in the Mekong basin. As membership is restricted to the riparian countries and excludes extra-regional countries, the LMC not only demonstrates Beijing's willingness to manage river-related issues with its downstream counterparts but is also a way of strengthening its influence on mainland Southeast Asia. The distinctiveness of the LMC, in contrast to other organisations on the Mekong River,[1] is China's substantial influence on water flows through the fait accompli tactic of dam construction. China's fait accompli tactics can be defined in terms of its unilateral actions which have irreversibly changed the status quo, leaving its neighbours with no feasible alternative. Despite the advantages of fait accompli tactics, certain challenges such as funding may, however, constrain the effectiveness of the LMC as well as China's geopolitical influence in the long term. Furthermore, the LMC's formation is based on specific geopolitical characteristics which are not present in other areas adjacent to China, thus suggesting the infeasibility of replicating the LMC's institutional form elsewhere.

Water resources management has been identified as the core issue confronting countries bordering the Mekong River due to the rapid increase in dam-building activities by all the riparian countries, especially China. The high potential of hydropower in the Mekong River has driven the riparian countries to build hydropower dams; Beijing took the lead ahead of its neighbouring counterparts back in the 1980s and set the precedent for them (Biba 2018b, pp. 76–7). Following Beijing's gradual commission of large dams on the river, it has been blamed for related flooding and droughts by the mass media, non-governmental organisations and other non-official sectors (International Rivers 2014; *The Economist*

2019). Although the official positions of the downstream countries have been cautious towards China—probably due to trade, investment and the latter's involvement in the former's dam-building activities (Urban *et al.* 2018, pp. 43–4, 49–53)—water resources management remains a contentious issue between China and the rest of the Mekong countries, given the significant amount of water that flows from China (Biba 2018b, p. 71).

China's attitude to its dam-building projects on the Lancang River has been complicated. Despite its strong belief that water is a sovereign issue—thus accounting for its objection to participating in the Convention on the Law of the Non-navigational Uses of International Watercourses (commonly referred to as the UN Watercourses Convention—UNWC)—China has engaged in some forms of cooperation such as data sharing and fisheries management with other Mekong countries and organisations (Feng *et al.* 2019, p. 60; Mekong River Commission n.d.(b); UN Watercourses Convention 2019). Thus, the establishment of the LMC in 2016 represents a further step by China to improve the water management of the Mekong, in addition to other kinds of cooperation in political and security issues, economic and sustainable development, and social, cultural and people to people exchanges (Lancang-Mekong Cooperation China Secretariat 2017a). The timing of Beijing's foundation of the LMC could also be seen as a fait accompli tactic given that the main Chinese dams on the Lancang River had already been commissioned. The direct impact of China's dams on the downstream countries of the Mekong River makes the LMC essential for the five riparian countries (Wu 2018). The LMC is also Beijing's first attempt to build a multilateral or minilateral organisation without accommodating other major or regional powers. Before we discuss this matter further, it is necessary to survey the current literature on the LMC.

Literature review

Since the Mekong River has been significant for academic research, the LMC naturally attracts other researchers' attention. Relying on long-term observation, Biba (2018a) compares China's foreign policies on the Mekong before and after the establishment of the LMC, and points out the mechanism's attraction for the Southeast Asian riparian member countries. The LMC has institutionalised the benefits of cooperation while reducing the cost of challenges such as droughts and damage to the dams. Nevertheless, the success of the sensitive and difficult issue of water resources management is critical for the LMC (Biba 2018a, pp. 625–6, 628–38). Guo (2018, pp. 73–85) also reviews the background and motives of the LMC before making some policy recommendations. Yang (2019, pp. 108–10, 121–5) focuses on the LMC's background and offers policy suggestions, but pays specific attention to international cooperation, particularly with the Association of Southeast Asian Nations (ASEAN) and existing organisations focusing on the development of the Mekong River, such as the Greater Mekong Subregion (GMS) Economic Cooperation Program and the Mekong River Commission. Xing (2017) addresses the LMC's importance through water security while paying specific attention to China's role. Middleton and Allouche (2016) concentrate on power generation and the related political impact on the three major markets, namely China, Thailand and Vietnam. They add that the LMC also reflects China's competition with other powers for regional influence (ibid.).

Work by both Chinese and non-Chinese researchers covers a broad variety of perspectives, such as river management, international cooperation, and hydropower, but the significance of the LMC in China's overall foreign relations is insufficiently addressed. While international cooperation is undeniably part of Beijing's foreign policy, the LMC also reflects the major power's fait accompli tactics and their impact on the geopolitical sphere. When Chinese Premier Li Keqiang proposed the framework of the LMC at the seventeenth China-ASEAN Summit in November 2014 (Lancang-Mekong Cooperation China Secretariat 2017b), its largest hydropower plant, Nuozhadu, had already been commissioned five months previously in the wake of earlier projects such as Xiaowan (Harris 2014). The coincident timings qualified as a fait accompli tactic to involved states because the construction and operation of these dams was irreversible. Pursuing such tactics is not rare in China's foreign policies, with other examples being the Air Defence Identification Zone (ADIZ) in the East China Sea, and the building of artificial islands in the South China Sea. For the LMC, nevertheless, it seems different from other cases as regards the type of responses which might be appropriate; what these differences are will be the first question that this chapter seeks to answer. The second question involves how the LMC will affect the regional geopolitical landscape, while the third question examines how the LMC 'minilateral' formula will work in China's foreign policy.

China's fait accompli tactics

As part of its foreign policy China has taken a number of unilateral actions, such as its dam-building activities in the Lancang-Mekong and the construction of artificial islands in the South China Sea, that have had an irreversible impact and have thereby given China the upper hand in dealing with its counterparts. Of course, such measures are not physically irreversible, because all these structures could be demolished or abandoned. However, Beijing's rising power—based on its economic might and military capability—is enough to deter other countries' attempts to reverse such developments. For instance, even though some US military flights have defied China's ADIZ, most civil airlines and other users still cooperate with ADIZ requirements, demonstrating the success of China's fait accompli policies (Green et al. 2017). In contrast, resisting China's fait accompli tactics, such as Vietnam's struggle against the Chinese oil rig in 2014, is more likely for other countries to preserve the status quo (Douglas et al. 2017). Despite the inability to nullify China's fait accompli tactics, affected countries usually protest, but this pattern does not apply to those in the Mekong basin. In contrast, the five Mekong countries' participation in the LMC could be interpreted as their acceptance of China's already built dams.

Sovereignty and dependence are two key factors making China's fait accompli tactics on the Lancang River distinct from that of other occasions. Due to the contested territorial claims in the South China Sea, the construction by China of artificial islands on top of existing coral reefs and rocks, as well as the installation of sophisticated weapons systems, has naturally resulted in criticism from other claimants and countries with a vested interest in the area, such as the United States (Borger and Phillips 2015). Contrary to the maritime arena, China's sovereignty on the Lancang River in its Yunnan province is not in doubt. Construction there is thus less likely to be a cause of protest, and even less likely to result in any demands for restoring the pre-construction situation.

Dependence is also the distinguishing factor in the fait accompli tactics employed in these two cases. Although the Southeast Asian territorial claimants in the South China Sea rely on sea lines of communication (SLOCs) for trade, the Chinese artificial islands are not chokepoints to their SLOCs. Investment from China indeed resulted in some claimants' adoption of a cautious attitude towards the former's island-building activities and militarisation in the South China Sea, but none of these countries have given up their territorial claims (IISS 2019a, pp. 136 9). In contrast, in the Mekong basin, not only are the downstream countries generally silent on the subject of the Chinese dams upstream (Biba 2018b, pp. 115–17), but indeed they have joined the China-led LMC. This bandwagon-style response could be attributed to their mutual dependence on the water flow and investment from China. The water flow in the Mekong River from the Chinese Lancang River makes up between 16 and 24 per cent of the total flow depending on the wet or dry season (Mekong River Commission n.d.(a)), and this significant amount of water flow is controlled by the Chinese dams. Substantial removal of the dams would be both politically infeasible and physically difficult, because any act of sabotage or military attack on the structures might not succeed and/or invoke serious retaliation from China. In the absence of physically removing the dams, mere protests or criticisms from the Southeast Asian Mekong countries would not affect Beijing's control of the river. For the former, a change of water flow from upstream could cause considerable damage to their agricultural and other sectors. Thus, the only practical option left for the downstream countries is to engage China by joining the LMC, despite their weaker positions. As such, the geopolitical landscape may change in the Mekong basin, Southeast Asia, and beyond.

(Re)shaping the geopolitical landscape

Enhancing its influence in Indochina is China's geostrategic goal for the LMC. After more than two decades of engagement backed by its rising economic might, Beijing has built strong bilateral relations with its mainland Southeast Asian counterparts, mainly through trade and investment. China is either the largest origin of imports, the largest destination for exports, or both for the five Mekong countries (World Trade Organization 2019). In terms of investment, Beijing's role may be less dominant but it is nevertheless still considerable (ASEAN Secretariat 2018, pp. 11,

14, 17, 21), more so in light of the expansive Belt and Road Initiative (BRI). Cambodia, Laos, Myanmar and Thailand have hosted BRI projects (Belt and Road Initiative n.d.), and Vietnam has also been integrated into the rail network on the Eurasia continent (Le 2019). Militarily, the Chinese defence industry supplies various sophisticated weapons systems, munitions and sensors to Cambodia, Laos, Myanmar and Thailand (SIPRI 2019). Given these close ties, it is natural for China, as a rising great or superpower, to work towards a certain level of hegemony, whether intentional or not, in its neighbourhood.

Among all the adjacent regions, mainland Southeast Asia is the most feasible area for Beijing to pursue its hegemony. Unlike Central and South Asia which accommodate Russia and India, respectively, and maritime Southeast Asia within which Indonesia is considered a regional power, there is no similar power in mainland Southeast Asia (Shekhar 2018, pp. 243–6). However, Japan, the United States and other powers have some presence through regional organisations, such as the US-led Lower Mekong Initiative and the Mekong-Japan Summit (Lower Mekong Initiative n.d.; Ministry of Foreign Affairs of Japan 2019). Unless it excludes the influence of other powers or makes itself stand out in some way, Beijing will not qualify as a regional hegemon.

Given its concentration on the Mekong River the LMC presents a natural excuse to exclude extra-regional powers. The unique focus of the LMC, on managing the river flow through Chinese-owned dams, makes it impossible for other powers to participate in the strategy. In addition to river management, Beijing applies BRI elements of infrastructure building and other cooperation to the LMC, thus enhancing the mechanism's appeal to the riparian countries. Consequently, the LMC has the potential to gradually surpass existing Mekong-related organisations with other extra-regional powers. It must be noted that the transition may not be immediate because the other Mekong-related organisations still hold certain projects and funds. The LMC's current aim would be to take the lead in new agendas as well as to strengthen the respective sets of bilateral relations.

Using the LMC, China could further enhance its special role vis-à-vis the Mekong countries in at least two directions: Vietnam and the whole of Southeast Asia. Drawing on its long bilateral history, Hanoi has carefully managed relations with its northern neighbour through hedging and diversifying its security and economic ties with other countries. Although their land borders have been agreed upon by both sides (Ministry of Foreign Affairs of the People's Republic of China 2000), the disagreement on maritime territorial disputes is unlikely to be resolved in the foreseeable future (Manyin 2018, pp. 211–17). Vietnam has subsequently focused its resources, particularly military modernisation, on its maritime front (SIPRI 2019; Wu 2019, p. 114), but this strategic outlook may be outflanked by the LMC. Through the LMC, Chinese influence in Laos and Cambodia may put pressure on Vietnam, with an outcome similar to Hanoi's deteriorating position in the South China Sea disputes since the China-friendly Rodrigo Duterte administration took office in the Philippines from 2016 (IISS 2019a, pp. 137–8). However, the changing political landscape in the Mekong basin would be more challenging to Hanoi than Manila's shifting attitude in the South China Sea.

The Chinese presence in Laos and Cambodia is mainly economic so far, but such geo-economic efforts may reshape these two countries' relations with Vietnam. For Vientiane, its friendly ties with Hanoi may be undermined by Beijing's rising influence (Parameswaran 2018; *Tuoi Tre News* 2017). Given that the expensive high-speed rail (HSR) project as well as the construction of hydropower plants have strained Laos' financial capacity (Hong Kong Trade Development Council 2017; Lindsay 2019), China's soaring influence through loans and investments would be expected. Furthermore, Chinese contractors for the dams in Laos under the build-operate-transfer (BOT) arrangement will enjoy the right of operation for three decades (Hong Kong Trade Development Council 2017), and this will enhance China's control of the water flow to the downstream countries, including Vietnam. Moreover, China could also be a major contractor in the Laos-Vietnam connection of the GMS-proposed East-West Economic Corridor, with the LMC consequently becoming a platform to promote this project (Greater Mekong Subregion 2017). Considering these developments, Hanoi may face a dilemma between economic development and potential vulnerability when considering further integration into BRI networks.

A closer Sino-Cambodia relationship could prove to be of greater concern than a Sino-Lao one due to Cambodia's location and relationship with Vietnam. Prime Minister Hun Sen returned to power in Phnom Penh in 1997 (Vachon and Roeun 2017), and his personal ties with Hanoi have not stabilised the bilateral relationship. Anti-Vietnam sentiments from the invasion, border disputes, China's involvement and other factors have caused the relationship between these two mainland Southeast Asian countries to fluctuate (Chheang 2017; Chhengpor 2019). There are a number of projects under the LMC in Cambodia that could strengthen the relationship. First, additional Cambodian dams and other hydropower constructions on the upper reaches of the Mekong and other rivers flowing into Vietnam could have a direct impact on the latter (International Rivers n.d.). The BOT contracts of such dams will allow the Chinese to operate the dams for several decades, which affects the river flow into Vietnam more than that in Laos (*China Daily* 2017). Phnom Penh's holding back of a report containing negative analysis of the Chinese dams until the end of the elections of 2018 suggests the administration's cooperative attitude towards such issues (Elten 2018).

Second, if some Phnom Penh-accepted projects from the LMC are dual-use for military and civilian purposes, such as a deep-water harbour, the strategic message to Hanoi is clear, particularly considering that Chinese BRI projects such as Hambantota and Gwadhar have aroused concern (Kondapalli 2018, pp. 115–16). While Cambodia has officially denied that a Chinese naval base is under construction on its land (Heath 2019), the building of a dual-purpose facility in the future followed by regular or more long-term visits by the Chinese armed forces is still feasible. Third, the LMC's involvement in the security domain may facilitate some projects that are designed to strengthen the Cambodian armed forces. The present state of the Cambodian armed forces is weak in some critical capabilities, such as airpower (IISS 2019b, pp. 254–5), and such weakness may be addressed through arms transfers in the name of security cooperation with China. With better capabilities, any border conflicts or confrontations that Cambodia has with Vietnam would attract more attention and military resources from the latter. Finally, a Sino-Cambodian joint project for the development of an economic corridor comprising the HSR and other land transportation lines could reach southern Vietnam. Based on the economic and agricultural importance of the Mekong Delta (Piesse 2019), an economic corridor running between southern Vietnam and Cambodia would have a greater geo-economic impact than one between central Vietnam and Laos.

In the face of its gradual strategic outflanking facilitated by the LMC, Vietnam would not have effective counter-measures. Given that the water flow in the Mekong is influenced by the dams in China and other upstream countries, withdrawing from the LMC is not a feasible option. Yet, with bilateralism as the main form of cooperation in the LMC (Lancang-Mekong Cooperation China Secretariat 2019), Hanoi would not be able to exert much influence in terms of countering those projects. Based on its strong nationalism and long history of dealing with China, Vietnam may not give up its territorial claims in its East Sea (South China Sea) (Hutt 2019), but some softening of its attitude may occur if Chinese influence is particularly significant in Laos and Cambodia. It must be noted that without the LMC, cooperation between China and Vietnam's two neighbours is still possible, but the LMC's comprehensive aims could make such joint effort projects more convenient. A softened Hanoi would accord more advantages to Beijing as regards its activities in the South China Sea and the whole of Southeast Asia, both issues which are associated with ASEAN.

The LMC may facilitate China's regional influence by dividing ASEAN. Prior to the LMC's establishment, mainland Southeast Asian countries, except for Vietnam, had adopted a cautious attitude towards China, such as in the matter of the South China Sea (National Institute for Defence Studies, Japan 2019, pp. 37, 41). Now that the LMC has helped to enhance relations between China and the other Mekong countries, this may deepen the division between maritime and mainland Southeast Asia in ASEAN. On the one hand, the consolidated ties with China under the LMC would constrain the position of the mainland ASEAN member states regarding the issues related to China (Busbarat 2018, p. 6). On the other hand, rising concerns and doubts about China in the public opinion of maritime Southeast Asian countries may result in them adopting a tougher approach towards the former (Heydarian 2019). The increasingly distinct attitudes towards China between the LMC and non-LMC countries could create a division in ASEAN. If Vietnam's position were to be altered as a result of the previously mentioned strategic move through the LMC, the division would be further deepened. Consequently, an increasingly divided ASEAN may gradually lose its ability to collectively engage China. Many important issues between ASEAN and China, such as the negotiations for the Code of Conduct in the South China Sea, could be either prolonged or even postponed, with bilateral negotiations subsequently appearing as an alternative—this is favoured by Beijing given its power advantage over the ASEAN member states (Hoang 2019, p. 17; IISS 2019a, p. 140). In other words, the LMC has the potential to assist China to build up its hegemony in and beyond Indochina.

Challenges and limits

Despite the significant prospects of the LMC, the path from the present to the eventual goals could encounter some obstacles, such as in water resources management and funding. Replicating the same LMC formulation elsewhere would be impractical.

To retain the deep engagement of mainland Southeast Asian countries in the LMC will require a fair or acceptable joint mechanism for water management and sufficient cooperation in matters such as data sharing and releasing water to increase flow during dry seasons (Biba 2018a, pp. 636–7). The Lancang-Mekong Water Resources Cooperation Center (LMWRCC), which was established along with the LMC secretariat in Beijing, is responsible for coordinating water flow and related issues, but the core of cooperation is still reliant upon the interactions between upstream and downstream member states in the LMC. Despite the priority on equality in the LMC, the superiority of Beijing's upstream location and national power as well as its rejection of the UNWC due to sovereignty concerns suggests that Beijing would be unlikely to allow other LMC members to wield strong determining power at the LMWRCC. The lack of available information about the LMWRCC means that its processes could essentially be a black box (Lancang-Mekong Cooperation China Secretariat 2019). Nevertheless, while we expect that the LMWRCC's decision making would not reflect complete equality among the member states, it is also unlikely that China would dominate across all aspects of cooperation (i.e. maintaining the pre-LMC status quo). In this sense, the downstream LMC members would generally still benefit from the LMWRCC. In addition, Southeast Asian LMC members may not have high expectations of China's willingness to collaborate with them over water resources management, based on their cautious responses to China during previous crises of abnormal water flows in the Mekong River (Biba 2018b, p. 121). Furthermore, the absence of a dispute-solving mechanism in the LMC implies a lack of effective means for member states to challenge the LMWRCC's operations.

However, Beijing cannot hold up the flow of river water forever, and some reasons suggest that releasing the water flow may not damage its interests. China's reliance on the Mekong River's hydro-source for its domestic power generation may be reduced due to additional power generation from a series of nuclear power plants that have already been commissioned (Gil 2017; Hu 2013). Furthermore, Yunnan province—through which the Lancang-Mekong river flows—is not suitable for irrigation systems from a few major dams due to the rugged terrain of many watersheds (Liang 2011). Finally, China could sacrifice its domestic needs for improved foreign relations as it has done previously; take for example the Tanzania Railway that was built for diplomatic purposes during the 1970s when China was poor and lacking in infrastructure (Sued 2012). Therefore, it can be expected that Beijing will make compromises up to a certain extent, but that China may prove to be obstinate about granting requests by other parties, as was the case when it displayed its ignorance of the Code for Unplanned Encounters at Sea in the South China Sea (IISS 2019a, p. 133). In short, unless China makes a serious mistake such as total denial of coordination which is against the LMC's mandate, the LMWRCC would retain its linkages and engagement with the other riparian countries.

The substance and sustainability of China's investment in the remainder of the LMC countries could be more critical than the LMWRCC. A fair or acceptable sharing of water resources could be adequate for the downstream countries to cooperate on issues related to the Mekong River, but to serve Beijing's other geopolitical interests more incentives may be required. Given their developing economies, all mainland Southeast Asian countries rely heavily on large foreign investment from China, which endows the latter with influence and leverage on the former's foreign policies. In addition, LMC membership could strengthen the grounds for Beijing's funding to the five riparian countries, in contrast to other countries involved in the BRI. However, it is not certain whether the bilateral projects will proceed or not for several reasons, such as the dynamics during negotiations, execution and financial availability. Bilateral negotiations on a joint project between China and a recipient state may not be smooth if financial and other conditions become obstacles that lead to significant delays. For example, the Chinese HSR project in Thailand has been postponed for several years due to the conditions imposed by loans, land development and other issues (Wu and Chong 2018, pp. 512–13). Even if a bilateral agreement is achieved, subsequent progress could be impeded due to various problems at the executive level. For instance, the commission of the Chinese metro project in Hanoi has encountered a setback due to technological flaws (Nguyen 2019), and the Chinese HSR line in Indonesia once fell into a sluggish state owing to complications in land acquisition in the local context (Wu and Chong 2018, pp. 516–17). In other words, it is easy to conceptualise many projects but realising them could be difficult.

Aside from projects per se, Beijing's financial capacity and preference for funding would be decisive in its support for the LMC members. In recent years, China's economic growth has slowed down for various reasons such as rising costs, financial policies and the trade war with the United States (Townsend and Daurat 2019). Although Beijing has managed the decline of foreign exchange reserves in the mid-2010s, the current amount of around US$ 3 trillion occupies a lesser percentage of its general domestic product compared to the past, and this change indicates less capacity to respond to economic upheavals (Babones 2018; Bloomberg 2019; Kwan 2016). Chinese foreign exchange reserves are a major foundation for BRI projects (Wolff 2016, p. 10). In this sense, a lesser portion of foreign exchange reserves in China's economy suggests that the funding for the projects in the LMC member states could be less reliable than before. In terms of distribution of the available capital, the LMC has to compete with at least 173 BRI projects across 40 countries (Hillman 2018). While the proximity of the LMC to China gives it an advantage over many other countries under the BRI, the availability of energy resources, geopolitics and alliance relations may elevate some relatively remote projects, such as the China–Pakistan Economic Corridor, to the level of the LMC's significance. Moreover, a lack of funding will fundamentally obstruct China's geopolitical influence through the LMC.

Establishing a multilateral or minilateral organisation similar to the LMC—with its exclusive nature—somewhere else is not feasible either. In North Asia, China, Mongolia and Russia are unlikely to form any organisation, not to mention one excluding Russia. As for Central Asia, Beijing's influence is indeed expanding in the Shanghai Cooperation Organisation (SCO), but Moscow, another powerful member, also works hard to retain its prestige. Furthermore, the addition of New Delhi as a SCO member in 2017 would reshape the dynamics within the organisation (Grossman 2017). As such, it is nearly impossible for China to either make the SCO exclusive to other powers, or to establish another minilateral organisation similar to the LMC in Central Asia. In terms of South Asia, the situation is more unfavourable for Beijing because New Delhi retains a major, if not dominant, role in all the regional organisations, such as the South Asian Association for Regional Cooperation, the Indian Ocean Rim Association, and the Bay of Bengal Initiative for Multi-Sectoral Technical and Economic Cooperation (BIMSTEC 2019; Indian Ocean Rim Association 2017; South Asian Association for Regional Cooperation 2018). This leaves almost no room for Chinese activities, not to mention any attempts by that country to establish an exclusive regional organisation. Beyond China's adjacent neighbourhood, in Africa for example, it may be possible to replicate an LMC-like organisation but the geopolitical value of doing so would be relatively low.

Conclusion

The LMC demonstrates Beijing's attempt to engage in international cooperation and geopolitical expansion based on its fait accompli tactics on the Lancang River. The participation of the riparian countries in the LMC suggests that China's influence on mainland Southeast Asia would be further enhanced through the proper management of water resources and the promotion of bilateral cooperation. Therefore, Vietnam, ASEAN and the whole of Southeast Asia could be affected by China through the LMC. Although the LMWRCC could help to retain the riparian countries' interest in the LMC, the critical factor for the LMC's success will be whether Beijing can inject sufficient capital into the region, while simultaneously focusing on other BRI projects and handling its own challenging economy. Thus, the substantial bilateral projects and their execution will be key indicators of the LMC's progress.

Note

1 In this chapter, the Lancang River refers to the section of the water that flows through China, and the Mekong River refers to the downstream section that courses through the five Southeast Asian countries.

References

ASEAN Secretariat 2018, *ASEAN Investment Report 2018*, Jakarta, ASEAN Secretariat.

Babones, S 2018, 'China is sitting on $3 trillion in currency reserves, but is that enough?' *Forbes*, 24 May, viewed 28 September 2019, www.forbes.com/sites/salvatorebabones/2018/05/24/china-is-sitting-on-3-trillion-in-currency-reserves-but-is-that-enough/#5af8b69b5fce.

Belt and Road Initiative n.d., 'BRI projects', viewed 16 September 2019, www.beltroad-initiative.com/projects/.

Biba, S 2018a, 'China's "old" and "new" Mekong River politics: the Lancang-Mekong Cooperation from a comparative benefit-sharing perspective', *Water International*, vol. 43, no. 5, pp. 622–641.

Biba, S 2018b, *China's Hydro-Politics in the Mekong*, London, Routledge.

BIMSTEC 2019, 'About BIMSTEC', viewed 30 September 2019, https://bimstec.org/?page_id=189.

Bloomberg 2019, 'China monthly foreign exchange reserves', September, viewed 28 September 2019, www.bloomberg.com/quote/CNGFOREX:IND.

Borger, J and Phillips, T 2015, 'How China's artificial islands led to tension in the South China Sea', *The Guardian*, 27 October, viewed 11 September 2019, www.theguardian.com/world/2015/oct/27/tensions-and-territorial-claims-in-the-south-china-sea-the-guardian-briefing.

Busbarat, P 2018, 'Grabbing the forgotten: China's leadership consolidation in mainland Southeast Asia through the Mekong-Lancang Cooperation', *Perspective*, no. 7.

Chheang, V 2017, 'Cambodia–Vietnam ties turn 50', East Asia Forum, 21 June, viewed 22 September 2019, www.eastasiaforum.org/2017/06/21/cambodia-vietnam-ties-turn-50/.

Chhengpor, A 2019, 'Border spat shows Cambodia-Vietnam relations tested, while Chinese influence grows', *Voice of America*, 23 January, viewed 22 September 2019, www.voacambodia.com/a/border-spat-shows-cambodia-vietnam-relations-tested-while-chinese-influence-grows/4754214.html.

China Daily 2017, 'Chinese-built biggest dam in Cambodia to start operation in November', 25 September, viewed 22 September 2019, www.chinadaily.com.cn/business/2017-09/25/content_32462600.htm.

Douglas, J, Green, M, Hicks, K, Cooper, Z and Schaus, J 2017, 'Counter-coercion series: China-Vietnam oil rig standoff', Asia Maritime Transparency Initiative, 12 June, viewed 11 September 2019, https://amti.csis.org/counter-co-oil-rig-standoff/.

Elten, H 2018, 'Cambodia's Chinese dam conundrum', East Asia Forum, 15 August, viewed 29 September 2019, www.eastasiaforum.org/2018/08/15/cambodias-chinese-dam-conundrum/.

Feng, Y, Wang, W, Suman, D, Yu, S and He, D 2019, 'Water cooperation priorities in the Lancang-Mekong river basin based on cooperative events since the Mekong River Commission establishment', *Chinese Geographical Science*, vol. 29, no. 1, pp. 58–69.

Gil, L 2017, 'How China has become the world's fastest expanding nuclear power producer', International Atomic Energy Agency, 25 October, viewed 27 September 2019, www.iaea.org/newscenter/news/how-china-has-become-the-worlds-fastest-expanding-nuclear-power-producer.

Greater Mekong Subregion 2017, 'Economic corridors in the Greater Mekong Subregion', 25 August, viewed 21 September 2019, www.greatermekong.org/content/economic-cor ridors-in-the-greater-mekong-subregion.

Green, M, Hicks, K, Cooper, Z and Schaus, J 2017, 'Counter-coercion series: East China Sea air defense identification zone', Asia Maritime Transparency Initiative, 13 June, viewed 11 September 2019, https://amti.csis.org/counter-co-east-china-sea-adiz/.

Grossman, D 2017, 'China will regret India's entry into the Shanghai Cooperation Organization', *The Diplomat*, 24 July, viewed 30 September 2019, https://thediplomat.com/2017/07/china-will-regret-indias-entry-into-the-shanghai-cooperation-organization/.

Guo, Y 2018, 'The evolution of China's water diplomacy in the Lancang-Mekong river basin', in H Zhang and M Li (eds), *China and Transboundary Water Politics in Asia*, London, Routledge, pp. 72–88.

Harris, M 2014, 'Last turbine unit in operation at China's 5,850-MW Huaneng Nuozhadu hydropower plant', *Hydro Review*, 30 June, viewed 10 September 2019, www.hydrowor ld.com/articles/2014/06/last-turbine-unit-in-operation-at-chian-s-5-850-mw-huaneng-n uozhadu-hydropower-plant.html.

Heath, TR 2019, 'The ramifications of China's reported naval base in Cambodia', *World Politics Review*, 5 August, viewed 22 September 2019, www.worldpoliticsreview.com/a rticles/28092/the-ramifications-of-china-s-reported naval base-in-cambodia.

Heydarian, R 2019, 'China's overreach provokes backlash across Southeast Asia', *Nikkei Asian Review*, 31 July, viewed 23 September 2019, https://asia.nikkei.com/Opinion/China-s-overreach-provokes-backlash-across-Southeast-Asia.

Hillman, JE 2018, 'China's belt and road is full of holes', Center for Strategic & International Studies, 4 September, viewed 28 September 2019, www.csis.org/analysis/chinas-belt-a nd-road-full-holes.

Hoang, TH 2019, 'From declaration to code: continuity and change in China's engagement with ASEAN on the South China Sea', *Trends in Southeast Asia*, no. 5.

Hong Kong Trade Development Council 2017, 'Hydropower investment sees Laos aligned with BRI objectives', Belt and Road, 22 August, viewed 21 September 2019, https://beltandroad.hktdc.com/en/insights/hydropower-investment-sees-laos-aligned-bri -objectives.

Hu, X 2013, 'The battle over Yunnan's hydropower', *China Dialogue*, 10 September, viewed 27 September 2019, www.chinadialogue.net/article/show/single/en/6347-The-b attle-over-Yunnan-s-hydropower.

Hutt, D 2019, 'Vietnam takes a stand in the South China Sea', *Asia Times*, 6 August, viewed 23 September 2019, www.asiatimes.com/2019/08/article/vietnam-takes-a-stand-in-the-south-china-sea/.

Indian Ocean Rim Association 2017, 'Member states', viewed 30 September 2019, www.iora.int/en/about/member-states.

International Institute for Strategic Studies (IISS) 2019a, *Asia-Pacific Regional Security Assessment 2019*, London, International Institute for Strategic Studies.

International Institute for Strategic Studies (IISS) 2019b, *The Military Balance*, London, International Institute for Strategic Studies.

International Rivers n.d., 'Cambodia', viewed 22 September 2019, www.internationalrivers. org/campaigns/cambodia.

International Rivers 2014, 'Understanding the impacts of China's upper Mekong dams', December, viewed 9 September 2019, www.internationalrivers.org/resources/8477.

Kondapalli, S 2018, 'China's evolving naval presence in the Indian Ocean region: an Indian perspective', in D Brewster (ed.), *India and China at Sea: Competition for Naval Dominance in the Indian Ocean*, Oxford, Oxford University Press, pp. 111–124.

Kwan, CH 2016, 'Why are China's foreign exchange reserves declining sharply? A reflection of valuation losses and capital outflow', Research Institute of Economy, Trade and Industry, 28 January, viewed 28 September 2019, www.rieti.go.jp/en/china/15122801.html.

Lancang-Mekong Cooperation China Secretariat 2017a, '3+5 cooperation framework', 14 December, viewed 9 September 2019, www.lmcchina.org/eng/zyjz_3/35hz/t1519481.htm.

Lancang-Mekong Cooperation China Secretariat 2017b, 'A brief introduction of Lancang-Mekong Cooperation', 13 December, viewed 10 September 2019, www.lmcchina.org/eng/gylmhz_1/jj/t1519110.htm.

Lancang-Mekong Cooperation China Secretariat 2019, 'Bilateral cooperations', viewed 23 September 2019, www.lmcchina.org/eng/sbhz_2/.

Le, D 2019, 'Vietnam-Europe railway link opens', *Vietnam Economic Times*, 13 March, viewed 16 September 2019, http://vneconomictimes.com/article/vietnam-today/vietnam-europe-railway-link-opens.

Liang, L 2011, 'Biodiversity in China's Yunnan province', United Nations University, 26 April, viewed 27 September 2019,https://unu.edu/publications/articles/biodiversity-in-chinas-yunnan-province.html.

Lindsay, S 2019, 'China-Laos railway marred by compensation issues and pollution', *ASEAN Today*, 11 June, viewed 21 September 2019, www.aseantoday.com/2019/06/china-laos-railway-marred-by-compensation-issues-and-pollution/.

Lower Mekong Initiative n.d., 'LMI overview', viewed 16 September 2019, www.lowermekong.org/about/lower-mekong-initiative-lmi.

Manyin, M 2018, 'Vietnam among the powers: struggle and cooperation', in G Rozman and JC Liow (eds), *International Relations and Asia's Southern Tier*, Singapore, Springer, pp. 207–227.

Mekong River Commission n.d.(a), 'Hydrology', viewed 13 September 2019, www.mrcmekong.org/mekong-basin/hydrology.

Mekong River Commission n.d.(b), 'Upstream partners', viewed 9 September 2019, www.mrcmekong.org/about-mrc/upstream-partners/.

Middleton, C and Allouche, J 2016, 'Watershed or powershed? Critical hydropolitics, China and the "Lancang-Mekong Cooperation framework"', *International Spectator*, vol. 51, no. 3, pp. 100–117.

Ministry of Foreign Affairs of Japan 2019, 'Japan-Mekong cooperation', 13 September, viewed 16 September 2019, www.mofa.go.jp/region/asia-paci/mekong/cooperation.html.

Ministry of Foreign Affairs of the People's Republic of China 2000, 'China and Vietnam sign land border treaty', 15 November, viewed 21 September 2019. www.fmprc.gov.cn/mfa_eng/wjb_663304/zzjg_663340/yzs_663350/gjlb_663354/2792_663578/2793_66358 0/t16247.shtml.

National Institute for Defence Studies, Japan 2019, *NIDS China Security Report 2019*, Tokyo, National Institute for Defence Studies.

Nguyen, H 2019, 'Transport Ministry to blame for Hanoi metro delays: state auditors', *VN Express*, 6 July, viewed 27 September 2019, https://e.vnexpress.net/news/business/economy/transport-ministry-to-blame-for-hanoi-metro-delays-state-auditors-3948738.html.

Parameswaran, P 2018, 'What's next for Vietnam-Laos military ties in 2018?' *The Diplomat*, 28 March, viewed 21 September 2019, https://thediplomat.com/2018/03/whats-next-for-vietnam-laos-military-ties-in-2018/.

Piesse, M 2019, 'The Mekong delta: land subsidence threatens Vietnam's "food basket"', Future Directions International, 18 July, viewed 23 September 2019, www.futuredirections.org.au/publication/the-mekong-delta-land-subsidence-threatens-vietnams-food-basket/.

Shekhar, V 2018, 'Indonesia as a regional power: a pan-Indo-Pacific worldview', in S Ganguly, A Scobell and JC Liow (eds), *The Routledge Handbook of Asian Security Studies*, London, Routledge, pp. 243–254.

South Asian Association for Regional Cooperation 2018, 'About SAARC', viewed 30 September 2019, http://saarc-sec.org/about-saarc.

Stockholm International Peace Research Institute (SIPRI) 2019, Arms transfers database, 11 March, viewed 21 September 2019, www.sipri.org/databases/armstransfers.

Sued, HK 2012, 'TAZARA: how the great Uhuru Railway was built', Embassy of the People's Republic of China in the United Republic of Tanzania, 11 April, viewed 27 September 2019, http://tz.china-embassy.org/eng/media/t921927.htm.

The Economist 2019, 'Why are water levels of the Mekong at a 100-year low?' *The Economist*, 7 August, viewed 9 September 2019, www.economist.com/graphic-detail/2019/08/07/why-are-water-levels-of-the-mekong-at-a-100-year-low.

Townsend, M and Daurat, C 2019, 'How bad is China's economic slowdown? It depends what you sell', Bloomberg, 6 February, viewed 28 September 2019, www.bloomberg.com/news/articles/2019-02-06/how-bad-is-china-s-economic-slowdown-it-depends-what-you-sell.

Tuoi Tre News 2017, 'Vietnam, Laos fortify special relationship', *Tuoi Tre News*, 20 December, viewed 21 September 2019, https://tuoitrenews.vn/news/politics/20171220/vietnam-lao-fortify-special-relationship/43249.html.

UN Watercourses Convention 2019, 'Global relevance', viewed 9 September 2019, www.unwatercoursesconvention.org/global-relevance/south-and-east-asia/.

Urban, F, Siciliano, G and Nordensvard, J 2018, 'Transboundary river management in Southeast Asia: the role of Chinese dam-builders', in H Zhang and M Li (eds), *China and Transboundary Water Politics in Asia*, London, Routledge, pp. 43–71.

Vachon, M and Roeun, V 2017, 'Return to war', *Cambodia Daily*, 30 June, viewed 22 September 2019, https://english.cambodiadaily.com/features/return-to-war-131980/.

Wolff, P 2016, 'China's "Belt and Road" Initiative: challenges and opportunities', German Development Institute, viewed 12 October 2019, www.die-gdi.de/uploads/media/Belt_and_Road_V1.pdf.

World Trade Organization 2019, 'Members and observers', viewed 16 September 2019, www.wto.org/english/thewto_e/whatis_e/tif_e/org6_e.htm.

Wu, S 2018, 'The trouble with the Lancang-Mekong Cooperation forum', *The Diplomat*, 19 December, viewed 10 September 2019, https://thediplomat.com/2018/12/the-trouble-with-the-lancang-mekong-cooperation-forum/.

Wu, S 2019, 'Vietnam: a case of military obsolescence in developing countries', *Pacific Review*, vol. 32, no. 1, pp. 113–130.

Wu, S and Chong, A 2018, 'Developmental railpolitics: the political economy of China's high-speed rail projects in Thailand and Indonesia', *Contemporary Southeast Asia*, vol. 40, no. 3, pp. 503–526.

Xing, W 2017, 'Lancang-Mekong river cooperation and trans-boundary water governance', *China Quarterly of International Strategic Studies*, vol. 3, no. 3, pp. 377–393.

Yang, X 2019, 'The Lancang-Mekong Cooperation mechanism: a new platform for China's neighbourhood diplomacy', *China: An International Journal*, vol. 17, no. 2, pp. 106–126.

6

THE QUADRILATERAL SECURITY DIALOGUE AND ASEAN CENTRALITY

Huong Le Thu

Introduction

This chapter looks at the relationship between the Association of Southeast Asian Nations (ASEAN) and the re-emerging minilateral arrangement—the Quadrilateral Security Dialogue (also known as the Quad or QSD)—comprising the United States, Japan, Australia and India. In examining ASEAN's views on the QSD, it looks at two levels: the conventional wisdom that sees the QSD as challenging ASEAN centrality, and also at the real state of perceptions among the policy community across the region—tested by a quantitative study. This chapter is based on an original survey that was conducted between April and July 2018 and collected 276 responses from all ten ASEAN member countries. The chapter seeks to answer the following questions:

1. What are ASEAN's concerns about the emerging minilaterals in the region?
2. How will minilateralism affect ASEAN unity and centrality in the regional security architecture?

Not all emerging minilaterals are framed as competing with or as mounting a challenge against ASEAN-centred regionalism. These are, however, often left out of the conversation and instead other initiatives are discussed as if they are contentious and are the only form of minilateralism. This is a popular perception of the QSD. It has been widely argued that the QSD is able to challenge or sideline ASEAN centrality. A commonly disseminated perception is that ASEAN member states view the QSD 'with concern, as they fear the informal body could eclipse the bloc's leading role in regional affairs' (Singh 2018). One commentator has said, '[h]owever, as tempting as this Quad-plus may look, it will mean further deterioration of an ASEAN-centred institutionalized system in Asia' (Tsvetov 2017).

Interestingly, often the voices of those who emphasise the QSD's challenge to ASEAN and ASEAN-centred architecture are amplified by echoes expressed beyond the ASEAN member states.

The reality is that the concept and implementation of minilateralism is much older than the QSD and has not been framed as something that can challenge ASEAN-led regionalism. A classic example is the Five Power Defence Arrangements (FPDA), which originated in 1971 and includes the United Kingdom, Australia, New Zealand and two ASEAN members—Malaysia and Singapore (Emmers 2012).

China's embrace of minilateralism is relatively new. Beijing's White Paper in January 2017 stated that China has a formative role in a number of minilateral initiatives, including the Shanghai Cooperation Organisation (SCO), the Six-Party Talks, the Lancang-Mekong Cooperation (LMC) mechanism, and the new China-Afghanistan-Pakistan-Tajikistan counter-terrorism mechanism (Ministry of Foreign Affairs of the People's Republic of China 2017). US-led minilateralism has been largely built on its existing 'hub-and-spokes' network. This has also included a range of major trilateral dialogues that cooperate through military exercises and intelligence-sharing mechanisms, such as US-Japan-Australia, US-Japan-India and US-Japan-South Korea cooperation (Wuthnow 2018).

ASEAN itself has instigated several selective cooperation mechanisms that do not include all the ASEAN member states and do not put ASEAN at the core of their operations. These include dialogues on counter-terrorism and extremism—issues that are of interest to only some of the ASEAN countries. Indeed, the very concept of 'ASEAN minus X' puts emphasis on the value of selective membership that is better tailored to a particular issue for cooperation. The idea behind 'ASEAN minus X' is to create an alternative to the ASEAN style of consensus-based decision-making mechanism that is not effective. Rather than suggesting unanimity, this practice of negotiation requires willingness by members to compromise on their own national interests for the sake of the larger region. Emmers (2017) observes that:

> This approach to decision-making has long been seen as the only option to consolidate the national interests and domestic legitimacy of the member states while at the same promoting regional interests. The consensus decision-making model is still necessary to address the differences that exist across ASEAN.

While this approach sounds like a revolution in ASEAN processes, it actually has long-established origins. In fact, the expansion of ASEAN membership was based on dividing the economies into different tiers reflecting the different development levels and timelines for the attainment of goals. The 'ASEAN minus X' formula is proposed for specific agendas, like counter-terrorism, that are priorities only for some in the ASEAN region. Although 'ASEAN minus X' is not a concept that seems to threaten ASEAN centrality, nevertheless it was not promoted by ASEAN.

Despite its ambivalent reception, the necessity to narrow down the number of participants in specific instances is understood and accepted.

The LMC mechanism is relatively new as an institution, but not as an idea. Geography determines the membership of this selective grouping. Only countries that share the river are involved, together with China, and this has not been a subject of objection, despite the fact that the agenda of such minilateral cooperation extends to infrastructure, energy and economic initiatives that arguably draws the ASEAN Mekong countries much more towards China than to the maritime ASEAN members.

Another example of a positive and clearly beneficial advantage of exclusivity in cooperation is the Sulu Sea Trilateral Patrols—one of Southeast Asia's minilateral security initiatives that involves Indonesia, Malaysia and the Philippines. The three ASEAN states cooperate in maritime and air patrols of a tri-border area measuring some one million square kilometres in order to monitor and prevent conflict, crime and terrorist threats. The initiative was welcomed both by individual ASEAN neighbours as well as by ASEAN as a whole with little reservation about challenging ASEAN centrality.

There are many similar examples of cooperation, which demonstrate that ASEAN neither opposes the concept of minilateralism nor considers it competitive to its 'centrality' by design. For the QSD, it is the membership (comprising of the United States, Japan, Australia and India) and the fact that the four countries came together that are the sources of contention. More interestingly, while ASEAN centrality is not seen as being challenged in the context of existing trilaterals involving some of the QSD countries (for example, existing US-Japan-Australia or US-Japan-India trilaterals), it becomes an issue with the QSD.

The QSD: a form of minilateralism

Based on membership patterns, from the ASEAN regional perspective there are three types of minilaterals:

1.   Those that include only ASEAN members (for example, ASEAN minus X);
2.   Those that include some of the ASEAN member states (for example, the FPDA, Sulu Sea Trilateral Patrols);
3.   Those that do not include any ASEAN countries (for example the QSD, SCO).

This chapter focuses on the third type of minilaterals—the QSD does not include any members of ASEAN, and perhaps this is why concerns have been voiced.

The origins of the QSD were never detached from ASEAN—from the physical location of its first meeting, to its regional role and relationship to this regional body. Whether the QSD engages with ASEAN as a collective, or expands to include some or all of the ASEAN member states, it would appear that the fate of the quadrilateral is linked to ASEAN. QSD meetings have taken place on the sidelines of ASEAN gatherings; in the Philippines in 2017 (the year in which it was revived) and in Singapore in 2018 (Sharma 2018). This means that ASEAN, and its nested network, has in fact facilitated the meetings by means of diplomatic assembly. Even in its first iteration in 2007, the QSD countries met on the sidelines of a regional security gathering led by ASEAN—the ASEAN Regional Forum (ARF).

The QSD originated in December 2004, when Japan, India, Australia and the United States responded to the catastrophic Indian Ocean earthquake and tsunami in a coordinated multilateral disaster relief and humanitarian assistance operation. This was followed in 2007 by the first informal meeting between the four countries, which took place on the sidelines of the ARF in Manila. However, soon afterwards, the first naval exercise involving all of the QSD members drew Chinese diplomatic protests (Thakur 2018). This resulted in Prime Minister Kevin Rudd pulling Australia out of the QSD, and the quadrilateral fell into lethargy. Some accused Rudd of 'getting cold feet' because of the potential risks attached to bilateral Australia-China relations (Rej 2018). Later, Rudd denied this and alleged that behind closed doors, uncertainties within the group had spread and that India was the first to pull out (Rudd 2019).

Thus, despite the benign nature of the original proposal, perceptions about the QSD—or more precisely the anticipation of the impact it might have—played a detrimental role and contributed to the initial false start.

The current revival of the QSD—the so-called QSD 2.0—has been justified by an even more compelling strategic environment that calls for such a minilateral. After all, the key driver behind a minilateral initiative is the search for cost and operational efficiency. Minilateral activities involving a relatively small number of states are especially useful in avoiding the cost of unilateral action on the one hand, and the problems of coordination among a larger, more diverse group of states on the other.

In October 2017, the Japanese Minister for Foreign Affairs Taro Kono publicly proposed during an interview that the QSD should be revitalised (Hayashi and Onchi 2017). In the following month, the first QSD meeting took place on 12 November 2017 when the four 'like-minded' partners debated seven key issues: rules-based order in Asia; freedom of navigation and overflight in the maritime commons; respect for international law; enhancing connectivity; maritime security; the North Korean threat and non-proliferation; and terrorism. This meeting sparked a debate about the revival of the QSD 2.0.

Since then, there have been modest developments, with only one more meeting having taken place at the time of writing this chapter—but the wording of a number of policies suggests that there might be a desire for the QSD 2.0 to succeed. For example, the first National Security Strategy published in December 2017 under the auspices of US President Donald Trump referred to the importance of cooperation with Japan, Australia, and India (The White House 2017). More specifically, when speaking about the tentative revival of the QSD, US Assistant Secretary of Defense for East Asia and the Pacific, Randall Schriver, declared: 'I detect interest [among the four nations], combined with some concern. I'm optimistic that it will come into being in some meaningful way' (Hartcher 2018).

An appetite for the revival of the QSD was felt keenly across the four nations (Le Thu 2019). In the decade following its initial inception, the strategic environment has become tenser, and concerns about China's actions and position in the region, as well as globally, continue to deepen, justifying the revival of the concept. It was Japanese Prime Minister Shinzo Abe's concept of a 'democratic security diamond', unveiled in December 2012, that first brought the QSD to life. And in November 2017, Kono gave an interview that focused attention back on the idea of a revitalised QSD.

Unlike the QSD 1.0, the QSD 2.0 seems to have gained Australia's bipartisan support. The government's 2017 Foreign Policy White Paper confirmed Canberra's strong commitment to trilateral dialogues with the United States and Japan and, separately, with India and Japan: 'Australia is open to working with our Indo-Pacific partners in other plurilateral arrangements' (Department of Foreign Affairs and Trade, Australian Government 2017).

India has reportedly been the most ambivalent of all of the four countries, but a more nuanced approach has been developed under Prime Minister Narenda Modi. India's vital interests in the Indian Ocean and China's activities in the area can make the QSD more compelling as a framework for strengthening Delhi's security.

Official policy documents affirm full US commitment to the QSD 2.0 as one of Washington's key security avenues. The Asia Reassurance Initiative Act, which Trump signed at the end of 2018, reads in part:

> (1) the security dialogue between the United States, Australia, India, and Japan is vital to address pressing security challenges in the Indo-Pacific region in order to promote—
> (A) a rules-based order;
> (B) respect for international law; and
> (C) a free and open Indo-Pacific; and
> (2) such a dialogue is intended to augment, rather than replace, current mechanisms.
>
> *(US Congress 2018)*

However, the two key reactions the QSD has gained thus far is that the four countries are too divergent to be able to come up with a concrete agenda; and even if the QSD can sustain criticism about its value, it needs to respond to the perception that it challenges ASEAN. ASEAN, having been at the centre of multilateral regional frameworks, is often said to be uncomfortable about the emergence of new multilateral mechanisms. This (mis)perception needs to be addressed not only for the wellbeing of the QSD, but also regional multilateralism in general. Yet, given that there have been warnings that the QSD could sideline ASEAN, such perceptions have increasingly gained in popularity through repetitive commentary.

What do Southeast Asians really think of the QSD? Survey findings

In order to validate the abovementioned view, I conducted primary research that allowed me to identify the prevailing perceptions of the QSD across the region, how they differ and what the distribution of opinions looks like (Le Thu 2018). One of the preferred methods of testing perceptions is by collecting quantitative data. One advantage of surveys is that they are anonymous and may better reflect the views that otherwise can be politically sensitive.

In my study which employed a quantitative survey, I tested expert opinions, rather than general public perceptions, of the QSD through targeting specific samplings. The research collected 276 responses to multiple questions from people working for government agencies, the armed forces, academia, think tanks, businesses and the media, as well as from university students in all ten ASEAN member countries. A considerable number of responses came from the ASEAN secretariat staff as well. The response rate was high at 87 per cent. More than 190 respondents declared that they were citizens of an ASEAN country, while 43 selected the citizenship category of 'Other', including those who chose not to disclose their citizenship (but who worked in an ASEAN member country). The origins of the collected responses were uneven. There was a relatively large number of responses from Indonesia, Malaysia, Philippines, Vietnam and, to a lesser extent, Thailand, and hence these have received particular attention in this report. There were fewer responses from Brunei, Cambodia, Laos and Myanmar. The unequal distribution of responses is not unusual and can be both a reflection of intensity of engagement of these four countries as well as potentially indicating the relatively lower interest of those countries in the QSD.

The survey found that quantitatively more respondents from the ASEAN region supported the QSD than opposed it (see Figure 6.1).

Indeed, the principles and goals of cooperation that dictate the work of ASEAN as well as guiding the QSD's cooperation are mutually complementary and should not provoke controversy. According to Ong Keng Yong, former ASEAN Secretary-General, Singaporean diplomat and head of the influential think tank the S. Rajaratnam School of International Studies, as long as the QSD, or indeed any other regional initiative, is in step with the ASEAN Charter—with the rule of law and the non-use of force in particular—then there is no reason why ASEAN members should not support it (Le Thu 2018).

The majority of respondents believed that the QSD could complement ASEAN, rather than challenge or sideline it. The latter opinion is certainly one possible view, but it is not the only one, nor even the prevalent one. In fact, most of the respondents (45 per cent) thought that the QSD complements the existing ASEAN-centred regional security frameworks—and this view is common (with a 3 per cent difference) to all the respondents as well as citizens of ASEAN countries. About 20 per cent thought that the QSD challenges ASEAN, 20 per cent thought that the QSD sidelines ASEAN, and 12 per cent thought that it does not affect ASEAN at all. The opinion that the QSD complements ASEAN was strongest among the

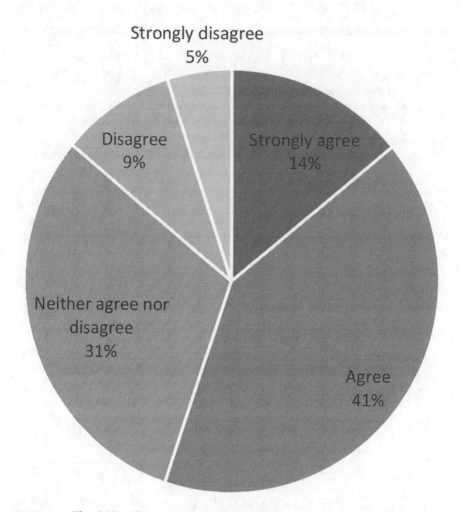

FIGURE 6.1 The QSD will contribute to stability and peace of the Indo-Pacific region
Source: Le Thu (2018).

Vietnamese, Filipino and Malaysian respondents (around 60 per cent), while the
Indonesian, Singaporean and Cambodian respondents appeared the most sceptical
about this view. The Indonesians and Cambodians were most concerned about the
QSD challenging ASEAN centrality, while the Singaporeans were most concerned
about it sidelining the ASEAN architecture (Le Thu 2018). A number of factors
may have contributed to the differing views of the Singaporean respondents—the
country that took over the ASEAN chairmanship for the year in which the
research was conducted—who remain firmly committed to ASEAN centrality. The
Singaporean respondents' views on the QSD, as an emerging pillar of the regional
architecture, are affected by their recognition that the QSD is an amalgamation of
extra-regional partners and does not involve any members of ASEAN. Moreover,
the QSD is often associated—whether correctly or not—with military cooperation

with the United States, Japan, Australia and India, something that Singapore sees as contributing more towards balancing China rather than to the region's development. Above all, the lack of clarity about what the QSD is and what it is committed to is deterring the Singaporeans' support (Le Thu 2018).

It is not only that more experts in the ASEAN region support the QSD and disagree that it would challenge ASEAN, but they also recognise the value of its limited membership. On the question of including ASEAN members in the QSD, there was a clear preference to avoid ASEAN-style inclusivity. Qualitatively, the interviewees and respondents offered reasons why they took this view. Some considered that ASEAN would be compromised from within and therefore cannot be counted on in regional security matters. Others thought that the value of the minilateral is precisely that it is not ASEAN. Moreover, a large grouping would seem counterproductive for such functional cooperation (Le Thu 2018).

ASEAN centrality: a contested concept

The discussion about challenging ASEAN centrality needs to be set in context. The view that the QSD sidelines ASEAN centrality is imprecise and based on a number of assumptions that need clarification themselves. The key assumption here is that ASEAN centrality is a well-recognised and uncontested concept. In reality, it has always been strongly contested and challenged. Moreover, doubts about ASEAN centrality had emerged long before the revival of the QSD 2.0. In fact, ASEAN centrality has been undermined by its track record of refusing to address the major regional security challenges. These include the South China Sea, the Rohingya crisis, and the transboundary haze problem, to name but a few. In fact, in recent years, criticism about ASEAN being ineffective and indecisive in the wake of major crises outweighs public confidence in its ability to resolve Southeast Asian issues. It is clear that ASEAN's pattern of responses towards Beijing's coercion of Southeast Asian claimant states in the South China Sea has shaped its reputation of being a mere 'talkshop' and that its alleged centrality is geographical—mostly as a summit convenor—rather than strategic. Therefore, the doubts about ASEAN centrality had been in place long before the revival of the QSD. In fact, one could also argue that if a couple of informal meetings (not even at ministerial level) not ending in any concrete statements or commitments can challenge ASEAN's centrality, it only testifies to its fragility. Hence, this rhetoric that the QSD presents a challenge to ASEAN centrality risks oversimplification, if not inaccuracy.

Respondents to my survey living in the ASEAN region have, however, a clear view of the challenges that lie ahead for the QSD (see Figure 6.2). About 73 per cent of the respondents identified the QSD's challenges as being internal, while 24 per cent saw the challenges as external (such as coming from China and ASEAN). In total, only 2 per cent thought that criticism from ASEAN could be a challenge for the QSD. So, despite the (mis)perceived thorny relationship between ASEAN and the QSD, the former is the least of the latter's problems.

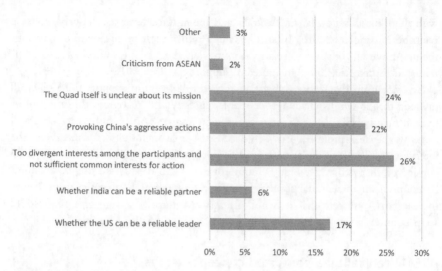

FIGURE 6.2 What are the biggest challenges facing the QSD?
Source: Le Thu (2018).

In fact, ASEAN-style multilateralism has been experiencing setbacks for some time. The debate over ASEAN multilateralism vis-à-vis minilateralism, whether in the form of the QSD or not, diverts attention away from the core problem of ASEAN—its diminishing unity, which ultimately poses an obstacle to ASEAN centrality. ASEAN multilateralism is affected by domestic as well as external factors. China's preference for bilateral negotiations has had an impact on ASEAN and regional dialogue overall. Beijing's insistence on holding exclusively bilateral talks about the South China Sea has made the multilateral settings less salient. This stepping back from multilateralism also coincides with the current inward-looking tendency in some of Southeast Asia's major democracies. An overall weakened commitment to multilateralism is certainly having an impact on the concept of ASEAN centrality. The tendency for each member state to promote, above all, its own national interests has contributed to a sense of zero-sum competition among the ASEAN states who fear being left out if they do not have at least as much connection with China as their counterparts. Each of the ASEAN members is keen to receive an economic or/and infrastructural boost from China accompanied by preferential access to the Chinese market or a favoured supply of resources and materials. Hence, there is almost a race among the Southeast Asian countries to deepen their bilateral relations with Beijing.

None of those factors are new to the region: economic nationalism, security bilateralism and political authoritarianism have been shaping Southeast Asian architecture since the era of decolonisation. ASEAN has never been immune to the impact of powerful global forces. The debate over whether, and to what extent, the great powers and their rivalry undermines the region's coherence continues as the ASEAN community-building process develops. But the very perception of the presence of external forces militating to provoke internal divisions has its role in the overall sense of Southeast Asian (dis)unity. The Southeast Asian countries' continuous nightmare is about being caught between the grindstones of competing superpowers. While American engagement seems to be more constructive, Chinese support for a strong ASEAN is less obvious. Indeed, China's practice of pressuring some ASEAN members not to take a stance on the South China Sea has proved to be an effective mechanism in emasculating the association's solidarity.

In this regard, a number of developments took place in 2016 that reconfirmed the image of Phnom Penh's client-patronage relationship with Beijing (Ciorciari 2013). Once again, Cambodia blocked an ASEAN statement on the Permanent Court of Arbitration ruling at the leaders' meetings. Along with Brunei and Laos, Cambodia also agreed to China's four-point consensus on the South China Sea disputes in April (Ministry of Foreign Affairs of the People's Republic of China 2016). In June regional leaders issued a communiqué that expressed ASEAN member countries' concerns about the rising tensions in the South China Sea; however, it was retracted the next day due to Cambodian opposition. This incident seemed to epitomise a divided ASEAN. China's 'divide and rule' tactics have proved to be working. The current deadlock in regard to the South China Sea disputes can be explained by the lack of a shared perception of a direct security threat. While some claimants have experienced increased levels of vulnerability vis-à-vis China in the South China Sea, for others such a threat remains indirect. If ASEAN's role in resolving the Cambodian conflict in the 1990s was hailed as a success, the inability to achieve a consensus on the South China Sea dispute epitomises ASEAN's failure. By effectively blocking ASEAN's decision-making process and sowing the seeds of disunity, confusion and even mutual distrust, China has been able to prevent any collective regional actions in what the country considers as its 'periphery' vital regional space. Thus, China has been successful in diminishing the efficacy of an 'institutionalized hedging' strategy, in which institutions become instruments in balancing against more powerful countries (Beeson 2015). Cambodia's behaviour signals that not all ASEAN members realise that without unity ASEAN cannot maintain its central position in the Asia Pacific.

The argument that other minilaterals are put in juxtaposition with ASEAN centrality assumes that ASEAN centrality is widely understood and accepted. This assertion is far from true. Acharya (2017), for example, who was once one of the most vocal proponents of the ASEAN institution, points out that ASEAN centrality

> is related to a number of similar concepts: ASEAN as the 'leader', the 'driver', the 'architect', the 'institutional hub', the 'vanguard' the 'nucleus; and the 'fulcrum' of regional processes and institutional designs in the Asia-Pacific region. A second popular misconception about ASEAN centrality is that it is about ASEAN itself. More accurately, it is really about the larger dynamics of regionalism and regional architecture in the Asia Pacific and even beyond. The third myth about ASEAN centrality is that it is the exclusively handiwork of ASEAN members—it is not.

With this in mind, the changes in the geostrategic environment suggest that the era of ASEAN being in the driver's seat has gradually passed. Some members of ASEAN have recognised this, but others prefer not to.

The notion of ASEAN centrality has a number of inter-related dimensions. In its most direct and limited sense, ASEAN centrality means that ASEAN is, and must remain, at the core of Asia's regional institutions—through ASEAN Plus mechanisms such as the ARF and the East Asia Summit, among many others. ASEAN provides an institutional platform to which the wider Asia Pacific and East Asian regional institutions are anchored. To put it another way, without ASEAN it would not have been possible to construct these wider regional bodies.

ASEAN's role as an institutional anchor is not likely to be overshadowed. Even if it is challenged, it can be a positive challenge. ASEAN centrality needs to be earned, rather than taken for granted. It is no surprise that ASEAN would resist the presence of another institution in the region for a number of reasons. One often-echoed reason is that it would risk sidelining ASEAN-centred institutions. Another reason is that given the rapid proliferation of regional institutions, there is no need for yet another one. While these arguments are logical and put ASEAN's interests at the core, they can be misleading and indeed hamper regional interests.

The conflation between ASEAN centrality and ASEAN unity is also conceptually misguiding, although one could also argue that ASEAN centrality is impossible to achieve without ASEAN unity. Clarity on what ASEAN centrality is, as well as its application and manifestation, is still absent, as is a common agreement across all ASEAN members on the concept. By now, it is clear that the QSD leaders do not harbour intentions of sidelining ASEAN centrality, as policy documents and speeches have paid due recognition to the principle. Whether the QSD can really achieve that is another matter, but that does not mean that such expectations do not exist. If ASEAN is not willing to deal with hard security, it needs to come to terms that there is a need for others to do so. Again, strategic and diplomatic centrality need to be exercised, not just claimed. Neither can it be achieved by simply obstructing or preventing other institutions from emerging. ASEAN centrality needs to be earned. Indeed, the late Surin Pitsuwan, the former ASEAN Secretary-General, distinguished between the 'centrality of goodwill'—that is, lip service—and 'centrality of substance' which includes setting the regional agenda, providing directions and resolving disagreements (Pitsuwan 2009).

While Southeast Asians are unsure whether the QSD will ever become a fully developed institution, their perceptions about the challenges facing it are accurate. The lack of commitment of the QSD members themselves is the main obstruction to the QSD's success. The longer their hesitation, the worse it is for the QSD's image.

Another clarification is that any multilateral or minilateral security cooperation is only supplementary to national strategies. As such, the QSD, or any other minilateral, is far from taking up a central security role in the Indo-Pacific. This is not a purpose for the QSD either. After all, any multilateralism or minilateralism has to complement other forms of security cooperation: '[n]one of the countries can entrust their national security to multilateral security cooperation' (Ohara 2015).

Unpacking ASEAN centrality

To go back to the basics before deliberating further, one question needs to be posed: what kind of centrality are we talking about—diplomatic, strategic, geographical, or institutional? While the aspired centrality would encompass all four dimensions, in reality no one can claim comprehensive centrality of ASEAN at all levels.

The presumption that the QSD, or indeed any other minilateral without any ASEAN member states, would challenge ASEAN needs to be assessed against each of these levels. This is discussed below. Diplomatically, could the QSD replace ASEAN, or function as a summit facilitator like ASEAN? The answer is not likely—and it is also unlikely that the QSD members would even have such an intention. Institutionally, through over half-a-century of existence, ASEAN's institutional strength has provided international relations with a unique but lasting model of regional cooperation. ASEAN has invented its own institutional personality that is not replicable by other regional organisations and has earned an important place on the map of global institutions. It has also created and sustained a network of relationships with other global and regional bodies, such as the United Nations, the European Union, Mercosur, and so on. The QSD, thus far, has neither the potential nor aspiration to convert into an institutionalised body. So, by this token, it is not likely to compete over ASEAN's institutional centrality.

ASEAN's strategic centrality has always been contested. ASEAN's inability and reluctance to deal with regional crises has raised doubts over its relevance and strategic centrality for a long time. By virtue of its position, institution and diplomatic weight, it was anticipated that ASEAN would play a much stronger role in addressing political and security crisis situations within Southeast Asia. Within the wider Indo-Pacific region, however, it will be difficult for ASEAN to claim strategic centrality when much larger and more active players are involved. In contrast, the geographical centrality of ASEAN will remain uncontested; in fact, it will be amplified in the current context of the Indo-Pacific. If great power competition continues, and it is most likely to be a long game, Southeast Asia and regional hotspots will again find themselves in the frontline.

The argument about the QSD potentially overshadowing ASEAN is dismissed by one regional observer thus: '[i]f a couple of informal meetings with no institutionalisation intent, or even joint statements, can make ASEAN—which conducts over 1,000 meetings a year and has an institutional history of over 50 years, then it tells more about ASEAN than the Quad' (personal communication, September 2018). In fact, the level of signalled alarm seems disproportionate to the real impact of the QSD meetings. I agree with the assessment that overemphasising the QSD's potential to sideline ASEAN says a great deal about ASEAN's confidence in its own centrality. Such a narrative is asserting a fallacy of comparison, because the QSD does not have the capacity, support, tradition or even appetite for institutionalisation in the same way that ASEAN does. Moreover, QSD members, who acknowledge such reservations, have repeatedly and explicitly reaffirmed ASEAN's centrality at almost every opportunity, ranging from policy documents and official speeches.

The binary fallacy also risks putting too much pressure on the QSD which eventually may affect perceptions of its effectiveness and utility. By framing it as a challenge for ASEAN, it suggests that the QSD will be able to overshadow ASEAN as it is likely to be more effective than the diplomatic gathering of Southeast Asian leaders. As the survey results proved, expectations of the QSD are high and commentaries as well as personal views expressed the anticipation that the QSD will be able to go beyond being a talkshop and have more of enforcing role (Le Thu 2018). These expectations need to be managed carefully as they may precede or even diverge from the intentions of the QSD members.

But a far more important question than whether the QSD, or other minilaterals for that matter, challenge ASEAN, is the question of how durable is the current regional architecture?

It is clear that we are currently heading towards a more tense situation in which existing institutions, norms, practices, arrangements and even laws are contested. In such an environment, can a regional architecture based on informality, goodwill of discussion and consultations manage stressful, and at times intense, confrontations? If ASEAN is not interested in stepping up, can it prevent other regional initiatives from emerging? The answer is probably not. ASEAN's concerns alone will not suffice to prevent other regional actors from becoming more active in the current strategic environment. For these reasons, it is in ASEAN's best interests to sustain its relevance through its relationships with the emerging minilaterals, including those that do not include any of its members.

Conclusion

This chapter has attempted to highlight that ASEAN's anxiety about one particular iteration of minilateralism—the QSD—has little rational basis. First, the perception of ASEAN being against the QSD is imprecise and inconsistent. The majority of the policy and security community, as the survey found out, are supportive of the QSD and see the value of this cooperation. This parallels the relative lack of diplomatic reservation voiced about other minilateral initiatives, including those whose membership does not involve any ASEAN countries, like the SCO. Second, the argument that minilateral initiatives, such as the QSD, challenge ASEAN centrality is flawed. The concept of ASEAN centrality can by no means be taken for granted; in fact, it is as contested as any other concept. Centrality needs to be earned, both nominally and functionally. Moreover, ASEAN does not reject other minilateral networks, thus making the argument less consistent.

ASEAN has taken the view that smaller countries engaged in the multilateral management of regional issues prevent or at least minimise tensions ensuing from major power competition. The QSD evokes concerns that the major powers are taking over and potentially even dictating regional power dynamics. The QSD's exclusiveness in its membership as a minilateral by design might suggest to the ASEAN leaders that its own long-term diplomatic capacity to include or exclude countries in major forums is being taken away from it.

One thing is certain—the global environment has changed significantly since ASEAN's inception when it was the 'only player in the game'. ASEAN needs to adapt to the new conditions and develop more constructive relationships with other multilaterals and minilaterals. If ASEAN wants to assert its centrality, it needs to maintain it amid other regional initiatives that are likely to continue to emerge, such as the QSD. To be able to maintain its central role, ASEAN needs to ascertain its utility despite the plethora of more agile, efficient and focused minilaterals.

References

Acharya, A 2017, 'The myth of ASEAN centrality', *Contemporary Southeast Asia: A Journal of International and Strategic Affairs*, vol. 39, no. 2, pp. 273–279.

Beeson, M 2015, 'Can ASEAN cope with China?' *Occasional Paper*, no. 26, September, Southeast Asian Studies at the University of Freiburg, Baden-Württemberg.

Chan, F and Soeriaatmadja, W 2017, 'Joint Sulu Sea patrols launched; info-sharing from Singapore next', *Straits Times*, 20 June, www.straitstimes.com/asia/joint-sulu-sea-patrols-launched-info-sharing-from-spore-next.

Ciorciari, J 2013, *Limits of Alignment in Southeast Asia since 1975*, Washington, DC, Georgetown University Press.

Department of Foreign Affairs and Trade, Australian Government 2017, *2017 Foreign Policy White Paper*, www.fpwhitepaper.gov.au/foreign-policy-white-paper.

Emmers, R 2012, 'Five Power Defence Arrangements and defence diplomacy in Southeast Asia', *Asian Security*, vol. 8, no. 3, pp. 271–286.

Emmers, R 2017, 'ASEAN minus X: should this formula be extended?' *RSIS Commentary* no. 199, 24 October.

Hartcher, P 2018, 'The powerful combination that gives US the edge over China', *Sydney Morning Herald*, 16 July, www.smh.com.au/world/north-america/the-powerful-combination-that-gives-us-the-edge-over-china-20180716-p4zrqn.html.

Hayashi, S and Onchi, Y 2017, 'Japan to propose dialogue with US, India and Australia', *Nikkei Asian Review*, 26 October, https://asia.nikkei.com/Politics/Japan-to-propose-dialogue-with-US-India-and-Australia2.

Le Thu, H 2018, 'Southeast Asian perceptions of the Quadrilateral Security Dialogue: survey findings', *ASPI Special Report*, October, www.aspi.org.au/report/southeast-asian-perceptions-quadrilateral-security-dialogue.

Le Thu, H (ed.) 2019, 'Quad 2.0: new perspectives for the revived concept', *ASPI Strategic Insights*, February, www.aspi.org.au/report/quad-20-new-perspectives.

Ministry of Foreign Affairs of the People's Republic of China 2016, 'Wang Yi talks about China's four-point consensus on South China Sea issue with Brunei, Cambodia and Laos', 23 April, www.fmprc.gov.cn/mfa_eng/zxxx_662805/t1358478.shtml.

Ministry of Foreign Affairs of the People's Republic of China 2017, 'China's polices on Asia-Pacific security cooperation', 11 January, www.fmprc.gov.cn/mfa_eng/zxxx_662805/t1429771.shtml.

Ohara, B 2015, 'Maritime multilateral security cooperation in East and South Asia', in W Lohman, RK Sawhney, A Davies and I Nishida (eds.) *The Quad Plus: Towards a Shared Strategic Vision for the Indo-Pacific*, New Delhi, Wisdom Tree, pp. 39–50.

Pitsuwan, S 2009, 'Building an ASEAN Economic Community in the heart of East Asia', www.ide.go.jp/library/Japanese/Event/Sympo/pdf/2009/surin_en.pdf.

Rej, A 2018, 'Reclaiming the Indo-Pacific: a political-military strategy for Quad 2.0', *Observer Research Foundation Occasional Paper*, no. 147.

Rudd, K 2019, 'The convenient rewriting of the history of the Quad', *Nikkei Asian Review*, 26 March.

Sharma, K 2018, '"Quad" seen to discuss ways to curb China's influence in the Indo-Pacific', *Nikkei Asian Review*, 14 November, https://asia.nikkei.com/Politics/International-Rela tions/Quad-seen-to-discuss-ways-to-curb-China-s-influence-in-Indo-Pacific.

Singh, S 2018, 'Is India shifting the goalposts in Indo-Pacific debate?' *Asia Times*, 9 July.

Thakur, R 2018, 'Quad isn't a knight in a shining armour to slay the dragon', *Japan Times*, 9 July.

The White House 2017, *National Security Strategy*, December, www.whitehouse.gov/wp -content/uploads/2017/12/NSS-Final-12-18-2017-0905.pdf.

Tsvetov, A 2017, 'Will the Quad mean the end of ASEAN centrality?' *The Diplomat*, 15 November.

US Congress 2018, 'The Asia Reassurance Initiative Act of 2018', https://www.congress. gov/bill/115th-congress/senate-bill/2736/text.

US Department of Defense 2018, *Summary of the 2018 National Defense Strategy of the United States of America: Sharpening the American Military's Competitive Edge*, https://dod.defense. gov/Portals/1/Documents/pubs/2018-National-Defense-Strategy-Summary.pdf.

Wuthnow, J 2018, 'US minilateralism in Asia and China's responses: a new security dilemma?' *Journal of Contemporary China*, vol. 28, no. 115, pp. 133–150.

7

MINILATERALISM IN SOUTHEAST ASIA

Facts, opportunities and risks

Vannarith Chheang

Introduction

As multilateralism is under threat, mainly due to rising protectionism and transactional politics in the United States, minilateralism appears to be more receptive and resilient. Some argue that 'minilateralism could overshadow and eventually challenge multilateralism' (Teo 2018). Here, minilateralism refers to functional cooperation on specific issues at the sub-regional level between countries or localities in a geographically defined area or region. Minilateralism, which is informal and flexible in its nature and characteristics, is therefore appealing to countries that are sceptical about multilateralism (Tow 2018). In Southeast Asia, minilateralism has expanded since the early 1990s and focuses on economic cooperation and practical cooperation on non-traditional security issues such as piracy, the environment, and human and drug trafficking.

Arguably, if it is properly utilised, minilateralism is a bonus for the Association of Southeast Asian Nations (ASEAN) as it offers a more effective decision-making process to overcome the shortcomings of the consensus-based decision making of this inter-governmental organisation, especially on regional sensitive security matters, such as the South China Sea issue (Gnanasagaran 2018). Heydarian (2017, p. 1) argued that '[t]o save the principle of ASEAN centrality, the regional body should transcend its unanimity/consensus-based decision-making and embrace minilateral arrangements on divisive issues'. However, there are risks and concerns deriving from minilateral mechanisms that might adversely affect the centrality and unity of ASEAN if the minilateral frameworks are dominated or dictated by any major power.

This chapter discusses two dimensions of minilateralism: economic minilateralism and political-security minilateralism. It then examines minilateralism in mainland Southeast Asia and analyses associated risks and concerns over externally driven minilateralism. It argues that economic minilateralism is complementary to ASEAN multilateralism but that political-security minilateralism potentially weakens the centrality and unity of ASEAN especially within the context of heightening geopolitical rivalry between major powers, particularly for the minilateral frameworks that are driven by geopolitical agendas.

Economic dimension

Economic minilateralism can be viewed as cooperation among three or more countries on economic issues to promote cross-border trade and investment, tourism, infrastructure development and connectivity. It is widely believed that through regional economic cooperation and integration, peace and development can be sustained and further enhanced. Economic minilateralism has proved to be more effective than multilateralism, especially with regards to the process of decision making and the actual implementation thereof (Naim 2009).

Minilateralism is driven by both state and market forces, and seeks to promote cross-border trade and investment cooperation between member countries and localities. Local governments also play an important role in facilitating cross-border cooperation. Minilateral mechanisms have proved to be relatively effective in facilitating cooperation among all the parties concerned, and to help to reduce poverty and to narrow the development gaps at the sub-regional level, especially in the border regions. The development of several growth triangles (such as the Indonesia-Malaysia-Singapore Growth Triangle and the Cambodia-Laos-Vietnam Development Triangle) is a case in point to demonstrate political will and cross-border cooperation to strengthen the regional economic links and border development, and to combine the competitive strengths and complementarity between the adjacent border areas (Chheang 2018c).

The concept of sub-regional cooperation, which is mainly driven by economic interests, has been developed so that it is part of regional integration in Southeast Asia. Cross-border cooperation is necessary for strengthening the flow of goods, services, investment capital and tourists. Minilateralism is complementary to regional integration and connectivity in Southeast Asia. First, it facilitates the implementation of the ASEAN Economic Community blueprints especially in the field of cross-border trade and investment, and regional connectivity. Second, minilateralism promotes economic development particularly along the border areas that are relatively remote, as well as in the less developed regions.

The Singapore-Johor-Riau Growth Triangle was created in 1989 and later expanded to become the Indonesia-Malaysia-Singapore Growth Triangle in 1994. It is the first growth triangle in Southeast Asia and seeks to take advantage of members' geographical proximity to facilitate cross-border trade and investment flow (Ooi 1995). The growth triangle is complementary to regional economic cooperation and integration efforts and it can co-exist with more formal regional arrangements such as free trade agreements and 'closer economic partnerships' (Heng 2006).

In 1994, the Brunei-Indonesia-Malaysia-Philippines East ASEAN Growth Area (BIMP-EAGA) was established to 'accelerate economic development in areas that are geographically distant from their national capitals, yet in strategic proximity to each other' (Asian Development Bank 2019). The aim of BIMP-EAGA was to increase trade, tourism and investment by facilitating the free movement of people, goods and services, making the best use of common infrastructure and natural resources, and taking the fullest advantage of economic complementation.

In mainland Southeast Asia, the Greater Mekong Subregion (GMS) was founded in 1992 with technical and financial support from the Asian Development Bank (ADB). Cambodia, China, Laos, Myanmar, Thailand and Vietnam are members of the GMS which is the sub-regional mechanism designed to enhance economic relations among the countries. The GMS has contributed to the development of infrastructure to enable the development and sharing of the resource base, and to promote the freer flow of goods and people in the sub-region. The strategic plan for 2012–22 covers multi-sector cooperation schemes including developing the major GMS corridors as economic corridors; strengthening transport linkages; developing an integrated approach to deliver sustainable, secure and competitive energy; improving telecommunications linkages and information and communication technology applications among the GMS countries; developing and promoting tourism in the Mekong as a single destination; promoting competitive, climate-friendly and sustainable agriculture; enhancing environmental performance in the GMS; and supporting human resources development and initiatives that facilitate the process of GMS integration while addressing any negative consequences of greater integration (Asian Development Bank 2012).

The Cambodia-Laos-Vietnam Development Triangle (CLV-DT), which was founded in 1999, is the most dynamic growth triangle in mainland Southeast Asia. Vietnam has taken a de facto leadership role in the CLV-DT not only to promote sub-regional economic cooperation and integration, but also to check the rising influence of China in Indochina (Chheang 2018c). The cooperation areas under the CLV-DT include infrastructure development, connectivity, trade and investment facilitation, and human resource development. At the biannual summit in 2018, for the first time there were representatives from ASEAN, the World Bank and the ADB—demonstrating that the CLV-DT has drawn more interest from these regional and international institutions.

Thailand has beefed up its role in promoting the Ayeyawady-Chao Phraya-Mekong Economic Cooperation Strategy (ACMECS) in order to strengthen its leadership role in mainland Southeast Asia (Busbarat 2014). In 2018, a funding mechanism was proposed that would facilitate the implementation of the master plan of ACMECS, which focuses on seamless connectivity (multi-modal transport links); software connectivity (trade, investment and industrial cooperation, and financial cooperation); and the development of human capital. The Bangkok Declaration that was adopted after the eighth ACMECS summit in 2018 encourages the 'active engagement of ACMECS member countries, potential development partners, regional and international organisations, as well as international financial institutions in the setting up of the ACMECS Fund' (Ministry of Foreign Affairs of Thailand 2018).

An extended sub-regional cooperation mechanism, the Bay of Bengal Initiative for Multi-Sectoral Technical and Economic Cooperation (BIMSTEC) involves Bangladesh, India, Myanmar, Sri Lanka and Thailand. The mechanism could play a bridging role between Southeast Asia and South Asia, and between ASEAN and the South Asian Association for Regional Cooperation. Similarly to other economic minilateral mechanisms, BIMSTEC aims to utilise regional resources and geographical advantages to facilitate regional growth. It is a sector-driven cooperative mechanism. The key areas of cooperation are trade, technology, energy, transport, tourism and fisheries. However, BIMSTEC is less effective compared with other economic minilaterals in Southeast Asia. One analyst argued:

> [W]ith access to the Indian Ocean and the Himalayas, BIMSTEC is becoming the theatre of convergence and competition for China's Belt and Road Initiative, India's Act East policy and the Asia–Africa Growth Corridor. It remains to be seen if BIMSTEC can seize the day and utilise the momentum to remodel itself as a grouping to be reckoned with.
>
> *(Hussain 2018)*

These economic minilateral mechanisms complement ASEAN multilateralism through three pathways. First, they narrow the development gaps within the country and between the member countries of ASEAN especially through the development of the border areas. Second, they facilitate practical and sector-driven cooperation between the ASEAN member countries. Third, they strengthen political will and strive to embed norms of regional economic integration within ASEAN.

Political and security dimension

Security minilateralism involves security cooperation and defence coalition among a few like-minded countries to address and deal with common non-traditional security threats and issues such as terrorism, transnational crimes, natural disasters and water resources management. Minilateralism has become more attractive due to the fact that the existing security multilateral mechanisms are unable to provide expeditious and effective solutions to increasing security challenges and issues in the region. The slowness of decision-making processes, which are usually based on consensus, is the main reason for some countries opting for minilateral initiatives.

Due to the complexity of the regional security environment, some countries have opted for minilateral cooperation. They believe that minilateral cooperation in the security and defence sector is more flexible and more effective and 'offers a valuable means' to deal with non-traditional security issues and threats (Nilsson-Wright 2017). In maritime Southeast Asia, the Five Power Defence Arrangements (FPDA), founded in 1971, is the first '"mini-lateral" defence coalition' with a focus on specific security issues and needs of the member countries (Malaysia, Singapore, Australia, New Zealand and the United Kingdom) (Emmers 2010). The FPDA remains relevant in addressing common security threats such as terrorism and maritime security, and is an integral part of the regional security architecture.

In 2004, the littoral states in Southeast Asia (Indonesia, Malaysia and Singapore) conducted the Malacca Straits Sea Patrol to ensure the security of the straits, which are critical and strategic waterways in the regional and global trading system. A year later, the 'Eyes in the Sky' mechanism, which combined maritime air patrols between the three countries, was launched. In 2006, the Malacca Straits Patrol Joint Coordinating Committee Terms of Reference and Standard Operating Procedures was signed. In 2008, Thailand became a member of the Malacca Straits Patrol. The first Malacca Straits Patrol exercise was held in 2011. The Malacca Straits Patrol consists of the Malacca Straits Sea Patrol, the 'Eyes in the Sky' Combined Maritime Air Patrols, and the Intelligence Exchange Group (Ministry of Defence of Singapore 2015).

In 2016, Malaysia, Indonesia and the Philippines agreed to set up trilateral patrols in the Sulu-Celebes Seas, following maritime attacks by the militant Abu Sayyaf group in early 2016. In 2017, the three countries launched coordinated naval patrols in the affected areas. Singapore supported these coordinated efforts through information sharing. Building the capacity of local maritime law enforcement agencies and protecting the economic interests of the marginalised coastal communities is of critical importance (Denson 2019). Due to the limited capacity of the three countries, capacity-building support from extra-regional countries, especially Japan and the United States to the Philippines, has helped regional states to deal with maritime security issues more effectively (Storey 2018).

In mainland Southeast Asia, the riparian states of the Mekong River (Cambodia, Laos, Thailand and Vietnam) signed the Mekong Agreement and created the Mekong River Commission (MRC) in 1995 to address water security issues. Compounded with climate change, population growth and urbanisation, the construction of a series of hydropower dams along the mainstream of the Mekong River has been a controversial issue and is potentially a source of conflict between the riparian countries (Chheang 2018b). During the period 2016–20 the MRC's work focused on the following four key areas: the enhancement of national plans, projects and resources based on basin-wide perspectives; the strengthening of regional cooperation; the improvement of monitoring and communication of the basin's conditions; and the enhancement of institutional effectiveness and efficiency.

Joint patrols between China and Lower Mekong countries including Laos, Myanmar and Thailand started in 2011 to ensure the safety of navigation along the Mekong River. Counter-terrorism, counter-trafficking (drug and human trafficking), and search and rescue are the three main areas of cooperation. China has taken a leadership role and sends the largest number of officers and vessels to participate in the patrols which take place regularly. From 2011 to 2018, there were 80 joint patrols. At March 2019, a total of 12,816 officers and 680 vessels were participating in the missions, covering a range of more than 42,000 kilometres (*Xinhua News* 2019).

Within the context of geopolitical rivalry between major powers, particularly between the United States and China, some Southeast Asian countries have been convinced to take part in minilateral security cooperation mechanisms that are initiated and led by the respective major powers. Some regional observers have argued that '[t]he Asia–Pacific to Indo-Pacific shift is really an instance of an emerging minilateral security regionalism, rather than the predominant forms of bilateral and multilateral security and economic regionalism that have dominated Asia in recent decades' (Lee-Brown 2018). This reflects the new dynamics of security minilateralism in the region which is driven by major powers. The US–China rivalry could potentially lead to the weakening of multilateral institutions such as ASEAN, which in turn forces weaker states to look for alternative minilateral mechanisms.

An interesting development is the creation of the informal security coalition (known as the Quadrilateral Security Dialogue—QSD) among the four key members of the Indo-Pacific Strategy, namely Australia, India, Japan and the United States. The QSD has not won support from ASEAN, and has been largely perceived by Southeast Asian observers and policymakers as a threat to ASEAN centrality, which refers to the power and capacity of ASEAN to set and drive the regional agenda (Ng 2018). Furthermore, within the context of an evolving Indo-Pacific Strategy, ASEAN has initiated its self-styled concept of an 'Indo-Pacific Outlook' aiming to maintain the centrality role of ASEAN in shaping the Indo-Pacific regional architecture. ASEAN stresses the principles of inclusiveness, openness, transparency and complementarity.

Security minilateralism that purely focuses on practical cooperation—particularly in capacity building and information sharing—on non-traditional security issues such as terrorism, piracy and resource security are complementary to the realisation of the ASEAN Political-Security Community. However, security minilateralism that embeds a geopolitical agenda, accompanied with the risk of creating geopolitical divide, poses a risk to ASEAN centrality.

Externally driven minilateralism

The Mekong region is a new growth centre and a strategic frontier of the Indo-Pacific region. It is the most dynamic region in terms of minilaterals that are driven by major and middle powers. Currently, there are five main cooperation mechanisms led by India, Japan, South Korea, the United States and China. These mechanisms can potentially weaken ASEAN centrality and unity if ASEAN does not take effective measures and provide a certain degree of leadership role in building synergies between these mechanisms with ASEAN community-building projects.

There is a risk that greater divisions will emerge between mainland and maritime Southeast Asia if ASEAN does not develop an effective engagement strategy with minilaterals in the Mekong region (Ho and Pitakdumrongkit 2019). There is also concern, particularly from Vietnam, that these mechanisms do not provide effective solutions to transboundary water resources management, and that power competition between China and the United States will largely shape the region's development trajectory (Nguyen 2019).

The minilaterals in mainland Southeast Asia have not been integrated or syner-gised to make full use of these mechanisms. It is suggested that for the member countries to realise their ambitious development goals and to narrow the development gap yet further, they need to build synergy across these various minilaterals and to strengthen coordination and cooperation between key agencies (the public sector, the private sector, civil society organisations, the research and academic community, and local people) (Sok 2019).

Mekong-Ganga Cooperation

India has been actively involved in the Mekong sub-region since the early 1990s. In 1989, India introduced the 'Look East Policy' to engage with ASEAN. In 2014, President Narendra Modi upgraded the 'Look East Policy' to the 'Act East Policy' to give more impetus to India's regional integration strategy with ASEAN and East Asia. In 2000, the Mekong-Ganga Cooperation (MGC) mechanism was established to promote regional cooperation. The MGC has six members, namely Cambodia, India, Laos, Myanmar, Thailand and Vietnam. The MGC focuses on several cooperation areas, including tourism, culture, capacity building, education and connectivity.

However, due to the lack of leadership and resources, the MGC has produced limited results. At the sixth MGC Ministerial Meeting in 2012, India announced the establishment of Quick Impact Projects with an annual budget of US$ 1 million to fund the projects in areas such as connectivity, education, social infra-structure, health, agriculture, farming and livestock rearing. In 2018, India expressed an interest in becoming the partner of the MRC, in order to share expertise on water resources management. Moreover, both India and the Mekong countries agreed to explore ways to enhance cooperation in areas such as natural resource management, especially management of water and related resources, environmental protection and climate change response (Ministry of External Affairs of India 2018).

At the tenth MGC Ministerial Meeting in August 2019, a new MGC Plan of Action 2019–22 was adopted. The plan envisaged project-based cooperation in seven areas: tourism and culture; education; science and technology; public health and traditional medicine; agriculture and allied sectors; transport and communica-tion; and micro, small and medium-sized enterprises. Three new areas of coop-eration were proposed, namely water resources management; science and technology; and skill development and capacity building. Moreover, India announced a US$ 1 billion line of credit for connectivity projects in ASEAN and pledged US$ 72.5 million under a Project Development Fund to facilitate Indian investments in Cambodia, Laos, Myanmar and Vietnam (Ministry of External Affairs of India 2019).

Japan-Mekong cooperation

Japan reached out to the Mekong countries in 2007 through the Japan–Mekong Regional Partnership Program. Japan–Mekong cooperation has been institutionalised and intensified since 2008 when the first foreign ministers' meeting between Japan and the Mekong countries took place in Tokyo. A year later, the Japan-Mekong exchange year was organised and the first Japan-Mekong summit was held. In 2015, Japan and the Mekong countries adopted the Tokyo Strategy 2015, with a financial commitment of US$ 10 million from Japan over a five-year period. The Tokyo Strategy 2015 emphasises four 'pillars' of cooperation: 'hard efforts' concentrating on industrial infrastructure development and strengthening hard connectivity; 'soft efforts' to advance industrial structures and human resources development, and strengthening soft connectivity; sustainable development and green growth in the Mekong; and coordination with various stakeholders (Ministry of Foreign Affairs of Japan 2015).

In 2018, Japan and the Mekong countries adopted the Tokyo Strategy 2018 with the emphasis on the strengthening of synergies between Mekong-Japan cooperation, the 2030 Sustainable Development Goals, the Free and Open Indo-Pacific (FOIP), and ACMECS. The three new pillars of cooperation comprise vibrant and effective connectivity (hard connectivity, soft connectivity and industrial connectivity); people–centred society (human resource development, health-care, education, legal and judicial cooperation); and realisation of a 'green Mekong' (disaster risk reduction and climate change, water resources management, circular economy, conservation and sustainable use of aquatic fishery resources) (Ministry of Foreign Affairs of Japan 2018b).

The co-chair's statement released on the occasion of the twelfth Mekong-Japan Foreign Ministers' Meeting in Bangkok in August 2019 stressed two areas of cooperation. First, enhancing partnership to achieve the 2030 Agenda for Sustainable Development under the three approaches, namely a region–wide approach, an open approach, and a public–private cooperative approach. Second, reinforcing the synergy between Mekong cooperation and the FOIP that emphasises a 'free and open order based on the rule of law to maintain peace, stability and prosperity in the Mekong region' (Ministry of Foreign Affairs of Japan 2019).

Mekong-South Korea cooperation

South Korea started engaging with the Mekong region in 2011 to contribute to reducing the development gap in ASEAN through support for the development of the Mekong region, and to facilitate economic cooperation between South Korea and the region. In 2011, ministers of foreign affairs from South Korea and the Mekong countries adopted the 'Han River Declaration on Mekong-Korea

Comprehensive Partnership for Mutual Prosperity' which emphasised connectivity, sustainable development and people-oriented development. The Mekong-Korea Plan of Action (2014–17) prioritises six areas: infrastructure, information technology, green growth, water resources development, agriculture and rural development, and human resources development. As of 2019, South Korea has provided a total of US$ 3.4 billion to ASEAN, 72 per cent of which goes to the less developed economies in the Mekong region (Cambodia, Laos, Myanmar and Vietnam) with a focus on capacity building and infrastructure development.

In 2018, both sides agreed to elevate their cooperation to a higher level through the nascent New Southern Policy, which focuses on three pillars (people, prosperity and peace) and four connectivity areas (transportation, energy, water resources, and information and communication technologies) (Lee 2018). In early 2019, South Korea and the Mekong countries agreed to hold their first summit in November 2019 alongside the ASEAN-Republic of Korea Commemorative Summit (Choi 2019).

At the ninth Mekong-Republic of Korea Foreign Ministers' Meeting, South Korea underlined the importance of the Mekong region, a geographical pivot connecting ASEAN, China and India as well as an area that is drawing attention as a future growth engine of the global economy with abundant natural resources, a young population and a high economic growth rate. South Korea stressed that the cooperation projects that it is carrying out with the Mekong countries are part of its New Southern Policy, including the expansion of official development assistance for the Mekong countries (Ministry of Foreign Affairs of Republic of Korea 2019).

Lower Mekong Initiative

The United States initiated the Lower Mekong Initiative (LMI) in 2009, with cooperation areas focusing on agriculture and food security, connectivity, education, energy security, water security, environmental issues, and public health. The US approach is to strengthen public institutions, empower civil society, promote social justice and human rights, and support sustainable and inclusive development. In 2016, the United States also emphasised sustainable infrastructure and narrowing the development gap within ASEAN. At the foreign ministers' meeting in 2018, the United States and the Lower Mekong countries agreed to streamline cooperation areas under two pillars: the water, energy, food and environment nexus; and human development and connectivity (which also includes activities related to connectivity, health and education). Moreover, the member countries are expected to integrate the themes of gender equality and women's empowerment, connectivity and public-private partnership across all LMI projects and activities (Lower Mekong Initiative 2018).

In terms of water resources management and information sharing, member countries agreed to strengthen the individual capacity of the Lower Mekong countries to collect, analyse and manage water, land and weather data, and to promote sustainable economic development across the water, food, energy and environment nexus; and to strengthen the capacity of the MRC to collect and analyse globally accessible datasets, remote sensing and other real-time data for support flood, drought and extreme event forecasting, basin-wide water resources, hydrological modelling, and impact analysis tools (Lower Mekong Initiative 2018).

To counter the increasing influence of China in the Mekong region, especially under the framework of the Lancang-Mekong Cooperation mechanism, the United States began to promote the linkage between the LMI with its revised Indo-Pacific Strategy in early 2019. The United States launched the LMI Public Impact Program and three new initiatives, namely the Digital Connectivity and Cybersecurity Partnership, the Infrastructure Transaction and Assistance, and the Enhancing Development and Growth through Energy (or Asia EDGE).

At the LMI ministerial meeting in Bangkok in August 2019, US Secretary of State Mike Pompeo took the opportunity to criticise China for exercising water hegemony over the downstream countries. He stated:

> We see a spree of upstream dam building which concentrates control over downstream flows. The river has been at its lowest levels in a decade—a problem linked to China's decision to shut off water upstream. China also has plans to blast and dredge riverbeds. China operates extra-territorial river patrols. And we see a push to craft new Beijing-directed rules to govern the river, thereby weakening the Mekong River Commission.
>
> *(US Department of State 2019)*

The issue of the LMI is the lack of funding, which makes it less attractive to the Lower Mekong countries. To stay relevant, the United States plans to provide an initial US$ 14 million in assistance to the Mekong countries to counter transnational crime and trafficking. The United States also announced its intention to provide an initial US$ 29.5 million under Asia EDGE to support the Mekong countries' pursuit of energy security and their citizens' reliable access to electricity. In 2019, the United States rolled out new initiatives to help Mekong nations in the infrastructure, energy, and digital sectors. The LMI member countries also launched a new Mekong water data-sharing platform and a new LMI Public Impact Program in 2019 (US Department of State 2019).

Lancang-Mekong Cooperation

The Lancang-Mekong Cooperation (LMC) mechanism was launched in 2015, with a focus on three areas of cooperation including politico-security issues, economic affairs and sustainable development, and social affairs and people-to-people exchanges. The LMC is one of the core elements of China's neighbourhood diplomacy to strengthen its presence and influence in the Mekong region and to further connect the Mekong region with its less developed regions in China in order to generate more opportunities in these regions. At the first LMC Summit in

2016, China committed US\$ 1.54 billion in preferential loans and a credit line of US\$ 10 billion to support infrastructure and production capacity projects in the Mekong countries (Blanchard and Meng 2016). As an upstream country, China has a responsibility to better manage the Mekong River with a view to the improvement of living conditions for the people living downstream.

The second LMC Summit in 2018 elaborated on the three pillars of sub-regional cooperation, namely political and security issues (with the focus on maintaining high-level exchanges, political dialogues and cooperation, exchanges among political parties, and non-traditional security cooperation); economy and sustainable development (with a focus on connectivity, production capacity, economy and trade, financial cooperation, water resources management, agriculture, forestry, poverty reduction, environmental protection, and customs and quality inspection); and social and cultural cooperation (with a focus on cultural exchanges, tourism development, education, health, media, people-to-people exchanges and local government cooperation) (Mu 2018).

The LMC has generally been perceived as the most important minilateral in the Mekong sub-region, due to the relatively large financial commitment that China is prepared to inject into comprehensive and interconnected connectivity projects. Development cooperation is the priority of the LMC. A Cambodian analyst and government adviser, Sok (2019) argues that China's leadership in promoting the growth of the LMC allows the Mekong countries to chart the sub-region's development. He opined that

> [t]he Mekong countries can feel assured about the trajectory of LMC, owing to the familiarity of the pillars of cooperation and knowing that promoting sustainable development and the protection of the Mekong's cultures are shared values that are important to all member countries.
>
> *(Ibid., p. 3)*

Risks and concerns

Minilateralism helps to facilitate international cooperation at the sub-regional level on specific issues as it has certain advantages (see above). However, there are limits to this. According to one observer, '[i]f minilateral institutions in Southeast Asia are framed as being competitive rather than complementary to existing multilateral institutions and subsequently garner more interest from outside powers, they can contribute to further weakening the centrality of wider ASEAN-led institutions' (Parameswaran 2018).

Minilateralism might potentially lead to political or strategic fragmentation and division within ASEAN if the mechanism and agenda of minilateral initiatives are driven and dominated by external major power(s). For instance, strategic competition between China and Japan in mainland Southeast Asia is on the rise, which potentially causes a certain degree of strategic challenge for the Mekong countries to adjust and balance their external relations with both Asian powers. One

Cambodian analyst argued, '[w]hile Mekong cooperation mechanisms are considered as complimentary to regional economic development and integration, Mekong countries seem to lack ownership over how they are run—with development partners having the upper hand' (Doung 2018).

China has effectively exerted economic inducement and coercion strategies to achieve its geopolitical goal. Under the LMC, China has shored up its leadership role, as well as its economic and political influence in the Mekong region. There are five main areas of LMC cooperation: connectivity; production capacity; cross-border economic cooperation; water resources management; and agriculture and poverty reduction (Chheang 2018a). China's mounting geopolitical clout in mainland Southeast Asia might prevent ASEAN from taking a united position against China's interests particularly in the South China Sea (Wong 2018). Mainland Southeast Asian countries, especially Cambodia, Laos and Myanmar, are reluctant to take any position that might harm their good relationship with China, which is their key economic partner.

Japan has also strengthened its engagement with mainland Southeast Asia. In the 2018 Tokyo Strategy the Mekong countries notably expressed their common position of support for the Japan-initiated FOIP, even though ASEAN has not taken a clear position on the FOIP. The statement reads:

> Leaders of the Mekong countries welcomed Japan's policy to realize a free and open Indo-Pacific to contribute to the peace, stability and prosperity in the region and the world. Leaders expressed their determination to steadily implement the Mekong-Japan Cooperation projects which contribute to and complement the promotion of a free and open Indo-Pacific.
>
> *(Ministry of Foreign Affairs of Japan 2018b)*

Remarkably, Cambodia, which is widely perceived as a close strategic partner of China in Southeast Asia, was the first country to register support for the Japan-proposed FOIP (ibid., 2018a).

US influence in mainland Southeast Asia is in relative decline in comparison with that of China and Japan. The LMI does not have its own financial resources to implement projects and activities. Moreover, India has not taken concrete measures to invest more resources in its Mekong-Ganga initiative. In such a geopolitical context, rising China-Japan competition will largely shape the geopolitical landscape in the region (Leng 2019). The engagement of the United States and India in the Mekong region will help to leverage Japan's position vis-à-vis China. The Lower Mekong countries will need to adjust their foreign policy postures accordingly given that they are implementing hedging strategies at varying degrees. For small states like Cambodia, the challenge is how to maintain trust and good relations with its two strategic partners—China and Japan. (Cambodia signed a strategic partnership agreement with China in 2010 and another with Japan in 2013. So far, these countries remain Cambodia's sole strategic partners.)

The escalating US-China tensions pose a significant threat to regional peace and stability in Southeast Asia. These two major powers will use their minilaterals to build their own sphere of influence. Within the context of increasing tensions, Southeast Asian countries are likely to be forced to choose sides against their wishes and interest. These two major powers will use all means available to them, including the minilateral mechanisms under their leadership, to impact policy changes. The US-led security minilaterals (under the form of policy coordination and interoperability, exercises and intelligence-sharing agreement) in the South China Sea have exacerbated China's fears of 'containment' or 'encirclement'. Such moves have caused China to take counter-moves, which in turn pose a security dilemma for Southeast Asian countries (Wuthnow 2019).

The Mekong region has become a new strategic frontier in Southeast Asia. Chongkittavorn (2019) argues that it has become a region that needs to reckoned with—it is no longer a strategic backyard but a strategic frontyard. Currently, there are more than ten minilateral mechanisms in operation, largely initiated and driven by external middle and major powers. At present, the institutions governing the Mekong are unable to provide the necessary sub-regional governance of the Mekong River (Murg 2019). The revival of the United States' LMI guided by the Indo-Pacific Strategy and the fast-expanding LMC led by China will be the two competing minilaterals in the Mekong region. The United States will strengthen its coordination and partnership with Japan and the Friends of the Lower Mekong—a coordinated donor group led by the United States to counterbalance China. Robinson (2019, p. 53) observes that

> intensifying rivalry among big powers for influence in the nascent Mekong region has generated new interest from donor countries and organizations since 2017 after decades of relative neglect. A key driver has been the rise of the U.S.-led 'Free and Open Indo-Pacific' strategy.

Conclusion

Minilateralism is becoming more attractive due its relative flexibility and because it provides effective decision making. It has gained renewed interest from Southeast Asian countries. In the field of economic cooperation and integration, minilateral mechanisms are complementary to ASEAN, rather than competitive with it, given that they generally aim to facilitate cross-border trade and investment, strengthen connectivity and narrow the development gap especially through poverty reduction in the border areas. The Mekong region is the most dynamic region in terms of the development of minilaterals, with development-focused cooperation.

Minilateral cooperation on non-traditional security issues complement existing multilateral mechanisms as minilaterals are more able to offer more practical and effective solutions to specific security issues such as counter-terrorism. Minilaterals that have been founded and led by the ASEAN member states are complementary to and an integral part of ASEAN community building.

Minilateralism is a two-edged sword in that it could either undermine or complement multilateralism. If it is not managed carefully, minilateralism could damage the centrality and unity of ASEAN. In the realm of politics and security, minilateralism poses certain risks to ASEAN given that the security agenda is usually influenced by external major power(s). If any of the ASEAN member states that have joined the minilateral mechanisms led by certain major power(s) were to lose their balanced position and decide to align with a major power for their economic and security interests, ASEAN unity and centrality would certainly be compromised.

Amid heightening geopolitical rivalry especially between the United States and China, ASEAN risks being divided. In order for minilateral mechanisms to be a plus for ASEAN, they must align their projects with ASEAN Community blueprints, and integrate the principles of ASEAN unity and centrality into the institutionalisation of minilaterals in the region. The proposed 'ASEAN minus X' formula for decision making remains a controversial and sensitive issue. The geopolitical divide between maritime and mainland Southeast Asia still exists and minilateralism can potentially widen rather than narrow the geopolitical gaps. ASEAN must pay close attention to the issues that mainland Southeast Asian countries are facing and forge a common position on those issues and challenges in order to strengthen ASEAN unity and centrality.

References

Asian Development Bank 2012, *The Hanoi Action Plan 2012–2022*, March, viewed 10 March 2019, www.adb.org/sites/default/files/institutional-document/409086/ha-noi-action-plan-2018-2022.pdf.

Asian Development Bank 2019, 'Brunei Darussalam-Indonesia-Malaysia-Philippines East ASEAN Growth Area (BIMP-EAGA)', viewed 10 March 2019, www.adb.org/countries/subregional-programs/bimp-eaga.

Blanchard, B and Meng, M 2016, 'China offers 11.5 billion in loans, credit to Southeast Asia', Reuters, 23 March, viewed 10 June 2019, https://uk.reuters.com/article/uk-china-diplomacy/china-offers-11-5-billions-in-loans-credit-to-southeast-asia-idUKKCN0WP19Y.

Busbarat, P 2014, 'Thailand's foreign policy: the struggle for regional leadership in Southeast Asia', in BTC Guan (ed.) *Foreign Policy and Security in an Asian Century: Threats, Strategies and Policy*, Singapore, World Scientific, pp. 133–153.

Chheang, V 2018a, 'China's economic statecraft in Southeast Asia', *Perspective*, no. 70, viewed 13 September 2019, www.iseas.edu.sg/images/pdf/ISEAS_Perspective_2018_45@50.pdf.

Chheang, V 2018b, 'Mekong water security sets off alarm bells in the Mekong region', *Khmer Times*, 14 August, viewed 13 September 2019, www.khmertimeskh.com/50522249/mekong-water-security-sets-off-alarm-bells-in-the-region/.

Chheang, V 2018c, 'The Cambodia-Laos-Vietnam Development Triangle', *Perspective*, no. 30, viewed 10 March 2019, www.iseas.edu.sg/images/pdf/ISEAS_Perspective_2018_30@50.pdf.

Choi, H 2019, 'Korea-ASEAN, Mekong summits set for November in Busan', *Korea Herald*, 1 April, viewed 10 June 2019, www.koreaherald.com/view.php?ud=20190401000807.

Chongkittavorn, K 2019, 'Mekong region: indefinite endgame among major powers', *Journal of Greater Mekong Studies*, vol. 1, no. 1, pp. 89–96.

Denson, J 2019, 'The forgotten key to maritime security in the Sulu-Celebes Seas', *The Diplomat*, 21 March, viewed 10 August 2019, https://thediplomat.com/2019/03/the-forgotten-key-to-maritime-security-in-the-sulu-celebes-seas/.

Doung, B 2018, 'Dynamics of cooperation mechanisms in the Mekong region', *Khmer Times*, 23 October, viewed 10 March 2019, www.khmertimeskh.com/50543025/dynamics-of-cooperation-mechanisms-in-the-mekong/.

Emmers, R 2010, 'The role of the Five Power Defence Arrangements in the Southeast Asian security architecture', *RSIS Working Paper*, no. 195, 20 April, viewed 21 October 2019, www.rsis.edu.sg/wp-content/uploads/rsis-pubs/WP195.pdf.

Gnanasagaran, A 2018, 'Is minilateralism the way forward?' *ASEAN Post*, 27 May, viewed 20 March 2019, https://theaseanpost.com/article/minilateralism-way-forward.

Heng, TM 2006, 'Development in the Indonesia-Malaysia-Singapore Growth Triangle', *SCAPE Policy Research Working Paper Series*, no. 2006/06, Singapore, National University of Singapore, Department of Economics, viewed 10 March 2018, www.fas.nus.edu.sg/ecs/pub/wp-scape/0606.pdf.

Heydarian, R 2017, 'Time for ASEAN minilateralism', *RSIS Commentary*, no. 210, 7 November.

Ho, S and Pitakdumrongkit, K 2019, 'Can ASEAN play a greater role in the Mekong subregion?' *The Diplomat*, 30 January.

Hussain, N 2018, 'Re-modelling for a bigger role?' *RSIS Commentary*, no. 187, 12 November, viewed 7 January 2019, www.rsis.edu.sg/wp-content/uploads/2018/11/CO18187.pdf.

Korea.net 2014, 'Mekong-Republic of Korea Plan of Action (2014–2017)' 29 July, viewed 10 March 2018, www.korea.net/koreanet/fileDown?fileUrl=/upload/content/file/14067 80276688.pdf&fileName=Korea_Mekong_Action_Plan.pdf.

Lee, J 2018, 'Mekong-Korea cooperation spearheads sustainable development', *Korea Herald*, 24 December, viewed 8 March 2019, www.koreaherald.com/view.php?ud=2018122400 0254.

Lee-Brown, J 2018, 'Asia's security triangles: maritime minilateralism in the Indo-Pacific', *East Asia*, vol. 35, no. 2, pp. 163–179.

Leng, T 2019, 'ASEAN connectivity: a new battleground for Japan and China', *Khmer Times*, 24 May, viewed 10 March 2019, www.khmertimeskh.com/50607324/asean-connectivity-a-new-battle-ground-for-japan-and-china/.

Lower Mekong Initiative 2018, '11th Ministerial Joint Statement', 4 August, viewed 10 June 2019, www.lowermekong.org/news/11th-lmi-ministerial-joint-statement.

Ministry of Defence of Singapore 2015, 'Fact sheet: the Malacca Straits Patrol', 21 April, viewed 8 January 2018, www.mindef.gov.sg/web/portal/mindef/news-and-events/lates t-releases/article-detail/2016/april/2016apr21-news-releases-00134/.

Ministry of External Affairs of India 2018, 'Joint Ministerial Statement for the 9th Mekong-Ganga Cooperation Ministerial Meeting in Singapore', 4 August, viewed 8 March 2019, www.mea.gov.in/Speeches-Statements.htm?dtl/30237/Joint_Ministerial_Statement_for_t he_9th_Mekong_Ganga_Cooperation_Ministerial_Meeting_in_Singapore.

Ministry of External Affairs of India 2019, 'Joint Ministerial Statement of the 10th Mekong-Ganga Cooperation Ministerial Meeting in Bangkok', 2 August, viewed 10 August 2019, https://mea.gov.in/bilateral-documents.htm?dtl/31713/Joint+Ministerial+Statement+of+t he+10th+MekongGanga+Cooperation+Ministerial+Meeting.

Ministry of Foreign Affairs of Japan 2015, 'New Tokyo Strategy 2015 for Mekong-Japan cooperation (MJC2015)', 4 July, viewed 10 March 2018, www.mofa.go.jp/s_sa/sea1/pa ge1e_000044.html.

Ministry of Foreign Affairs of Japan 2018a, 'Japan–Cambodia Summit Meeting', 8 October, viewed 10 March 2019, www.mofa.go.jp/s_sa/sea1/kh/page3e_000943.html.

Ministry of Foreign Affairs of Japan 2018b, 'Tokyo Strategy 2018 for Mekong-Japan cooperation', 9 October, viewed 8 March 2019, www.mofa.go.jp/mofaj/files/000406731.pdf.

Ministry of Foreign Affairs of Japan 2019, 'Co-Chair's Statement of the 12th Mekong-Japan Foreign Ministers' Meeting', 3 August, viewed 10 August 2019, www.mofa.go.jp/files/000504081.pdf.

Ministry of Foreign Affairs of Republic of Korea 2019, '9th Mekong-ROK Foreign Ministers' Meeting', 8 August, viewed 10 August 2019, www.mofa.go.kr/eng/brd/m_5674/view.do?seq=319920.

Ministry of Foreign Affairs of Thailand 2018, 'Bangkok Declaration of the 8th Ayeyawady-Chao Phraya-Mekong Economic Cooperation Strategy Summit', 16 June, viewed 8 January 2019, www.mfa.go.th/main/en/information/8151/90566-BANGKOK-DECLARATION-OF-THE-8TH-AYEYAWADY-%E2%80%93CHAO-PHRAYA-%E2%80%93MEKONG-ECONOMIC-COOPERATION-STRATEGY-SUMMIT.html.

Mu, X 2018, '2nd LMC leaders' meeting concludes with declaration, 5-year action plan', *Xinhua News*, 10 January, viewed 13 September 2019, www.xinhuanet.com/english/2018-01/10/c_136886004.htm.

Murg, B 2019, 'Too many cooks? Biodiversity and institutional diversity in the Greater Mekong Subregion', *Journal of Greater Mekong Studies*, vol. 1, no. 1, pp. 45–52.

Naim, M 2009, 'Minilateralism: the magic number to get real international action', *Foreign Policy*, 21 June.

Ng, J 2018, 'The quadrilateral conundrum: can ASEAN be persuaded?' *RSIS Commentary*, no. 120, 17 July, viewed 10 March 2019, www.rsis.edu.sg/wp-content/uploads/2018/07/CO18120.pdf.

Nguyen, KG 2019, 'The Mekong region is caught in a tug-of-war', East Asia Forum, 7 February.

Nilsson-Wright, J 2017, 'Creative minilateralism in a changing Asia: opportunities for security convergence and cooperation between Australia, India and Japan', Research Paper, Asia Programme, London, Chatham House, viewed 8 March 2018, www.chathamhouse.org/sites/default/files/images/2017-07-28-Minilateralism.pdf.

Ooi, GL 1995, 'The Indonesia–Malaysia–Singapore Growth Triangle: sub-regional economic cooperation and integration', *GeoJournal*, vol. 36, no. 4, pp. 337–344.

Parameswaran, P 2018, 'The limits of minilateralism in Asean', *Straits Times*, 15 February, viewed 10 March 2019, www.straitstimes.com/opinion/the-limits-of-minilateralism-in-asean.

Robinson, G 2019, 'Metamorphosis of big power rivalry in the Mekong region', *Journal of Greater Mekong Studies*, vol. 1, no. 1, pp. 53–64.

Sok, S 2019, 'The indispensable role of intra-Asian cooperation in promoting Mekong development', *Mekong Connect*, vol. 1, no. 1, pp. 1–6, viewed 10 August 2019, https://static1.squarespace.com/static/5c1e0cbdf93fd4d532bff977/t/5c4e91f04ae237479fb8d7c6/1548653064780/Mekong+Connect+Issue+1+210119.pdf.

Storey, I 2018, 'Trilateral security cooperation in the Sulu-Celebes Seas: a work in progress', *Perspective*, no. 48, viewed 10 March 2019, www.iseas.edu.sg/images/pdf/ISEAS_Perspective_2018_48@50.pdf.

Teo, S 2018, 'Could minilateralism be multilateralism's best hope in the Asia Pacific?' *The Diplomat*, 15 December.

Tow, W 2018, 'Minilateral security's relevance to US strategy in the Indo-Pacific: challenges and prospects', *Pacific Review*, vol. 32, no. 2, pp. 232–244.

US Department of State 2019, 'Opening remarks at the Lower Mekong Initiative ministerial', 1 August, viewed on 10 August 2019, www.state.gov/opening-remarks-at-the-lower-m ekong-initiative-ministerial/.

Wong, C 2018, 'Is Mekong River set to become the new South China Sea for regional disputes?' *South China Morning Post*, 2 January, viewed 10 March 2019, www.scmp.com/ news/china/diplomacy-defence/article/2126528/mekong-river-set-become-new-south-c hina-sea-regional.

Wuthnow, J 2019, 'U.S. minilateralism in Asia and China's responses: a new security dilemma?' *Journal of Contemporary China*, vol. 28, no. 115, pp. 133–150.

Xinhua News 2019, '80th joint patrol on Mekong River concludes', 22 March, viewed 5 June 2019, www.xinhuanet.com/english/2019-03/22/c_137915672.htm.

8

ASEAN DEFENCE MINISTERS' MEETING-PLUS

Multilateralism mimicking minilateralism?

See Seng Tan

Introduction

Arguably, the ASEAN Defence Ministers' Meeting-Plus (ADMM-Plus), an eighteen-member arrangement centred upon the Association of Southeast Asian Nations (ASEAN), has achieved a level of success in regional cooperation hitherto unattained by other ASEAN-led forms of institutionalised multilateral mechanisms in the Asia Pacific (Tan 2017a, 2018b). However, whether the ADMM-Plus represents an effective security multilateralism is still unclear. This is because the ADMM-Plus shares many of the institutional qualities of its weaker counterparts such as the ASEAN Regional Forum (ARF). Against this backdrop, this chapter looks at some of the structural and institutional conditions behind the achievements of the ADMM-Plus. It is argued that despite its relatively large membership, the ADMM-Plus has hitherto avoided the obstacles and pitfalls that have plagued the ARF as a result of its having behaved just as might have been expected from a minilateral club. This is not to imply that minilateralism—small sub-groups of actors collaborating over specific concerns—is automatically better than multilateralism as distinct forms of institutionalised interstate cooperation, as suggested by the oft-cited contemporary examples of still immature minilateral collaboration in the Asia Pacific, the Trilateral Security Dialogue and more recently the Quadrilateral Security Dialogue (QSD) (Tow 2009). Nor does it mean that the ADMM-Plus is thereby problem-free (Tan 2018b). At most, it suggests that at a time when multilateralism as a whole appears to be on the wane (Laidi 2018), the ADMM-Plus has not only kept afloat but has flown high because of its willingness, for pragmatic reasons stemming from its stakeholders' collective quest for effective regional cooperation, to (quietly) challenge some of ASEAN-led multilateralism's most cherished conventions.

Recent scholarship on the contested nature of Asia Pacific multilateralism has sought to differentiate between ASEAN-led multilateral diplomacy, which emerged in the 1990s with the formation of the ARF in 1994, and newer multi-lateral forms initiated by non-ASEAN powers—the Shanghai Cooperation Orga-nisation, the Asian Infrastructure and Investment Bank, the QSD, inter alia—which either complement or compete against the former (Bisley 2019; He 2018). With-out exception and correctly so, that literature tends to locate minilateral groupings within the latter category of newer multilateral forms. In doing so, however, it indirectly and inadvertently places ASEAN-led multilateralism *in opposition to* minilateralism, at least where Asia Pacific security cooperation is concerned. In contrast, what this chapter contends is the apparent readiness of ASEAN to coun-tenance and even host what could conceivably be regarded, with qualifications, as minilateral groupings or, perhaps more appropriately, multilateral arrangements that function in ways not dissimilar to the way in which minilateral clubs work (or are expected to work). What this arguably implies is ASEAN's tacit endorsement—contra its long-standing advocacy and practice of open regionalism and inclusive multilateralism (Acharya 1997; Garnaut 1996)—of an arrangement, the ADMM-Plus, that is not only putatively exclusive in orientation and practice (without saying as much), but aims higher than the 'lowest common denominator' with which its ASEAN counterparts are typically associated. With these concerns in mind, this chapter begins by revisiting the key conceptual claims of minilateralism. It then sets the stage with a brief account of the debate about ASEAN and mini-lateralism before concluding with an assessment of whether the ADMM-Plus as a multilateral form nonetheless behaves in ways one might expect of a minilateral club.

Minilateralism: concept and praxis revisited

In recent times, multilateralism—that is, big or large-sized multilateral institutions such as the World Trade Organization or the United Nations (UN)—has taken a severe hit. Warning that the world is facing a 'trust deficit disorder', UN Secretary-General Antonio Guterres lamented that 'multilateralism is under fire precisely when we need it most' (*Daily Finland* 2018). And while US President Donald Trump's known aversion to multilateralism undoubtedly exacerbated the crisis facing multilateralism by depriving it of American leadership, the fact remains that multilateralism was already in serious trouble well before Trump and his 'America First' policy came into the picture (Boon 2017; *Financial Times* 2018). Multilateralism in the post-Cold War Asia Pacific is also facing a crisis of sorts, whereby the ability of ASEAN to hold the ring as the appointed custodian of the region's multilateral security architecture has come under challenge for a variety of reasons, not least the growing and destabilising rivalry between China and the United States. Nowhere is this more obvious than in the way ASEAN-led multi-lateral institutions, especially the ARF, have struggled to weather the tensions wrought by great power strategic competition (Tan 2018c). Indeed, the widely held perception that ASEAN's 'centrality' in the Asia Pacific multilateral archi-tecture can no longer guarantee an effective multilateralism that could deliver the outcomes desired by its stakeholders has led discontented participants to call for and/or create alternative arrangements, including minilateral clubs, more suited to their liking and aims (Bisley 2019; He 2018). In other words, while multilateral arrangements in the Asia Pacific are, in a sense, 'regional derogations' from international multilateralism (Kahler 1992, p. 296), it is also evident that the region's growing nod towards minilateralism shares similar points of concern vis-à-vis the perceived inefficacies of the region's established multilateral institutions.

A 2009 article by Naím revived an older debate from the 1990s on 'big' versus 'small' types of multilateralism. Naím's starting premise is that big multilateralism has either failed or has proved ineffective in delivering the promised peace and prosperity dividends. His contention is as follows. While the need for effective multinational collaboration on big concerns such as climate change and nuclear non-proliferation has grown, either multilateral efforts aimed at managing them have failed, or the implementation of agreed upon multilateral solutions has stalled (Naím 2009). The better solution in his view is to bring together a small 'magic number' of countries—a dozen to twenty, depending on the issue at hand—that could have the largest possible impact on solving a particular problem. Naím argued that although minilateralism could rightly be criticised for its seemingly undemocratic and exclusionary character—its emphasis being on efficacy and efficiency rather than on equity or representativeness (Porter et al. 2004)—its basic agreements could nonetheless provide the foundation on which more inclusive and feasible deals could be struck and, just as importantly, kept. In Naím's view, the G20, formed in 1999 following the Asian financial crisis in 1997, offers a compelling case given the inordinate combined impact on world trade of its member economies.

At least three points regarding the concept and practice of minilateralism are noteworthy for our purposes. The first is that group size matters: the smaller the multilateral grouping, the better. Naím's conception is predicated on numerical distinctions (Keohane 1990, p. 731; Ruggie 1993, p. 11). The logic behind his minilateralism (or 'small n' multilateralism) is not new. In his seminal work on group size and collective action, Olson (1965) contended that the larger the group ceteris paribus the less likely its members are to choose to cooperate for some joint gain. Emmers (2013) used this same logic with respect to the Asia Pacific to explain the purported remit and raison d'être of the Five Power Defence Arrangements, the security grouping comprising Australia, New Zealand, the United Kingdom, Malaysia and Singapore. Moreover, large groups that rely on the consensus principle, as opposed to majority voting, are more likely to find it difficult to reach agreement especially on challenging or complex issues where perspectives differ markedly among member countries. The larger the group, the more difficult it is for its members to achieve conditional cooperation (Taylor 1987, p. 12). However, others have noted that a number of multilateral institutions have gradually shifted from majority voting to consensus, or a flexible combination of the two (Footer 1997; Smith 1999). But to the extent that agreement is obtained by consensus, it is potentially diluted by the 'lowest common denominator' problem (Hardin 1982; Oye 1986; Taylor 1987). However, even institutions that rely on majority voting are susceptible to a prospective tyranny or domination by the majority, whereby the majority could conceivably opt against outcomes that they deem politically or socially risky to their respective national situations, no matter the promised benefits in the longer run (Kahn 1968, p. 523). The failure to achieve 'real international action', as Naím (2009) termed it, could therefore be attributed to the (in his view) flawed obsession with big or 'large n' multilateralism as the panacea for the world's ills.

Second, group composition matters. Naím's use of the G20 as a positive example implies that minilateralism involves not just numbers but, crucially so, the collective power of the world's twenty largest and most powerful economies and the norms and rules they promote. A related way to define minilateral groupings is that these are essentially coalitions capable of exerting economic and political influence (Rothkopf 2009). In order to ensure international stability, core groups of powerful actors and the multilateralisation of their agreements—which other states are invited to accept, indeed are socialised into—are required (Kratochwil 1993, p. 468). Put simply, minilateral clubs are essentially select decision-making groupings that comprise a small number of economically, diplomatically and/or strategically influential countries that enjoy inordinate say in and sway over global affairs or at least select sectors of it (Victor 2006, p. 101). Minilateralism highlights the importance of great power cooperation.[1] Regime stability arises because the actors whose actions have the most impact—the major powers within that regime—choose to cooperate rather than defect. Quite often it is defection by great powers from multilateral agreements, rather than any inherent inability to cooperate among large numbers of states, that constitutes a key barrier to multilateral cooperation. In his assessment of global trade, environmental and maritime regimes, Kahler (1992) concluded that in each of those cases, the principal barriers to cooperation appear to be great power defection. Thus understood, post-war international order and stability, not unlike the Concert of Europe from 1815 to the early twentieth century vis-à-vis European order, relied on a minilateral club of key powers led by the United States (Eichengreen 1989, p. 287). Moreover, as coalitions of not just the powerful but, perhaps more crucially, the influential, minilateral clubs could therefore also be groupings of emerging great powers, middle powers, or states that enjoy inordinate sway over international affairs incommensurate with their size. It is not enough to assume the indispensability of great powers. New or emerging powers are equally significant since it is difficult to imagine how major global challenges today can be dealt with by cooperative arrangements, whether multilateral or minilateral, without the participation, say, of the BRICS (Brazil, Russia, India, China and South Africa) countries. But as the Doha Round of world trade talks or the Copenhagen climate change talks in 2009 have shown, established and emerging powers do clash on matters both consider non-negotiable (Bremmer 2009).

Third, it is not just standalone groupings that matter, but equally caucuses and/or coalitions, informal or otherwise, that are 'nested' or 'embedded' within larger institutions (Aggarwal 1998; Ostrom 1990; Young 1999). Nested institutions are issue-specific arrangements that draw upon broader frameworks and/or regimes, and whose norms, rules, practices and behaviours are influenced—constrained, as it were—by the latter within which they are embedded. They are seen as complementing big multilateralism in that they are small self-selected sub-groups of countries that seek to complement bilateralism and region-wide multilateralism (Medcalf 2008, p. 25). For example, the 1980s and 1990s proved to be a fertile period for minilateral great power collaboration within multilateral institutions in the Asia Pacific (Kahler 1992, p. 296). Yet such developments are viewed by some as posing potential problems for big multilateralism. The concern over regionalism, for instance, focused on the perceived fragmentary and dilutive impact it could have on global institutions and agreements, whereas the concern over great and/or middle power minilateralism had to do with its potential contravention of the very rules of multilateralism (Lamy 2014; Yarbrough and Yarbrough 1994). For example, the prospective leading role that the Trilateral Summit comprising the 'Plus Three' countries of the ASEAN Plus Three—China, Japan and South Korea—could conceivably play in East Asian financial collaboration or, more challengingly, tripartite security cooperation over the Korean peninsula, raises intriguing possibilities for either a nested economic minilateralism within the ASEAN Plus Three and its ancillary frameworks such as the Chiang Mai Initiative Multilateralisation (CMIM) or a nested security minilateralism within the ARF or East Asia Summit (Kovrig 2018). Similarly, despite the penchant among analysts to treat the QSD—the quadrilateral club comprising Australia, India, Japan and the United States—as separate from ASEAN-led multilateralism, it bears reminding that QSD members have been meeting on the sidelines of ASEAN summits and meetings (Panda 2018).

Minilateralism: where ASEAN has not feared to tread?

Before evaluating the ADMM-Plus on the basis of the three points highlighted above—club size, club composition and nestedness within larger groupings—a preliminary look at how ASEAN has most recently engaged with the minilateral idea is in order. Notwithstanding its role as a standard bearer for open regionalism and inclusive multilateralism (Acharya 1997; Garnaut 1996), ASEAN has seen its fair share of debate over whether minilateralism ought to be considered as a solution to overcoming the deadlock and inaction typically associated with ASEAN where its approach to vexing security challenges such as the South China Sea disputes is concerned. For example, a number of observers have proposed that ASEAN should consider applying its 'ASEAN minus X' formula—the idea that economic liberalisation between two or more ASEAN states can and should proceed so long as it has the concurrence of all of the other member countries—to intra-ASEAN security cooperation (Emmers 2017; Heydarian 2017). Crucially, the formula is deemed acceptable because its application is sanctionable only by consensus. This form of ASEAN-endorsed cooperation at the sub-regional level arguably fits a characteristic of minilateralism (that is, issue-based collaboration among sub-groups nested within multilateral institutions). On the other hand, it has been argued that the enshrinement of this principle within the ASEAN Charter has complicated things since previous applications of the principle were conducted in a highly ad hoc and flexible way. The worry here is that the formal inclusion of the principle in the charter risks transforming the 'ASEAN minus X' into a rigid tenet based on unanimity rather than flexibility, which hypothetically complicates the process towards security cooperation (Tan 2017b). The reason behind this is that should the principle ever be applied to security collaboration, it is likely to prove even more challenging given ASEAN's cherished doctrine of non-interference, which member states readily invoke to ward off regional security initiatives they believe would impinge on their respective sovereignty. Another cause for concern is that should ASEAN permit the 'ASEAN minus X' to be applied with increasing frequency and regularity, it could inadvertently operate not unlike a majority-vote rule and end up making a mockery of ASEAN's consensus principle.[2]

However, the fact of the matter is that ASEAN members have been applying the formula to intraregional security cooperation, formally or otherwise. In 2004, Indonesia, Malaysia and Singapore formed Operation MALSINDO, comprising trilateral maritime patrols by the navies of the three littoral countries—but with each navy restricted to patrolling its own nation's territorial waters—aimed at interdicting piracy and smuggling in the Malacca Straits (Southgate 2015). An air element, the 'Eyes in the Sky' initiative, was included in 2005. Thailand joined the enterprise in 2008, whereupon MALSINDO became renamed as the Malacca Straits Sea Patrols. In 2011, the ASEAN Convention on Counter-Terrorism, established in 2007, entered into force upon ratification by just six members even though full ratification by all ten was achieved only in 2013 (Tan and Nasu 2016, p. 1220). Furthermore, in June 2017, Indonesia, Malaysia and the Philippines launched the Trilateral Maritime Patrol, which involves trilateral patrols in the Sulu and Sulawesi Seas, an area long renowned for transnational organised crime and militancy (Guiang 2017). These illustrations more or less satisfy the conditions of minilateralism: they are small sub-groups nested within ASEAN whose shared interest in the safety and security of their societies and their littoral waters render them appropriate collaborators. The illustrations also suggest that ASEAN states have not been loath to experiment with minilateral cooperation among themselves—as and when they believed regional circumstances warranted it.

ADMM-Plus: minilateralism in spirit?

The proposition that the ADMM-Plus constitutes the mimicry of minilateralism by a multilateral arrangement might seem far-fetched, but not unreasonable against a regional backdrop of 'frustrated' multilateral experiments (Nair 2009). Nowhere has this been more evident than in the ARF's lack of progress. Feted when it was launched in 1994, the ARF has since become a poster child for what many believe is fundamentally wrong about ASEAN-based multilateralism. The criticisms have also centred on the inability of ASEAN, despite its vaunted centrality in the regional architecture (Tan 2017c), to furnish the regional leadership needed to ensure a productive and effective multilateralism (Emmers and Tan 2011; Yuzawa 2006). As noted earlier, the ARF has floundered all the more in the light of its susceptibility to the destabilising impact wrought by great power rivalry (Acharya 2010; Goh 2012). Since its inception, the ARF has arguably contributed to regional security and stability through institutionalising and normalising ties among the great powers and regional actors within an ASEAN-led framework (Khong 2004). On the other hand, it has been beset by criticisms that it is merely a talkshop with a lacklustre record in multilateral cooperation. This is reflected in the ARF's inability to advance beyond confidence-building activities and implement preventive diplomacy, as promised in the 1995 ARF concept paper (Yuzawa 2006). For that matter, the reluctance of the ARF to get involved in regional flashpoints such as the Korean peninsula, the South China Sea and the Taiwan Straits—the very kinds of interstate security problems allowed for by the ARF's definition of preventive diplomacy—has raised serious objections concerning the relevance of the ARF to regional security, hence prompting demands for alternative regional architectures such as former Australian Prime Minister Kevin Rudd's proposal for an 'Asia Pacific Community' (Woolcott 2009). Its subsequent turn to non-traditional security issues, welcomed as an opportunity for the ARF to engage in practical cooperation, not only puts it in indirect competition with the ADMM-Plus, but risks disqualifying the ARF as a regional actor of consequence should it inadvertently recuse itself from the region's most important strategic challenges (Tan 2017a, p. 262). Others have also suggested that the institutional design and diplomatic protocols of the ARF, combined with the power-balancing gamesmanship of its members, effectively consign the ARF's efforts to lowest-common-denominator outcomes at best and outright failure at worst (Emmers and Tan 2011). Crucially, its ineffectiveness clarified, at least for some of its participants, the inappropriateness of grand security designs. For example, Rudd's proposal is illustrative of the belief that a minilateral club of great and regional powers furnishing collective leadership within larger multilateral arrangements is the way to manage the region's challenges. Ultimately, the idea was rejected by ASEAN not for its tacit minilateralism but its potentially negative ramifications for ASEAN's centrality in Asia Pacific multilateralism (Tan 2015a, pp. 165–75).

In contrast to the ARF, the fortunes of the ADMM-Plus have fared better. Formed only in 2010 as a triennial gathering (which became an annual event from 2017 onwards), the ADMM-Plus has been forging ahead with increasingly complex multilateral exercises and enhancing the capacity, cooperation and interoperability of the region's militaries in humanitarian assistance and disaster relief (HADR), maritime security and counter-terrorism (Tan 2018b). Between 2011 and 2018, a total of at least 64 Experts' Working Group (EWG) sessions, six tabletop exercises and seven 'full troop' exercises took place under the ADMM-Plus aegis. The scale and scope of some of these activities are by no means trivial; for example, in a combined maritime security and counter-terrorism full troop exercise held in Brunei Darussalam and Singapore (as well as in the waters between them) in May 2016, a total of 3,500 personnel, eighteen ships, 25 aircraft and 40 special forces teams from all eighteen members participated (Tan 2016). The ASEAN core of the ADMM-Plus has also formed an ASEAN Militaries Ready Group on HADR and endorsed standard operating procedures (SOP) for the utilisation of military assets for HADR under the framework of the ASEAN Agreement on Disaster Management and Emergency Response. The SOP augments the existing Standard Operating Procedures for Regional Standby Arrangements and Coordination of Joint Disaster Relief and Emergency Response Operations, a template that defines the roles and terms of reference for both provider countries and recipient countries as well as enhances HADR interoperability among ADMM-Plus members. Supporting infrastructures and assets include the Regional HADR Coordination Centre based in Singapore and the UN Humanitarian Response Depot based in Malaysia. In the area of counter-terrorism, ASEAN has launched the Our Eyes Initiative, an intelligence-sharing arrangement that, for the time being, draws together a select group of ASEAN members (Brunei, Indonesia, Malaysia, the Philippines, Singapore and Thailand, representing perhaps another example of 'ASEAN minus X' security cooperation) and a number of Plus powers (Australia, Japan, New Zealand and the United States). With these and other developments, the ADMM-Plus has significantly enhanced its capacity as a preventive diplomacy actor without declaring its intention to become one, not publicly at least—a suggestion, perhaps, that progress in regional security cooperation in the Asia Pacific is better done on the quiet, *sans* the exaggerated promises and extravagant expectations for which ASEAN-led multilateralism has come to be known for but not delivered (Tan 2019, pp. 86–7). According to one assessment:

> Activities in the [ADMM-Plus] imply ASEAN's strong will to differentiate the framework from the [ARF], which countries concerned have found to be ineffective for promoting conflict prevention and dealing with confrontational, sensitive issues of traditional security, like the South China Sea.
>
> *(Shoji 2013, p. 13)*

The foregoing list of achievements would probably not have been possible if the ADMM-Plus had stuck to the conventions that have presumably shackled the ARF and impeded multilateral cooperation (Emmers and Tan 2011; Tan 2017a). If the aim of minilateralism is to find a pragmatic solution to address the problems of multilateralism, then the architects of the ADMM-Plus presumably had in mind to establish an effective cooperation by consciously avoiding the mistakes made by the ARF. In this respect, size mattered because the ARF's 27 members made it exceedingly difficult to achieve consensus on decisions of significance,[3] since cooperation could proceed only 'at a pace comfortable to all participants', as the mantra goes. If the ARF has shown itself unwieldy in terms of its size and scale of its putative ambitions, the ADMM-Plus arguably reflects a more manageable number of relatively like-minded states with sufficiently common interests and aversions who have eschewed grandiose aspirations in favour of functional, practical and actionable cooperative activities. According to a notable US analyst, a complement of eighteen is a good size as the ADMM-Plus allows Asia Pacific ministers of defence to hold constructive discussions and for their militaries to undertake practical cooperation 'without being crippled by too many members' (Seawright 2018). On the other hand, the ADMM-Plus is by no means small. Although it is less than Naím's magic number twenty, it bears reminding that the context of reference for Naím was the world at large and not the Asia Pacific. That said, relative to a largely ineffectual ARF, the case could be made that the ADMM-Plus has hitherto exceeded expectations partly due to its smaller size. Owing to its perceived successes, overtures have been made by outsiders—among them Canada, France, the United Kingdom and the European Union—wishing to join the ADMM-Plus. Notably, there is no consensus yet among existing members to expand the grouping's membership.

Unlike group size, there is no equivocality where the group composition of the ADMM-Plus is concerned. Eschewing the ad hoc institution building that theretofore had characterised ASEAN-led multilateralism, the architects of the ADMM-Plus thought long and hard over who ought to be in the arrangement. According to Singapore's former top defence official who had a key role in the formation of the ADMM-Plus, he and his ASEAN counterparts were firmly convinced that the ADMM-Plus needed to 'start right and be inaugurated with the right configuration and composition of countries, and in one step, from the outset, rather than in a series of small incremental steps' (Chiang 2014, p. 6). Thus understood, the current eight 'Plus' powers—Australia, China, India, Japan, New Zealand, Russia, South Korea and the United States—were presumably invited by ASEAN to join the ADMM-Plus based on what and how they could contribute to helping the ASEAN states to build their requisite capacities to respond compellingly to maritime complexities, natural disasters, terrorism and the like.[4] Moreover, the lack of consensus among existing ADMM-Plus members on the prospect of enlarging the institution's membership base is due partly to their shared worry over the possible dilution of the focus and vitality of the ADMM-Plus. Paradoxically, owing to its very success, existing members today face the real prospect of participation fatigue stemming from the high level of activity and operational tempo and—should the ADMM-Plus prove incapable of handling hotspots like the South China Sea (Baldino and Carr 2016)—low (or worse, negative) returns on their investments (Tan 2019, p. 13).[5]

It should be said the ADMM-Plus has yet to prove its mettle in defusing South China Sea tensions. Indeed, its aims might not be as ambitious as imagining itself a peace process of any sort (Leifer 1999). Yet it succeeded in establishing a Code for Unplanned Encounters at Sea (CUES) for all its member countries; in 2018, the ASEAN states conducted maritime table-top cum full troop exercises with China based on CUES, and in 2019 the inaugural ASEAN-US maritime exercise was held. Finally, the ADMM-Plus is not immune to security dilemmas and deterrence dynamics played out among its members (Chang and Chong 2016; Chong and Lee 2018; Loh 2016). Indeed, given the participation of the Chinese and the Americans in the ADMM-Plus, the prospect that the arrangement might be negatively affected by great power rivalry—as happened at the third ADMM-Plus meeting in 2015, which scuttled the release of a planned joint statement (Tan 2015b)—cannot be discounted. If like-mindedness is an attribute of minilateralism, then the presence in the same institution of the world's two most powerful nations locked in a titanic wrestling match with one another undoubtedly complicates the proposition of the ADMM-Plus as a quasi-minilateral club. By this logic, minilateral groupings that include China and the United States within their exclusive memberships—the Permanent Five of the UN Security Council, the G20, take your pick—face a similar conundrum. However, as interest-based entities, minilateral groupings are presumably also places where strategic rivals can find sufficiently common ground to check their mutual disputes at the door and focus on cooperating towards the realisation of functional goals at hand. For the most part, both the Chinese and the Americans have kept faith with their ADMM-Plus counterparts and have eschewed any untoward rocking of the boat.

Third, as part of the suite of multilateral arrangements and initiatives that together make up ASEAN-led multilateral diplomacy, the ADMM-Plus can be said to be nestled within that broad multilateral security architecture (Tan 2015a). Indeed, nowhere is the idea of nesting more obvious than the fact that all members of the ADMM-Plus are also members of the ARF. If minilateral clubs are self-selected sub-groups of larger multilateral groupings in joint pursuit of specific collective economic or political aims—but, importantly, without undermining those larger multilateral groupings—then the ADMM-Plus fits the bill of a sub-group and component part within the wider ASEAN-led 'multiverse'. Notwithstanding (as argued here) its pragmatic focus to ensure the ADMM-Plus goes beyond just being a talkshop through delivering reasonably productive and effective cooperation, the ADMM-Plus is still very much an ASEAN-based institution in that it adheres more or less to ASEAN norms and conventions—at the very least, it does not fall far from the ASEAN tree—and seeks above all to ensure ASEAN's centrality in Asia Pacific multilateralism stays intact (Tan 2018a). However, the possibility that the continued success of the ADMM-Plus could well come at the expense of the ARF—if only through inadvertently exposing the latter's relative poverty of ideas and substance—cannot be ruled out.

Conclusion

At face value, the ADMM-Plus does not seem to fit with the core claims and expectations of minilateralism, not least the ones highlighted in this chapter. Yet as argued above, their collective quest for effective multilateral cooperation has led the member states of the ADMM-Plus towards pragmatically oriented conduct that seems to challenge some of ASEAN-led multilateralism's most cherished conventions, such as the long-standing support for open regionalism and inclusive multilateralism. To be sure, the trustees of the ADMM-Plus have no intention of fundamentally deviating from ASEAN's established practices. After all, the ADMM-Plus is well nested within the structures and customs of ASEAN-led multilateralism, even as its innovations in security cooperation continually stretch and test the outer limits of ASEAN-based diplomacy and security. But as this discussion has also shown, there is no shortage of obstacles which, given the right conditions, could trip up the ADMM-Plus and impede its progress. Paradoxically, the very success enjoyed by the ADMM-Plus today could well become its Achilles heel in time to come, as a consequence of progress on the ground becoming outstripped by rising expectations. Its custodians would do well to bear that in mind.

Notes

1 In this regard, the theory of hegemonic stability—whereby the stability and success of the international regime is underwritten by the preponderant power—is not particularly useful in explaining multilateral financial cooperation, not least when the hegemonic power to which the theory has mostly been applied—the United States—has arguably been a fervent and consistent supporter—indeed, progenitor—of multilateral institutions and norms in the post-war system (Ikenberry 2000).
2 As Anwar (2017, p. 24) has cautioned about unbridled applications of the 'ASEAN minus X' (or '10 minus X', as she calls it) formula to regional security: 'There are already those that have suggested that a more flexible sort of consensus should be taken in the realms of politics and security, similar to that in the economic realm that uses the 10-X formula, because the credibility of ASEAN will diminish if it too often fails to reach an agreement on strategic issues. Yet it must also be asked whether removing the consensus principle in politics and security matters, which are "high politics" and related to the core interests of a nation that are often not negotiable, will truly strengthen ASEAN or not? What would happen if Indonesia had a different view from all the other ASEAN members on an issue it feels strongly about on principle, but because consensus is no longer needed, ASEAN can still make a decision with majority-rule that overrides Indonesia's objections?'
3 As Richard Woolcott (2009, p. 3), the special envoy tasked by then Australian Prime Minister, Kevin Rudd, to promote the latter's Asia Pacific Community vision wrote in 2009, 'many believe [the ARF] is too large and has made insufficient progress since its inception'.
4 As a diplomat of a country that has publicly indicated willingness to join the ADMM-Plus told this author, the oft-heard response from ASEAN officials to their overtures goes along the lines of 'prove to us your readiness to do more for ASEAN and we will consider your request' (personal communication, 19 September 2018).
5 According to a senior defence official from an ADMM-Plus member country, a recent and rather ironic development is the proclivity of some co-leaders of the ADMM-Plus EWGs to eschew conducting combined exercises with other EWGs—as has been the past practice of the ADMM-Plus in 2013 (that is, a combined full troop exercise in HADR and military medicine) and in 2016 (that is, three combined full troop exercises in humanitarian mine action and peacekeeping, in maritime security and counter-terrorism, and in HADR and military medicine, respectively)—and insisting instead on conducting exercises exclusive to their own EWGs. Such a direction runs the risk of taxing member countries of their resources and military personnel in even greater measure, raising the likelihood of participation fatigue (personal communication, September and October 2018).

References

Acharya, A 1997, 'Ideas, identity, and institution-building: from the "ASEAN way" to the "Asia-Pacific way"?' *Pacific Review*, vol. 10, no. 3, pp. 319–346.

Acharya, A 2010, 'Asia-Pacific security: community, concert or what?' *PacNet*, no. 11, 12 March, viewed 9 August 2019, https://csis-prod.s3.amazonaws.com/s3fs-public/legacy_files/files/publication/pac1011.pdf.

Aggarwal, VK (ed.) 1998, *Institutional Designs for a Complex World: Bargaining, Linkages, and Nesting*, Ithaca, NY, Cornell University Press.

Anwar, DF 2017, 'Indonesia, ASEAN and regional stability', inaugural lecture presented at the Social Science Commission of the Indonesian Academy of Sciences, Jakarta, 16 February.

Baldino, D and Carr, A 2016, 'Defence diplomacy and the Australian defence force: smokescreen or strategy?' *Australian Journal of International Affairs*, vol. 70, no. 2, pp. 139–158.

Bisley, N 2019, 'Contested Asia's "new" multilateralism and regional order', *Pacific Review*, vol. 32, no. 2, pp. 221–231.

Boon, K 2017, 'President Trump and the future of multilateralism', *Emory International Law Review*, vol. 31, pp. 1075–1081.

Bremmer, I 2009, '20 is still a very big number', *Foreign Policy*, 23 June, viewed 9 August 2019, http://blog.foreignpolicy.comhttp//eurasia.foreignpolicy.com/posts/2009/06/23/20_is_still_a_very_big_number.

Chang, JY and Chong, A 2016, 'Security competition by proxy: Asia Pacific interstate rivalry in the aftermath of the MH370 incident', *Global Change, Peace & Security*, vol. 28, no. 1, pp. 75–98.

Chiang, CF 2014, 'Insights on the ADMM and ADMM-Plus: the road to realisation, and what lies ahead', speech given at the Goh Keng Swee Command and Staff College Seminar, Singapore, 9–10 October, viewed 9 August 2019, http://news.ntu.edu.sg/SAFNTU/Documents/Panel%203%20-%20Mr%20Chiang%20Chie%20Foo%20.pdf.

Chong, A and Lee, IW 2018, 'Asia's security competition by proxy: competitive HADR as a respectable arena?' in A Chong (ed.), *International Security in the Asia-Pacific: Transcending ASEAN towards Transitional Polycentrism*, Cham, Palgrave Macmillan.

Daily Finland 2018, 'Multilateralism is under fire when world needs it most: UN chief', 25 September, viewed 9 August 2019, www.dailyfinland.fi/worldwide/7170/Multilateralism-is-under-fire-when-world-needs-it-most-UN-chief.

Eichengreen, B 1989, 'Hegemonic stability theories of the international monetary system', in RN Cooper, B Eichengreen, G Holtham, RD Putnam and CR Henning (eds), *Can Nations Agree? Issues in International Economic Cooperation*, Washington, DC, Brookings Institution Press.

Emmers, R 2013, 'The role of the Five Power Defence Arrangements in the Southeast Asian security architecture', in WT Tow and B Taylor (eds), *Bilateralism, Multilateralism and Asia-Pacific Security: Contending Cooperation*, London, Routledge.

Emmers, R 2017, 'ASEAN minus X: should this formula be extended?' *RSIS Commentary*, no. 199, 24 October, viewed 9 August 2019, www.rsis.edu.sg/rsis-publication/cms/co17199-asean-minus-x-should-this-formula-be-extended.

Emmers, R and Tan, SS 2011, 'The ASEAN Regional Forum and preventive diplomacy: built to fail?' *Asian Security*, vol. 7, no. 1, pp. 44–60.

Financial Times 2018, 'Multilateralism without American leadership', 7 June, viewed 9 August 2019, www.ft.com/content/cc6c44c8-697f-11e8-b6eb-4acfcfb08c11.

Footer, ME 1997, 'The role of consensus in GATT/WTO decision-making', *Northwestern Journal of International Law & Business*, vol. 17, no. 1, pp. 653–680.

Garnaut, R 1996, *Open Regionalism and Trade Liberalization: An Asia-Pacific Contribution to the World Trade System*, Singapore, ISEAS-Yusof Ishak Institute.

Goh, E 2012, 'Institutions and the great power bargain in East Asia: ASEAN's limited "brokerage" role', in R Emmers (ed.), *ASEAN and the Institutionalisation of East Asia*, London, Routledge.

Guiang, G 2017, 'Are minilaterals the future of ASEAN security?' East Asia Forum, 30 September, viewed 9 August 2019, www.eastasiaforum.org/2017/09/30/are-minilaterals-the-future-of-asean-security/.

Hardin, R 1982, *Collective Action*, Baltimore, MD, Johns Hopkins University Press.

He, K 2018, 'Contested multilateralism 2.0 and regional order transition: causes and implications', *Pacific Review*, vol. 32, no. 3, pp. 1–11.

Heydarian, RJ 2017, 'ASEAN needs to move to minilateralism', East Asia Forum, 5 December, viewed 9 August 2019, www.eastasiaforum.org/2017/12/05/asean-needs-to-move-to-minilateralism/.

Ikenberry, GJ 2000, *After Victory: Institutions, Strategic Restraint, and the Rebuilding of Order after Major Wars*, Princeton, NJ, Princeton University Press.

Kahler, M 1992, 'Multilateralism with small and large numbers', *International Organization*, vol. 46, no. 3, pp. 681–708.

Kahn, AE 1968, 'The tyranny of small decisions: market failures, imperfections, and the limits of econometrics', in B Russett (ed.), *Economic Theories of International Relations*, Chicago, Markham Publishing.

Keohane, RO 1990, 'Multilateralism: an agenda for research', *International Journal*, vol. 45, no. 4, pp. 731–764.

Khong, YF 2004, 'Coping with strategic uncertainty: the role of institutions and soft balancing in Southeast Asia's post-cold war strategy', in PJ Katzenstein, JJ Suh and A Carlson (eds), *Rethinking Security in East Asia: Identity, Power, and Efficiency*, Stanford, CA, Stanford University Press.

Kovrig, M 2018, 'Trilateral North East Asia summit signals a return to cooperation', *International Crisis Group*, 23 May, viewed 9 August 2019, www.crisisgroup.org/asia/north-east-asia/trilateral-north-east-asia-summit-signals-return-cooperation.

Kratochwil, F 1993, 'Norms versus numbers: multilateralism and the rationalist and reflexivist approaches to institutions: a unilateral plea for communicative rationality', in JG Ruggie (ed.), *Multilateralism Matters: The Theory and Praxis of an Institutional Form*, New York, Columbia University Press.

Laidi, Z 2018, 'Is multilateralism finished?' *Project Syndicate*, 18 May, viewed 9 August 2019, www.project-syndicate.org/onpoint/is-multilateralism-finished-by-zaki-laidi-2018-05?barrier=accesspaylog.

Lamy, P 2014, 'Is trade multilateralism being threatened by regionalism?' *Adelphi Series*, vol. 54, no. 450, pp. 61–78.

Leifer, M 1999, 'The ASEAN peace process: a category mistake', *Pacific Review*, vol. 12, no. 1, pp. 25–38.

Loh, DMH 2016, 'ASEAN's norm adherence and its unintended consequences in HADR and SAR operations', *Pacific Review*, vol. 29, no. 4, pp. 549–572.

Medcalf, R 2008, 'Squaring the triangle: an Australian perspective on Asian security minilateralism', in WT Tow, M Auslin, R Medcalf, A Tanaka, F Zhu and SW Simon, *Assessing the Trilateral Strategic Dialogue*, NBR Special Report, no. 16, Seattle, WA, National Bureau of Asian Research, pp. 23–31.

Naím, M 2009, 'Minilateralism: the magic number to get real international action', *Foreign Policy*, no. 137, pp. 136–137.

Nair, D 2009, 'Regionalism in the Asia Pacific/East Asia: a frustrated regionalism?' *Contemporary Southeast Asia*, vol. 31, no. 1, pp. 110–142.

Olson, M 1965, *The Logic of Collective Action: Public Goods and the Theory of Groups*, Cambridge, MA, Harvard University Press.

Ostrom, E 1990, *Governing the Commons: The Evolution of Institutions for Collective Action*, New York, Cambridge University Press.

Oye, K 1986, 'Explaining cooperation under anarchy: hypotheses and strategies', in K Oye (ed.), *Cooperation under Anarchy*, Princeton, NJ, Princeton University Press.

Panda, A 2018, 'US, Japan, India, and Australia hold senior official-level quadrilateral meeting in Singapore', *The Diplomat*, 8 June, viewed 9 August 2019, https://thediplomat.com/2018/06/us-japan-india-and-australia-hold-senior-official-level-quadrilateral-meeting-in-singapore/.

Porter, RB, Sauvé, P, Subramanian, A and Zampetti, AB 2004, *Efficiency, Equity, and Legitimacy: The Multilateral Trading System at the Millennium*, Washington, DC, Brookings Institution Press.

Rothkopf, D 2009, 'Roll up your pants, time to wade back into "minilateralism"', *Foreign Policy*, 25 June, viewed 9 August 2019, http://blog.foreignpolicy.comhttp//rothkopf.foreignpolicy.com/posts/2009/06/25/roll_up_your_pants_time_to_wade_back_into_minilateralism.

Ruggie, JG 1993, 'Multilateralism: the anatomy of an institution', in JG Ruggie (ed.), *Multilateralism Matters: The Theory and Praxis of an Institutional Form*, New York, Columbia University Press.

Seawright, A 2018, 'ADMM-Plus: an ASEAN-led security forum', *Business Times*, 13 November, viewed 9 August 2019, www.businesstimes.com.sg/hub/asean-singapore-2018/admm-plus-an-asean-led-security-forum.

Shoji, T 2013, 'ASEAN Defense Ministers' Meeting (ADMM) and ADMM Plus: a Japanese perspective', *NIDS Journal of Defense and Security*, vol. 14, pp. 3–17.

Smith, CB 1999, 'The politics of global consensus building: a comparative analysis', *Global Governance*, vol. 5, no. 2, pp. 173–201.

Southgate, L 2015, 'Piracy in the Malacca Strait: can ASEAN respond?' *The Diplomat*, 8 July, viewed 9 August 2019, https://thediplomat.com/2015/07/piracy-in-the-malacca-strait-can-asean-respond/.

Tan, SS 2012, '"Talking their walk"? The evolution of defence regionalism in Southeast Asia', *Asian Security*, vol. 8, no. 3, pp. 232–250.

Tan, SS 2015a, *Multilateral Asian Security Architecture: Non-ASEAN Stakeholders*, London, Routledge.

Tan, SS 2015b, 'The media got the 3rd ADMM-Plus wrong', *PacNet*, no. 82, 1 December.

Tan, SS 2016, 'The ADMM-Plus: regionalism that works?' *Asia Policy*, no. 22, pp. 70–75.

Tan, SS 2017a, 'A tale of two institutions: the ARF, ADMM-Plus and security regionalism in the Asia Pacific', *Contemporary Southeast Asia*, vol. 39, no. 2, pp. 259–264.

Tan, SS 2017b, 'Minilateralism: a way out of ASEAN's consensus conundrum?' *ASEAN Focus*, no. 5/2017, p. 9.

Tan, SS 2017c, 'Rethinking "ASEAN centrality" in the regional governance of East Asia', *Singapore Economic Review*, vol. 62, no. 3, pp. 721–740.

Tan, SS 2018a, 'Defence and security cooperation in East Asia: whither ASEAN centrality?' in A Chong (ed.), *International Security in the Asia-Pacific: Transcending ASEAN towards Transitional Polycentrism*, London, Palgrave Macmillan.

Tan, SS 2018b, 'The ADMM and ADMM-Plus: regional security mechanisms that work?' in T Huxley and W Choong (eds), *Asia-Pacific Regional Security Assessment 2018*, London, International Institute for Strategic Studies.

Tan, SS 2018c, 'When giants vie: China-US competition, institutional balancing, and East Asian multilateralism', in H Feng and K He (eds), *US-China Competition and the South China Sea Disputes*, London, Routledge.

Tan, SS 2019, *The Responsibility to Provide in Southeast Asia: Towards an Ethical Explanation*, Bristol, Bristol University Press.

Tan, SS and Nasu, H 2016, 'ASEAN and the development of counter-terrorism law and policy in Southeast Asia', *UNSW Law Journal*, vol. 39, no. 3, pp. 1219–1238.

Taylor, M 1987, *The Possibility of Cooperation*, Cambridge, Cambridge University Press.

Tow, W 2009, 'Assessing the Trilateral Strategic Dialogue', East Asia Forum, 12 February, viewed 9 August 2019, www.eastasiaforum.org/2009/02/12/assessing-the-trilateral-strategic-dialogue/.

Victor, DG 2006, 'Toward effective international cooperation on climate change: numbers, interests and institutions', *Global Environmental Politics*, vol. 6, no. 3, pp. 90–103.

Woolcott, R 2009, 'Towards an Asia-Pacific community', *The Asialink Essays*, no. 9, November.

Yarbrough, B and Yarbrough, RM 1994, 'Regionalism and layered governance: the choice of trade institutions', *Journal of International Affairs*, vol. 48, no. 1, pp. 95–117.

Young, O 1999, *Governance in World Affairs*, Ithaca, NY, Cornell University Press.

Yuzawa, T 2006, 'The evolution of preventive diplomacy in the ASEAN Regional Forum: problems and prospects', *Asian Survey*, vol. 46, no. 5, pp. 785–804.

INDEX